CLEARING THE AIR

*This book is dedicated to my mother,
who died in January, 2001*

Clearing the Air

European advances in tackling
acid rain and atmospheric pollution

JØRGEN WETTESTAD
The Fridtjof Nansen Institute, Norway

Ashgate

Published by
Ashgate Publishing Limited
Gower House
Croft Road
Aldershot
Hampshire GU11 3HR
England

Ashgate Publishing Company
131 Main Street
Burlington, VT 05401-5600 USA

Ashgate website: http://www.ashgate.com

British Library Cataloguing in Publication Data
Wettestad, Jørgen, 1955-
    Clearing the air : European advances in tackling acid rain
    and atmospheric pollution
    1.Air - Pollution - European Union countries - Prevention
    2. Air - Pollution - Government policy - European Union
    countries 3. Air - Pollution - Law and legislation -
    European Union countries
    I. Title
    363.7'392'7'094

Library of Congress Control Number: 2001098850

ISBN 0 7546 0959 6

Printed and bound in Great Britain by MPG Books Ltd, Bodmin, Cornwall

Contents

List of Figures and Tables

Figures

Tables

Preface

This book has grown out of a decade-long interest in the politics of acid rain and air pollution. Initially I focused on the work of the Convention on Long-Range Transboundary Air Pollution (CLRTAP), this work being of great importance for the Norwegian environment. From the mid-1990s I became increasingly aware of the important further development of EU air pollution policy taking place. Hence, when I received the grant for this project from the 'SAMRAM' programme (on central factors affecting Norwegian energy and environmental policy-making) in the fall of 1998, I felt that this was really 'the right money at the right time' for me. I extend warm thanks to SAMRAM and the Norwegian Research Council.

This project has really been a pleasure from start to finish. I have been kindly received by a number of people who shared their experience and insight gratuitously with me. You will find their names in the list of interviews in the Bibliography. I would especially like to thank Lars Bjørkbom, Lars Nordberg, Mari Sæther and Magnar Ødelien. A very special thanks goes to Christer Ågren, who reviewed the whole manuscript thoroughly, helping me to avoid mistakes and offering invaluable insight from one who has served on various sides of the negotiating table.

Moreover, several people have provided splendid comments in various phases of this work: Marcus Amann, Steinar Andresen, Andrew Farmer, Ron Mitchell, Henrik Selin, Jon B. Skjærseth, Olav Schram Stokke, Arild Underdal and Rudi Wurzel. Thanks to John Taylor for language assistance, and warm thanks to Maryanne Rygg for all kinds of formatting and editing assistance.

I must also thank the Fridtjof Nansen Institute for excellent support; not least by granting the additional funds necessary for turning the initial, rough manuscript into a publishable book. Many thanks also to Kirstin Howgate at Ashgate for believing in this project.

Hats off to musical soulmates for fueling every line in this book: Guy Clark, Steve Earle, James Harman and Chris Isaak.

Polhøgda, October 15, 2001

Jørgen Wettestad

List of Abbreviations

ACEA	European Automotive Manufacturers Association
BAT	Best Available Technology
BATNEEC	Best available technology not entailing excessive costs
CAFE	Clean Air for Europe Programme
CLRTAP	Convention on Long Range Transboundary Air Pollution
CO	carbon monoxide
DETR	(British) Department of Environment, Transport and the Regions
DG ENV	Environment Directorate, EU Commission
EB	Executive Body (CLRTAP)
ECE	Economic Commission for Europe
ELV	Emission Limit Values
EMEP	Cooperative Programme for Monitoring and Evaluation of Long-range Transmissions of Air Pollutants in Europe
ENGO	Environmental Non-governmental Organisation
EPEFE	European Programme on Emissions, Fuels and Engine Technologies
EU	European Union
EUROPIA	European Petroleum Industry Association
HC	hydrocarbons
IIASA	International Institute for Applied Systems Analysis
IPPC	Integrated pollution prevention and control

LCP	Large Combustion Plants
MEPs	Members of European Parliament
NEC	National Emission Ceilings
NH_3	ammonia
NO_x	Nitrogen Oxides
PEMAs	Pollutants Emissions Management Areas
PM10	Particulate Matter
POPs	Persistent Organic Pollutants
RAINS	Regional Air Pollution Information and Simulation model (IIASA)
SO_2	Sulphur dioxide
TFACT	Trust Fund for Assistance to Countries in Transition (CLRTAP)
TFEAAS	Task Force on Economic Aspects of Abatement Strategies (CLRTAP)
TFIAM	Task Force on Integrated Assessment Modelling (CLRTAP)
UNEP	United Nations Environmental Programme
UNICE	European employers federation
VOC	Volatile Organic Compounds
WGS	Working Group on Strategies (CLRTAP)
WHO	World Health Organisation
μ/m^3	micrograms per cubic metre

Chapter 1

Introduction

The Changing Politics of European Air Pollution Control

The fight against air pollution, leading to acidification of nature and choking cities, has now become a global concern. Although Western Europe and North America experienced these problematic by-products of economic growth quite early, as pinpointed by John McCormick, 'emissions of many of these pollutants are increasing in much of Eastern Europe, Asia, and Latin America [and have] become a problem for newly industrialising countries as well' (McCormick 1998:17). In the face of this challenge, there is clearly a need for a strong political response to meet environmental and health needs. However, as such international policies affect high-valued economic growth and core national interests, how can they be established and strengthened over time? This is the general theme of this book.

The changing politics of European air pollution control provides an excellent opportunity for exploring this theme in depth within a regional context having had a comparatively long history of dealing with these problems. Both the European Union (EU) and the Convention on Long-Range Transboundary Air Pollution (CLRTAP) have experienced a recent and fascinating further strengthening of policies. Within CLRTAP, an innovative – and in several ways more ambitious multi-pollutant and multi-effects protocol – was adopted in Gothenburg on November 30, 1999. In contrast to earlier CLRTAP protocols which targeted a single substance (for example, sulphur dioxide) and one main environmental effect (initially, acidification), the 1999 Gothenburg Protocol targets the four substances of nitrogen oxides (NO_x), volatile organic compounds (VOCs), sulphur dioxide (SO_2), and ammonia (NH_3), and the three effects of acidification, tropospheric ozone formation and eutrophication. According to the CLRTAP Secretary at the time, Lars Nordberg, the agreement is 'the most sophisticated environmental agreement ever negotiated and will yield great benefits, for both our environment and health'.[1] Within the European Union, the Council of Ministers adopted a common position on a parallel directive on National Emission Ceilings (NEC) on June 22, 2000, targeting the same substances as the Gothenburg Protocol. Taken together, these developments are a clear indication that the policy ambitiousness – and overall 'strength' – of European air pollution policy increased considerably in the latter part of the 1990s. A first objective of this book is to substantiate this claim of increased policy strength through a closer review and assessment of the content and the political and environmental implications of the adopted policies. Does, for instance, the recent policy development mean that policies in line with environmental and public health needs are now finally in place?

The next and even more important aim is to shed light upon *how* this development has come about. In the wake of the rather reluctant establishment of CLRTAP in 1979, regulatory protocols on sulphur dioxide (1985), nitrogen oxides (1988), volatile organic compounds (1991) and again, sulphur dioxide (1994), were adopted. Moreover, policy development within the European Community received an impetus, leading among other things, to the adoption of the Large Combustion Plant (LCP) Directive in 1988 and important car emissions directives in 1989 and 1990.[2] Hence, by the early 1990s, although air pollution problems were far from solved, considerable policy developments had already taken place and it is reasonable to believe that the further development of abatement measures were becoming increasingly expensive. Moreover, the issue of climate change was rising quickly on the political agenda, replacing air pollution as the central environmental concern for many states. In addition, after the general heyday of green issues in the period between 1988 and 1992, the general political saliency of environmental concerns was on the decrease again.[3] So how was it possible to substantially develop policy even further? Given that several environmental and air pollution policy characteristics did not develop in a direction favourable for a strengthening of policy, *it is natural to focus attention on several interesting institutional changes in terms of membership and decision-making procedures both within CLRTAP and the EU.*

Within the East-West context of CLRTAP, an important change in the 1990s has been the break-up of the Soviet Union and the participation of a new group of Eastern countries. This made CLRTAP parties more homogenous, relaxed the policy-making atmosphere, and, dependent upon a greening of Eastern positions, opened up new possibilities for East-West coalition-building. Moreover, in terms of decision-making, regime-induced improvement in the knowledge relating to critical loads and the interplay of pollutants and their effects has paved the way for a new, broader and a potentially more integrative decision-making approach. Within the EU, Austria, Finland and Sweden became members in 1995, with their accession probably influencing the operation of all major EU institutions. Not least relevant, these countries were all relatively green and concerned about air pollution. Moreover, interesting procedural changes took place, with the 1992 Maastricht Treaty paving the way for a strengthened decision-making role for the comparatively green European Parliament. Both these developments may have contributed to a decision-making context more sympathetic to initiatives to strengthen air pollution policies from the mid-1990s onwards.

The third intention is to shed light upon several interesting questions related to the relationship between the EU and CLRTAP. First, when directly comparing the emission ceilings in the CLRTAP Protocol and the parallel EU NEC Directive, the EU ceilings are overall somewhat more ambitious. As the problems addressed are fairly similar, could it be that this difference stems from institutional contexts which differ in a number of ways? And given the wide-spread perception of the EU as a considerably stronger institution than traditional regimes, why are the differences in strength still so moderate? Moreover, although the institutions and policies have developed independently enough to warrant a comparison, there are also interesting *interplay* effects which require a closer study. Not least is this related to the developing similarity in the policy-making approach within the two contexts, with a common focus upon critical loads and emission ceilings. As the EU has traditionally favoured technology standards, how has this 'parallelism' come about?

The fourth and final aim of the book is to discuss important prospects ahead. Although this book is primarily focused on the *making* of international policies, the 'proof of the pudding' lies in effective and successful national implementation. What are the general prospects for successful implementation in key-emission countries such as the UK, Germany and France? Moreover, an important EU coordinating effort of air pollution policy-making was launched in May 2001, under the banner of 'Clean Air for Europe' (CAFE). This Programme was launched in May 2001, signalling EU policy dynamism. Add to this that the already institutionally stronger EU is expanding eastwards and gradually diminishing the differences in membership between the two institutions. In light of all this, will there be any remaining rationale for upholding the CLRTAP forum and room for continuing the constructive interplay witnessed between the two institutions in the 1990s?

These questions will be developed and addressed in the following manner in the following seven chapters. Chapter Two, *Studying European Air Pollution Politics: The Analytical Lenses*, will provide the analytical and methodological backbone of the study.

Chapter Three is titled *Background and baseline: main European air pollution processes in the 1980s.* The more specific 1980s processes which will be given most attention are, within CLRTAP, the negotiations on a nitrogen oxides (NO_x) protocol which took place from 1985 to 1988. Within the EU, the parallel negotiations on directives addressing emissions from large combustion plants (LCPs) and motor vehicles, which took place between 1984 and 1989/90, will be summed up.

The focused development in the 1990s will then be documented and discussed in chapters four and five. Chapter Four will introduce and discuss *CLRTAP air pollution politics in the 1990s: Negotiating the 1999 Gothenburg Protocol.* The negotiation process on a multi-pollutant/multi-effects protocol started in 1994, developing into a fascinating and complex interplay between scientists and policy-makers in the period up to the end of 1998. The final negotiation rounds took place in 1999 and the protocol was adopted in Gothenburg in the beginning of December 1999.

Chapter Five will zoom in on *How the EU took up the challenge of acidification and smog in the 1990s: The Acidification Strategy and NEC Directive.* Work on an Acidification Strategy was started in 1995. Over time, this work was broadened into an Acidification and Ozone Strategy and given regulatory flesh and blood through a proposal for a National Emissions Ceilings (NEC) Directive, covering the same four pollutants as the Gothenburg Protocol. The Council of Ministers agreed upon a common position in June 2000 and the Directive was finally adopted in September 2001.

Chapter Six will then turn to *Comparing the EU and CLRTAP: Explaining policy differences – and why they are so small.* Building upon the separate histories and case studies carried out in the previous chapters, this chapter seeks to shed light upon the difference in policy strength between the two contexts.

Chapter Seven will then address the important question of prospects for successful implementation. *'Will high hopes in Brussels and Geneva be dashed in London?'* In addition to the UK, the two other key-emission countries of Germany and France are singled out for special attention.

The concluding Chapter Eight will then be *Summing up and looking ahead,* discussing main findings and prospects for institutional interplay.

Notes

[1]   See UN/ECE Press Release ECE/ENV/99/11, 24 November 1999. As several of these substances are also greenhouse gases, the protocol also represented a little-noted step forward for the slow and painful international process of developing an effective response to the threat of global climate change.

2   Central references here are Lammers (1988), Boehmer-Christiansen and Skea (1991); Boehmer-Christiansen and Weidner (1995); and Liefferink (1996).

3   According to Sbragia in Wallace and Wallace (2000:294), 'the impact of German unification, the persistent problem of unemployment, and the very difficult choices implied by stringent environmental restrictions, at a time of increased global competition, all served to lower environmental protection on the EU's political agenda'.

Chapter 2

Studying European Air Pollution Politics
The Conceptual Lenses

Introduction

This chapter prepares the ground for the empirical investigation of the main questions raised in this study. First, a general discussion of the comparability of the EU and CLRTAP contexts is made. Is this a case of incomparable 'apples and oranges'?. This is followed by an analysis of the operationalisation and measuring of the main dependent variable in the study, namely 'policy strength'. The important issue of explaining policy strength is then taken up. After introducing 'institutionally flavoured inter-governmentalism' as the theoretical cornerstone of the study, the institutional issues covering changes in membership and decision-making procedures will be discussed, and some selected EU, CLRTAP and comparative propositions will be formulated. Thereafter, the important issue of rival explanations is taken up and some key rival propositions are introduced, along with a further clarification of the issue of case selection. The chapter concludes with a summary of the main perspectives of the study in the form of two simple models; one pertaining to the development of policy strength within the two contexts over time, and one to the 'synchronic' comparison of the two contexts.

'Apples and Oranges'? Comparisons within and between the EU and CLRTAP

A central methodological tool utilised in this study is diachronic and synchronic comparison. Although comparing air pollution policy-making *within* the EU and CLRTAP over time is in no way unproblematic, it has the distinct advantage of at least comparing different versions of the same 'creature', operating within roughly the same context. It can be assumed that many factors change only slightly over time, and in order to study the

specific impact of institutional changes, this facilitates the general challenge of holding control variables constant. However, as pointed out in
Chapter One, it is also interesting to compare EU and CLRTAP air pollution policy-making more directly and synchronically. First, EU's NEC
Directive and CLRTAP's Gothenburg Protocol develop country-specific
emission ceilings linked to the same four pollutants. Moreover, as the problems addressed by both institutions are quite similar and overlapping, this
provides a good opportunity to scrutinise the impact of several, at least
formal, institutional differences between the EU and international environmental regimes such as CLRTAP. Back in 1983, Wetstone and Rosencrantz
predicted that the EU was the organisation most likely to succeed in dealing
with Europe's transboundary air pollution problems.[4] This claim is echoed
much more recently by McCormick (1997) where he states that '[the EU]
has legislative tools and powers of persuasion that allow it to compel its
members to reach agreement in a manner that is far beyond the scope and
powers of a purely international organization such as the ECE'
(McCormick 1997:96). How do such general claims stand up in more elaborated and specific comparisons?

However, some would undoubtedly ask whether it is really meaningful to compare EU air pollution policy-making and policies with that of
within CLRTAP. Is this not a case of comparing apples with oranges? In
one sense these institutions are, of course, quite different in nature.
CLRTAP was established and has functioned as a 'classic' international
environmental regime, focusing on one specific and transboundary environmental problem (air pollution), within a traditional inter-state cooperative
context.[5] As in most international environmental cooperation, the main
regulatory instrument has been the adoption of protocols, subject to national ratification processes and subsequent (and often several years later) entry
into force.[6]

By contrast, the EU started as an European *Economic* Community
back in 1957, and the environment was not added to the agenda before the
1970s.[7] Hence, environmental policy-making in the EU, including air pollution, was initially based upon and still is significantly influenced by trade
harmonisation and internal market concerns. For instance, Duncan
Liefferink (1996:189) has put forward the proposition that 'EC environmental policy making is essentially about economics'.[8] Moreover, air
pollution is only one of a number of environmental problems addressed by
the EU. Further, as described in more detail below, EU institutions and
decision-making procedures have developed into a complex institutional
machinery, acquiring supra-national traits along the way. Finally, EU
'environmental' regulations take many forms, with directives as the main

instrument preferred so far. Directives are binding as to the results to be achieved, but leave to the Member States the choice of form and methods.[9] They are not subject to ensuing national ratification processes, but require a process of transposition into national law and policy before practical implementation can commence.

However, it can still be argued that there is a fundamental commonality which warrants comparative efforts. Seen from the perspective of any EU member state, EU environmental directives and CLRTAP are both international commitments requiring domestic attention and follow-up. Moreover, in this specific case the commonality is particularly striking, as the policies developed within both contexts are structured around emission ceilings targeting the same four substances. Hence, at the level of policies, it makes sense to talk about both EU directives and CLRTAP protocols as 'different sorts of apples'. Then there are clearly fundamental differences between the institutions EU and CLRTAP as such; the practical results of such differences being very interesting to scrutinise further. As pinpointed by Wallace and Wallace (2000:40): 'In most areas there is competition between the EU and other possible arenas'.

The Issue of Policy Strength: Political 'Bite' and Implications for the Environment

We can now turn the focus of our attention to the main dependent variable in this study, namely the concept of policy strength. There are several reasons why this concept is the predominant object in the study. First, at the time of writing the main processes under scrutiny have only recently been concluded, and little or no implementation has so far taken place. Second, and no less important, the strength of policies has important environmental problem-solving implications. Agreeing on policies which are in accordance with critical limits in the environment comes close to being a necessary condition for successful problem solving. However, achieving such strength cannot be seen as a sufficient condition for problem solving, as the crucially important and difficult phase of implementation can 'dash the high hopes in Brussels and Geneva' – to borrow a famous paraphrase.[10] Moreover, as we will return to, achieving strong policies by, for instance, voting down laggards may mean trouble in the implementation phase. Hence, important implementation perspectives need to be kept in mind also in a study of policy strength. The prospects for successful implementation will be discussed further in Chapter Seven.

How, then, measure policy strength? According to Underdal (1999:4), 'a "strong" regime is one whose substantive norms, rules and regulations significantly constrain the range of behaviour that qualifies as legal or appropriate'.[11] Hence, EU and CLRTAP policies must have national and sub-national behavioural 'bite' in order to reduce emissions and ultimately contribute to environmental problem-solving. The behavioural bite of policies can be measured by at least three central dimensions: legal bindingness, specificity, and ambitiousness.[12]

Turning first to the dimension of *bindingness*, and 'whether the commitments are binding within the framework of international law' (Skjærseth 1998:67), it can generally be argued that moving from political declarations of intent to legally binding instruments 'constrain the behaviour that qualifies as legal', and hence increases policy strength. However, evidence from international environmental politics indicates that the prospects in terms of implementation are much more open, and probably dependent upon several other issue-specific and organisational factors.[13]

Comparing the EU and CLRTAP, it is clear that there are formal differences in the way decisions are framed. As noted above, within the EU the use of directives is most common in the field of environment. Within CLRTAP, the establishment of protocols is the standard regulatory form. It is possible to argue that an EU directive is a politically stronger legal instrument than a regime protocol. This is primarily due to the fact that EU directives are directly enforceable on the Member States once they are adopted, and there is also the existence of the European Court of Justice as an EU institutional 'stick' and enforcer, with no direct counterpart in international regimes.[14] However, the impression of lacklustre EU follow-up and an 'implementation gap' indicates that the political 'weight' of EU directives may be not so different in practice from the case of regime protocols.[15]

With regard to *specificity* and the problem of vague obligations and the lack of 'operationality' (Young 1979:99), such vagueness may contribute to discretion due to interpretation problems; it tends to make other states' actions less predictable and makes verification of behavioural change more problematic.[16] In the environmental policy context, a central device for strengthening specificity is to introduce numerical targets and timetables. Hence, it can generally be argued that moving from less specific – for instance, a general ambition to reduce emissions sometime in the future – to more specific, quantified and time-limited regulations, constrains the range of behaviour that qualifies as legal or appropriate, and increases policy strength. Prospects in terms of implementation are more clear-cut than in the case of legal bindingness. Increased specificity and transparency make implementation more meaningful and easier for all parties involved to monitor. However, the relationship between bindingness and specificity may be somewhat inverse. Increasing the dimension of specificity, and hence providing treaty watchdogs with clearer policy benchmarks by which to monitor performance, may weaken the involved parties' willingness to accept legally binding obligations.

The central dimension of *ambitiousness* in this context will primarily refer to the level of standards and the 'amount' of behavioural change required. All other factors being equal, a policy calling for a 50 percent cut in emissions clearly constrains the range of behaviour that qualifies as appropriate, more so than a call for a 25 percent cut in emissions. Again, implementation prospects may be somewhat inverse. Increasing policy ambitiousness may mean decreasing possibilities for effective implementation. In principle, the issue of 'ambitiousness' can also include the very choice of policy approach. For instance, the broadening of policy scope to include substances and activities not previously targeted can be seen as a part of – and as an expression of – the increase in policy strength. However, one should be careful in this regard, given the weight given in this study to the broadening of scope and the development of the multi-pollutant and multi-effects approach as an *explanatory* perspective.

Policy ambitiousness is closely related to environmental problem-solving capability, but these concepts are not the same. Even if ambitiousness increases considerably, it may still be far from enough to ensure effective problem-solving 'on the ground'. Hence, we must find a way to measure *the rough distance and thereby 'match' between regulatory development and environmental challenges.* Due to developments in the thinking about 'critical loads' in the environment in the recent years, this matching exercise has become easier.[17] A critical load can be defined as 'the maximum amount of acid deposition that an ecosystem can experience without suffering adverse effects in the long run' (Tuinstra, Hordijk and Ammann 1999:36). The development of this issue over time can be illustrated nicely by the two CLRTAP sulphur dioxide protocols. With regard to the 30 percent reduction agreed to in the 1985 protocol, although both negotiators and observers had a clear feeling that this was 'not enough', the gap at the time was hard to pin down precisely. By comparison, in the follow-up sulphur negotiations at the beginning of the 1990s, developments in the thinking about critical loads allowed a much more precise and explicit measurement of the remaining short-comings of the 1994 Oslo Protocol.[18]

In summary, policy strength will in this study be measured both according to a political and an environmental perspective. The political perspective centres on the three concepts of bindingness, specificity, and (especially) ambitiousness – and the related implications in terms of domestic political bite. The environmental perspective centres on the distance and match between such political strength and critical loads in the environment.

Explaining Policy Strength: Approach and Focused Issues

Introducing 'Institutionally Flavoured Intergovernmentalism'

According to analysts such as Golub (1996), in spite of changes in the wake of the Single European Act, 'power ultimately lies with the national representatives in the Council of Ministers' (p.329).[19] Hence, adopting a fundamental 'intergovernmental' explanatory fundament for this study, in the most simple and direct sense, policy strength appears as the outcome of a final aggregation of preferences in the EU Council of Ministers or the CLRTAP Executive Body.[20] So this constellation and aggregation of interests and preferences can hence be seen as a central *intermediate* variable in this study; the 'medium' and mechanism around which the propositions have to revolve.

In principle, an increase in strength may either have as its immediate cause a more benign constellation of preferences, or a more powerful aggregation of preferences – or both. Hence, there are two principal 'routes' to a strengthening of policies. Given that especially the latter route is a procedural and institutional route, the explanatory approach adopted in this study is labelled 'institutionally flavoured intergovernmentalism'.[21] This is fitting also because institutional matters will be given specific attention in this study, due to interesting and striking changes having taken place within the EU and CLRTAP contexts in the last ten years. It is to these institutional matters we will now turn.

The Focused Institutional Issues: Changes in Membership and Decision-making Procedures

There are certainly good reasons why the role and importance of institutional factors will be focused in order to account both for outcomes within the different contexts and for differences in policy strength between the two contexts. As indicated in Chapter One, in the period under scrutiny here, other factors such as the public concern about the environment have developed in a way that does not point towards new policy development and increased policy strength. Moreover, the fact that the two contexts fundamentally address the same problems does little, at least at a first glance, to explain why the EU has developed a stronger policy. However, in terms of institutional changes and differences, there are a number of issues to focus upon. These range from simple differences in membership within the EU compared with CLRTAP, to fundamental differences in the policy scope and hence the very logic of the two institutions.

   In selecting the institutional dimensions for more specific detailed scrutiny in this context four main criteria have been utilised: first, the dimensions must figure in the theoretical literature as central institutional facets; second, they must link up to interesting, general institutional developments actually having taken place within the two contexts; third, they must be general enough to work within these somewhat differing contexts; and, fourth, they must not be too many, in order to reduce the ever-present problem of 'too many variables and too few cases' as much as possible.

   Against this background, the issues of membership and decision-making procedures have been chosen. First, both these issues are central characteristics defining the very nature of institutions.[22] Just consider the implications of important countries within the earlier Warsaw Pact joining the North Atlantic Treaty Organization in the 1990s, and the heated discussions over the possible extension of majority voting in connection with the December 2000 EU Nice summit.[23] Moreover, as pinpointed in the previous section, the procedural aspects shape one of the two important 'routes' to increasing policy strength. In addition, the dimensions are general enough to work within both contexts, and the number of two is not very high. Last, but not least, they clearly link up interesting developments which have actually taken place within both contexts in the course of the 1990s. These will be further elaborated in the following sections.

   Finally, policy-making within the two contexts has unfolded in a quite parallel way; possibly more closely intertwined than ever. Hence, in addition to institutional changes having taken place within the EU and CLRTAP, the very relationship between the two institutions has been changing. So there is a need to add specific institutional interplay propositions to the analytical point of departure.

The EU: Developments in Terms of Membership, Decision-making Procedures and Interplay with CLRTAP

The Membership Issue: The 1995 Accession and Possible Effects Within the Central EU Decision-making Bodies

The accession of Austria, Finland, and Sweden in 1995 generally meant a strengthening of the 'rich and green' group within the EU. As pinpointed by Andersen and Liefferink (1997:1), together with the traditional EU environmental 'pioneers' of Germany, the Netherlands and Denmark, these six countries acting together can form a blocking minority in the Council.[24] More specifically, in terms of air pollution it is well known that the Scandinavian countries, and especially Sweden, have long been affected by long-range transboundary air pollution and have given this issue high priority.[25] Moreover, although little documented so far, it is reasonable to assume that this accession of new Member States has influenced the composition, staffing and quite probably functioning of all the major EU institutions.[26] In the (environmental) policy-making context, the changes in the composition and functioning of three main EU institutions in particular stand out as important to scrutinise: the Commission, the European Parliament (hereafter: the Parliament), and the Council of Ministers (hereafter: the Council). Let us address these bodies in turn.

The general functioning of the Commission and its Environment Directorate (DG XI/DG ENV) is well-described elsewhere.[27] In essence, the main role of the Commission within the EU system is agenda-setting and policy-initiating, but the Commission also plays a central role in the supervision of the follow-up of EU legislation. In relation to these roles and tasks, the Commission has generally been characterised as a small organisation, with a permanent and temporary staff of under 20,000. There are 23 General Directorates (DGs), with DG ENV as particularly interesting in the environmental policy-making context. Compared to other Directorates, DG ENV has been among the smaller. The staff increased from 230 in 1987 to 430 in 1992, and the number in 1996 stood at 478.[28] The 1995 accession further changed and increased the staffing of all Directorates in the Commission. However, in terms of possible greening effects related to the accession of new Member States, the issue is somewhat ambiguous – especially compared with a fundamentally national and 'politicised' body as the Council, but also to some extent, the Parliament.

On the one hand, although staffed by bureaucrats and experts from the various Member States, the Commission is not formally a body composed of 'national' representatives. For instance, the Commissioners take

an oath to act in the 'European interest' and 'neither seek or take instruc-
tions from any government'.[29] On the other hand there are in practice
clearly national interests and priorities involved, both in terms of allocation
of Commissioners and the staffing of the DGs. For instance, with regard to
the latter, Wurzel (1999:126) maintains: 'The parachuting in of national
civil servants to strategic positions within the Commission is a well known
fact'. There has been a substantial use of temporary, seconded national
experts in DG ENV policy-making in the 1990s, and a figure close to 50
percent of the total staff has been indicated.[30] Hence, the pathways for
influence in accordance with special member state priorities are clearly
there. So, although somewhat qualified, it is not totally wrong to look for
greening effects of the 1995 accession also within the Commission,
contributing to increased policy strength in the field of air pollution.

As in the case of the Commission and DG ENV, the general policy-
making role and functioning of the Parliament is very well described and
analysed elsewhere.[31] In terms of composition of the EP, the accession of
Austria, Finland, and Sweden in 1995 has had clear effects – although the
Parliament is not formally organised according to nationality. Before the
1995 accession, the Parliament was composed of 518 representatives. The
accession increased the number to 626 representatives. Sweden has 22
representatives, Finland has 16 and Austria has 21.

This process may have greened the Parliament in several ways: first,
as was indicated in the previous section, the 1995 accession countries are
'rich and green', and comparatively quite concerned about air pollution.
Hence, representatives from all political parties from these countries may
be assumed to give comparatively high priority to environmental issues,
including air pollution.

Second, although the 1994 Parliamentary election meant a general
weakening of the Greens,[32] the three new countries provided the Greens
with six additional representatives.[33]

Third, in terms of strategic positions within the Parliament, it is
generally acknowledged that the positions of Committee Chairs and
Rapporteur (for specific policy-making processes and directives) are the
most important. The Parliament is organised into 17 committees, and the
Environment Committee has become one of the largest (around 60
members).[34] Given that the Chairs do not change that often (as for instance
Ken Collins chaired the Environment Committee for 15 years), the position
of Rapporteur is more within reach for policy entrepreneurs. The
Rapporteur prepares initial discussions, presents draft texts and reports, and
communicates with the Commission and the Council.[35] According to
Wurzel (1999:141), 'the Rapporteur is very important because he/she can

give a report a certain spin which may be difficult to change during the debate in the Environmental Committee and the Plenary Sessions'. Given the environmental policy interests of the 1995 accession countries, it would not be unnatural if representatives from these countries sought and acquired rapporteur positions in the air pollution processes.[36]

Turning finally to the Council, as the logic and implications of the 1995 accession are so tightly interwoven with procedural matters and developments, it makes sense to present the broader picture with regard to developments here. In terms of procedural development, the increasing room for majority voting is an obvious focal point.[37] Decision-making procedures requiring unanimity mean that a single environmental laggard may block the adoption of more ambitious environmental policies at the last minute of the decision-making process.

The introduction of majority voting means that the laggard has to look around for allies earlier in the decision-making process in order to form a blocking minority. Although 'environmental' majority voting in the Council of Ministers was introduced in connection with the Single European Act in 1987, it was considerably extended in the 1992 Maastricht Treaty and somewhat further extended in the 1997 Amsterdam Treaty. In terms of votes, before 1995 there was a total of 76 votes in the Council. The four key EU countries France, Italy, West Germany and the UK all had 10 votes each. A qualified majority meant at least 54 of the 76 available votes. In order to form a blocking minority of 23, a key environmental policy hesitant in the 1980s such as the UK required at least two allies.[38]

After 1995, a qualified majority is at least 62 votes out of a total of 87, and the threshold for a blocking minority has been raised to 26.[39] With regard to the 1995 accession countries, Austria and Sweden were each given four votes, and Finland was given three. Compared to the effects of the procedural changes, the addition of eleven votes seems a quite modest change in the overall operation of the Council. However, given the policy profile of these countries, it has generally increased the size of the 'rich-and-green' group in the Council. Moreover, according to Katharina Holzinger (1997:72), before the 1995 accession, the green front-runners (i.e. Germany, the Netherlands and Denmark) did not have enough votes to achieve a blocking minority (23 votes), and in no case were these states necessary for the formation of a winning coalition.[40] After the enlargement, power became distributed far more equally among the three groups of frontrunners, hesitants and in-betweens.[41] This leads Holzinger to maintain that '…in the eyes of the three original frontrunner states…the newcomers must be very welcome to the EU. With respect to environmental decision-making, their accession greatly improves the situation in the Council of

Ministers. Therefore it can be presumed that the environmental policy of the EU will become more progressive in the future than in the past' (ibid:80).

Hence, in sum, as the first proposition for further scrutiny it can generally be suggested that *the 1995 accession of a group of 'rich and green' new Member States specifically concerned about air pollution, has greened the staffing of both the Environment Directorate and other Directorates within the Commission, and also the composition of the Parliament and the Council – subsequently and together leading to a more benign constellation of preferences in the Council and ultimately increasing EU air pollution regulatory strength.*

Changing Decision-making Procedures: Increased Majority Voting in the Council and a More Prominent Role for the Parliament

In essence, up until the 1987 Single European Act (SEA), there was no specific 'environmental' decision-making within the EU. Given the uncertainty about the legal basis, environmental directives in the pre-1987 period were primarily based on generally formulated Common Market Articles requiring unanimity. The Parliament was routinely generally consulted in the course of policy-making. Then in the 1987 SEA, which contained a separate, specific environmental section (Articles 130r, s and t), several interesting changes were introduced. First, it was explicitly opened up for the limited use of qualified majority decisions for 'environmental' policy-making related to matters affecting the establishment of the internal market, as in the case of product standards (Article 100a). Moreover, in cases of votes taken in the Council by a qualified majority, a cooperation procedure with a specific 'second reading' by the Parliament was introduced. Given the developing green profile of the Parliament compared to other EU bodies in the 1980s, this was potentially important in the context of environmental acts based on Article 100a.

In the 1990s, and cutting a much longer story short, the Maastricht Treaty (in effect from November 1993) broadened the scope for qualified majority voting considerably, making it the standard procedure, with a few important exceptions.[42] Moreover, the potential for more frequent use of the cooperation procedure and the introduction of a new co-decision procedure increased the potential influence of the Parliament further by opening up for several rounds and readings by the Council and the Parliament. If the Council and the Parliament continued to disagree after the second reading, then a Conciliation Committee (with equal Parliament and Council representation) was instituted as a final mechanism to reach agreement.

The 1997 Amsterdam Treaty then broadened the application of the co-decision procedure also to Directives adopted on the basis of the 'environmental' paragraph 130s, hence increasing the decision-making role of the Parliament further. Keeping in mind the comparatively green profile of the Parliament in relation to other EU bodies,[43] it is clearly possible that this development has also influenced the course of specific air pollution policy processes focused upon in this context.

So what about the increased formal opportunities to use majority voting in the Council? Does this development imply a greening effect in itself? Not necessarily. As indicated in the previous section, going from consensus to majority voting certainly changes the logic of the decision-making game, and it surely also increases the very aggregation capacity of the decision-making system in question. But the effect in terms of the 'political colours' of the outcomes is entirely dependent upon the positions and preferences of the group members.

However, it is still clear that the position of the single, environmental laggard became more complicated after 1987. Moreover, a more indirect greening effect may also be envisaged, as the increased use of majority voting has automatically put the Parliament in a more prominent decision-making position, through the cooperation and co-decision procedures.[44] Hence, Wurzel (1999:141, 301) states that 'there can be little doubt that the EP's influence has increased at the expense of the Commission' and developments in the 1990s indicate that it 'no longer relies merely on a (negative) veto but has developed into a co-legislator'.[45]

Moreover, the increased room for majority voting means that, under certain conditions, the Commission and the Parliament working in tandem can exert considerable pressure on the Council.[46] If the Council's initial decision had led to critical amendments from the Parliament and subsequently a strengthened proposal from the Commission, the Council can only make unanimous decisions in the next round. Hence, the outcome may be that the Council has to choose between accepting a strengthened Directive or having no Directive at all.[47] In addition to this, in the cases where the Council and the Parliament continue to disagree after a second reading, there is the establishment of a Conciliation Committee (with equal representation from the Parliament and the Council) as a specific instrument. Although allegedly used sparingly hitherto, as an instrument the Conciliation Committee has also contributed to a changed inter-institutional balance, forcing the Council to accept compromises, while sidelining the Commission.[48]

In sum, there seem to be several reasons why it is interesting to scrutinise the following propositions further; examining first the possible effects of increased majority voting: *The 1995 accession cannot by itself explain regulatory strengthening. An increased possibility for majority-voting in the Council has to be brought into the picture. Majority-voting has meant a more 'powerful' aggregation of preferences and has given the 1995 enlargement a more decisive effect in the Council proceedings; ultimately leading to increasing regulatory strength.*

The third proposition in this study helps us to keep in mind the increasing role of the comparatively green Parliament in EU decision-making: *Other procedural changes are the ultimate cause of regulatory changes. A more prominent role for the Parliament in decision-making has more generally contributed to a greening of preferences in the Council, and especially the final round of conciliation has forced the Council to move in a policy strengthening direction.*

A Closer Interplay with CLRTAP Regulatory Development in the 1990s ?

In dealing with (transboundary) air pollution, the EU certainly does not operate in an organisational vacuum. From its establishment in 1979, policy development within the LRTAP Convention has stimulated air pollution policy-making in the EU; forming a benchmark to which EU policy entrepreneurs have been able to latch on to. However, in the 1980s CLRTAP was the clear forerunner and the interplay with EU policy-making was limited (as further elaborated in Chapter Three).

As will be further elaborated in Chapter Four, there is no doubt that CLRTAP regulatory development in the 1990s has been formidable. Starting in 1991 with a protocol on volatile organic compounds (VOCs), a second protocol on SO_2 was adopted in 1994. From the mid 1990s, processes on three new protocols were in fact on-going: on heavy metals; persistent organic pollutants (POPs); and not least a multi-pollutant protocol targeting the four substances NO_x, VOCs, SO_2 and ammonia (NH_3), and the three effects of acidification, tropospheric ozone formation and eutrophication. As will be further elaborated below, the multi-pollutant approach has been underpinned by a significant knowledge-improvement effort. Hence, it is possible that the development of EU air pollution policy in the 1990s has been positively and increasingly influenced by a partly parallel development of policies within CLRTAP – with EU policy entrepreneurs using policy development and knowledge improvement within CLRTAP as regulatory benchmarks and stimulants within the EU context.

The following proposition can act as a guide in the scrutiny of CLRTAP influence on EU policy-making: *The substantial knowledge improvement and policy development in the 1990s within the CLRTAP context has functioned as a regulatory inspiration and stimulant, strengthening the position of EU policy entrepreneurs in the field of air pollution, leading to a more benign constellation of preferences and ultimately increasing regulatory strength.*

CLRTAP: Developments in Terms of Membership, Decision-making Procedures and External Institutional Influences

Have Changes in the East-West Relationship had Positive Institutional and Policy Effects within CLRTAP ?

Within the CLRTAP context, an important formal change in the 1990s has been the break-up of the Soviet Union and the participation of a new group of Eastern countries. Has this change influenced the functioning of CLRTAP as an institution and CLRTAP decision-making in the 1990s? If so, has it led to measurable effects in terms of more progressive positions being taken by these countries this time around, compared to the negotiations in the 1980s?

It is clear that Russia and the new Eastern states are generally more open and democratic societies than the cold-war Soviet empire. Hence, this has clearly made CLRTAP parties overall more homogenous. Moreover, the changed East-West relationship has possibly led to more 'relaxed' policy-making, with an increased ability to push reluctants harder within the fundamental consensual CLRTAP decision-making context.[49] In addition, the break-up of the former Soviet bloc means that these countries have become much more free to adopt independent positions, opening up new possibilities for issue-specific East-West coalition building. On top of this, it is also possible that the prospects with regard to EU enlargement and the accession of several East European states may have contributed to more constructive and progressive Eastern positions within the CLRTAP context. Taken together, it is thinkable that all of these institutionally flavoured developments may have led to a greening of Eastern positions in negotiations under CLRTAP.

Hence, guiding this part of the analysis, the following proposition can be formulated: *The break-up of the old Soviet bloc and the changes in Eastern Europe have made CLRTAP parties more homogenous and led to more open and constructive CLRTAP decision-making. Combined with the 'pulling effect' of the EU enlargement process, this has contributed to a greening of the Eastern countries' positions in the negotiations and subsequently led to increasing CLRTAP regulatory strength.*

Decision-making Changes and the Development of a Multi-pollutant Approach: Facilitating Constructive Linkages or Slowing Things Down ?

As will be further described in Chapter Three, the NO_x process in the 1980s was underpinned by a considerable knowledge-improvement process. Still, the development of a multi-pollutant and multi-effects approach in the 1990s marks a substantial further development of the science-politics interface and the very decision-making approach. As opposed to earlier CLRTAP processes targeting one substance (e.g. sulphur dioxide) and one main environmental effect (e.g. acidification) at the time, the 'multi approach' targets several substances (such as nitrogen oxides, volatile organic compounds, sulphur dioxide, and ammonia), and several effects (such as acidification, tropospheric ozone formation and eutrophication).

How did this approach come about? From the late 1980s on, knowledge of the interplay of a variety of substances and several environmental effects was improving, and hence also the intellectual capacity to grasp this interplay was growing. Important tools were the concept of 'critical loads'[50] and the RAINS (Regional Air Pollution Information and Simulation) model. This model had been developed by The International Institute for Applied Systems Analysis (IIASA) from the late 1980s and tentatively utilised in the negotiations leading up to the 1994 Sulphur Protocol.

In terms of more specific institutional effects, it is reasonable to assume that such a comprehensive approach can both facilitate and complicate positions and negotiations.[51] Facilitating effects can stem from possibilities of linkage between positions and the establishment of integrative package-deals. If states offer higher emission reductions and lower ceilings on emissions of particular transboundary importance, they can be 'rewarded' by being allowed higher ceilings in relation to other substances. Conversely, complicating effects can arise from the resulting complexity related to such a comprehensive approach. Conflicts of interest and lacking progress on one issue can easily stall the very progress of the negotiations. However, within the context of shedding light on the increase in policy strength, it is reasonable to highlight the facilitating and positive institutional effects related to the multi-pollutant approach.

Hence, the following proposition can be formulated: *The development of a multi-pollutant approach in the 1990s has meant an increasing ability to address several pollutants together and develop broader, integrative policy packages, leading to a more benign constellation of preferences and ultimately increasing CLRTAP policy strength.*

Has Policy Development Within the EU Influenced CLRTAP ?

As indicated, development of the CLRTAP regime in the 1980s was increasingly supplemented with policy development within the EU context. For instance, with processes starting in 1983/84, the Large Combustion Plant (LCP) Directive was adopted in 1988 and important car emissions directives were adopted in 1988 and 1989.[52] However, as will be further elaborated in Chapter Five, EU air pollution policies have developed substantially in the 1990s. The EU has, for instance, developed new vehicle emissions regulations through an innovative Auto-Oil programme. Moreover, the LCP Directive has been renegotiated and an ambitious Acidification and Ozone Strategy has been produced, resulting in a proposal for a National Emissions Ceilings (NEC) directive. Hence, given that the EU and its members constitute a central part of CLRTAP's membership, it is very well possible that the development of CLRTAP regulatory strength in the 1990s has been positively influenced by the parallel development of more ambitious positions and policies within the EU.

The following proposition can act as a guide in the scrutiny of EU influence on CLRTAP policy-making: *The development in the 1990s of parallel and more ambitious air pollution policies within the EU context has led to more progressive positions being taken by EU members within the CLRTAP context and hence has contributed to increasing CLRTAP policy strength.*

Why is Policy Stronger Within the EU than Within CLRTAP? Institutional Propositions

Let us then turn to the more specific and direct 'synchronic' comparison of policy strength within the EU and CLRTAP, and possible institutional differences which may account for differences in such strength. As indicated in Chapter One, it can quite safely be concluded that policy strength within the EU is higher than within CLRTAP. In order to shed light upon this difference, the central issues of membership scope and decision-making procedures and capacity will again be used as central organising devices.

Membership Scope: Is an Expanding EU Still a Much More 'Handy'
Institution than CLRTAP ?

In a comparative perspective, the difference in membership scope is an
obvious candidate for accounting for differences in policy strength. Forty-
six parties as well as the EU have now joined CLRTAP, and the number of
parties participating in the CLRTAP negotiations, for instance on the POPs
protocol, was more than 30; in other words, more than double the number
of EU countries. Moreover, not only is the number of state actors much
larger within CLRTAP, but also the heterogeneity of actors is much more
striking in this context. First, this is related to the Eastern European participation in CLRTAP. In addition to aspiring EU member countries like
Hungary, the Czech Republic and Poland, large former republics within the
Soviet Union like Ukraine and not least Russia, take part in cooperation
within CLRTAP. The Russian territory is so large that in several protocols
the Soviets/Russians have gotten acceptance for exempting part of the
territory from the agreed targets, due to the argument that these (Eastern)
parts do not contribute to transboundary air pollution.

A second membership dimension which makes CLRTAP special is
the Northern American participation, i.e. the US and Canada. This participation is primarily related to the initial East-West confidence building
context in which the establishment of the regime took place. Hence, given
this 'contextual' motivation, and several differences between the US and
Europe in terms of regulatory philosophies and approaches, it is perhaps
not so surprising that in the issue-specific negotiation processes conducted
so far within the regime, the North American participation has had some
complicating effects.[53]

Against this background, the following proposition can be formulated: *Policy-making within the smaller and somewhat more homogenous EU*
group of countries is generally less complicated than policy-making within
the broader and more heterogeneous group of CLRTAP countries. This
difference has led to comparatively greater policy strength within the EU.

Differences in Administrative Strength: David and Goliath for Sure – but
Who is Who in Terms of Air Pollution Policy-making?

Thinking in formal terms, the David and Goliath metaphor is at first glance
clearly a fitting one. The policy-initiating and driving force within the EU
system, the Commission, is of course a totally different type of institution
than the CLRTAP Secretariat. Even if we only count the Environment
Directorate, DG ENV, its administrative capacity is around 480 employees,

compared to the CLRTAP Secretariat's 9-10 employees. However, in terms of air pollution policy-making more specifically, the comparative picture gets less clear-cut. There is only a small section within the DG ENV handling air pollution issues.[54] Still, in terms of 'systemic institutional forces' backing up decision-making processes, within the EU there is also the possibility of the green institutional forces within the EU joining forces. In addition to DG ENV, it may be assumed that at the least these forces include the Environment Committee in the Parliament. The difference in terms of budgetary resources is also, of course, quite vast.

On this background, the following proposition can be put forward: *Greater policy strength within the EU can be explained by more and stronger institutional resources and forces backing up regulatory propositions within the EU than within CLRTAP.*

Differences in Decision-making Procedures and Approaches: Majority Voting and Issue Linking

In general, the multi-institution and multi-layered EU is a much more complex and, especially in one sense, procedurally stronger institution than the more straight-forward CLRTAP international regime. As indicated, EU decisions are shaped through intricate bargaining, back-and-forth processes involving the policy-initiating Commission, the consultative Parliament, and the decision-making Council of Ministers. One of the aspects most clearly setting the EU apart from traditional international regimes is the increasing ability to make decisions by some sort of majority. In general, majority decisions increase the ability to cut through aggregation deadlocks easily caused by unanimity requirements, and hence also the ability to vote down policy laggards. If the majority of parties are green in nature, then the use of this procedure may also lead to greener outcomes than under rules of consensus. As discussed in the foregoing EU section, the 1995 accession of a group of 'rich and green' new Member States may have strengthened the general capacity to form green majorities within the EU.

Within CLRTAP, the requirement for consensus was written into the 1979 Convention.[55] This was quite in line with standard procedures in international cooperation, and politically absolutely essential both in light of the reluctant establishment of the regime and the underlying East-West confidence-building aspect. However, in practice, the requirement for consensus has been practised with some flexibility. For instance, Convention parties critical to the development of the regime in the form of the establishment of specific Protocols have chosen the exit option instead of blocking the majority's wish to develop the regime further. In a sense, such flexibility could enhance regulatory strength more within CLRTAP than the EU as there is less such 'opt-out' flexibility within the latter.[56] Hence, there are clearly several forces at play here. Still, the main task in this context is to pinpoint differences which may shed light upon higher policy strength within the EU than CLRTAP.

Thus, if we assume that in the latter part of the 1990s there has been a majority of parties positive to a strengthening of policy in this issue area within both the EU and CLRTAP contexts, then the following proposition for further scrutiny may be formulated: *A greater capacity to make decisions by majority and vote down environmental laggards within the EU than within CLRTAP has led to comparatively greater regulatory strength within the EU.*

Let us then turn to the possibilities for the constructive linking of issues. As discussed at the beginning of this chapter, the EU was established for broader economic and trade reasons, with the environment 'incidentally' added to the regulatory focus in the 1970s, and given formal legal footing first with the SEA in 1987 – in contrast to the issue-specific concern about acidification which led to the establishment of CLRTAP. In a comparative perspective, therefore, the EU covers a much broader set of issues than CLRTAP. As hinted earlier, such a broad scope may in principle imply both decision-making weaknesses and strengths.

On one hand, the 'adding on' of the environment as an issue over time indicates that economic and single market forces have been – and still to large extent are – the driving forces. Moreover, the very broadness of partly linked issues means that conflicts of interests and lacking progress on one issue can spill over and impede progress within related policy-making processes.

On the other hand, in principle, the EU's spanning of the main sectors *producing* environmental problems represents a unique opportunity for 'environmental policy integration'. More specifically, it may be envisaged that concessions that states will be willing to make within an 'environmental' policy-making process could be rewarded by concessions from other states in other environmental policy-making processes or even processes within other issue areas. Such possibilities can be assumed to be of less relevance within the more narrowly focused CLRTAP.

Hence, the following comparative proposition can be launched: *Greater capacity to put together integrative package deals within the EU than within CLRTAP has led to comparatively greater regulatory strength within the EU.*

Case Selection and the Important Issue of Rival Propositions

In order to fine-tune the rival propositions, let us first clarify the exact empirical focus of this study. Taking developments within CLRTAP as the point of departure, the process leading up to the adoption of the Gothenburg Protocol in November 1999 stands out as a natural choice. As indicated in Chapter One, this protocol has been characterised as 'the most sophisticated environmental agreement ever negotiated'. Against this background, within the EU context it becomes very natural to single out the process of developing an Acidification and Ozone Strategy and subsequently a directive on National Emission Ceilings (NECs). The NEC Directive targets the same four pollutants as the Gothenburg Protocol and roughly the same effects. A common position on this Directive was reached in the Council in June 2000.

Let us now turn to the issue of rival propositions, which deserves special attention. There is clearly a need to systematically check the institutional propositions in relation to central rival explanations. Especially within the EU context there are a number of potentially interesting and relevant developments. These range from the issue-specific public concern about air pollution in the Member States to developments in adjacent policy fields such as energy liberalisation – and ultimately to the broader EU debates in the 1990s about subsidiarity and new policy instruments.[57]

Luckily (in terms of analysis), some of these factors are quite neutral or even work in the opposite direction in relation to increasing policy strength, and can quite likely be eliminated from consideration. This is the case both with regard to processes of energy liberalisation/deregulation and the subsidiarity debate. So far, these processes seem not to have worked in favour of strengthening EU environmental policies; rather the contrary.[58] For instance, in terms of the interesting Auto-Oil I process, Collier (1997:18) maintains that 'the deregulation doctrine...has left the onus on the auto and oil industries to come up with their own reduction targets, an approach widely criticised by environmental organisations'.

Still, within both the EU and CLRTAP contexts, *other, more issue-specific policy developments* have taken place, which have potentially influenced the processes. Within the EU air pollution policy context, recent years have witnessed an interesting further development in both air quality legislation and requirements pertaining to Large Combustion Plants. Positive and policy-enhancing spill-over from these processes to the Acidification Strategy and NEC Directive process is not unlikely and should be investigated further. Such spill-over can take the form of policy goals being adopted in one context (for instance air quality goals) logically pointing to the need for stricter emissions reduction goals. But it can also take the form of integrative package deals being formed with progress in the field of emissions reduction policies becoming possible due to linkages to other processes. Also within the CLRTAP context, other policy processes have unfolded during the period in question; resulting in protocols on heavy metals and persistent organic pollutants (POPs) being established in 1998.

Hence, the first rival proposition can be formulated in the following way: *Other relevant policy developments within the EU and CLRTAP have had positive spill-over effects upon the focused policy processes, leading to more benign constellations of preferences and ultimately increasing policy strength.*

The logical main alternative perspective to the internationally focused institutional and policy development perspectives developed so far is a perspective pinpointing various *domestic developments.* This perspective highlights the possibility that a more benign constellation of preferences and increasing strength of policy have been caused by domestic developments having little or nothing to do with the activities of the international institutions. A full opening up of the 'black box' of domestic politics is beyond the scope of this study, but some important developments in key states which have changed positions and preferences over time will be summed up. Particularly the background for the movement of earlier indifferent states, and especially key laggards moving in a more green and constructive direction, will be given special attention.

Increasing public concern about air pollution is a central – and relatively easily measurable – possible driving force which will receive specific attention in this context; cf. the well-known and important 'Waldsterben' dynamic in German politics in the early 1980s.[59] There are, of course, numerous other possibilities, including economic recessions and energy switching having absolutely nothing to do with environmental politics as such.[60]

Hence, the following, second rival proposition can be formulated: *A domestically induced greening of laggards and those who are indifferent have lead to a more benign constellation of preferences and subsequently greater policy strength.*

With regard to the comparison of the EU and CLRTAP, it has been argued earlier in this chapter that the fundamental problem characteristics are quite similar, paving the way for an interesting and meaningful comparison of the institutional strengths and weaknesses of the two contexts. However, 'quite similar' in no way means *identical.* This acknowledgement provides us with the key to the main rival proposition in this context.

'Problem characteristics' can of course be defined in various ways.[61] Within the context of the RAINS (Regional Air Pollution Information and Simulation) model, which has come to underpin policy-making both in the EU and CLRTAP contexts, four main components are included: energy use and the emissions of pollutants; the costs of different options for reducing these; the geographical dispersion of those pollutants; and their environmental effects.[62] By combining the 'score' on these elements, it is possible to calculate the least expensive means of achieving a desired environmental improvement.

Given the EU and CLRTAP's different geographical coverage, it is inevitable that the scores on these four input elements will be different in the two contexts. For instance, the geographical dispersion and hence transboundary flows of pollutants are clearly different in the two contexts. Hence, it is perfectly thinkable that such differences in scores add up to a need for stronger abatement measures and lower emission ceilings in the EU context than in the CLRTAP context – in order to achieve similar environmental goals. If this is the case, then problem characteristics which at a cursory glance seem quite similar, may under closer scrutiny reveal important differences with related policy implications.

Hence, in the comparative context, the following rival proposition can be put forward: *Remaining differences in problem characteristics have led to greater policy strength within the EU than within CLRTAP.*

Winding Up: The Models Introduced

All in all, in order to understand the increase in policy strength over time within the two contexts, the thinking underlying this study is summed up on the following page in Figure 2.1.

Pondering upon Figure 2.1, some would undoubtedly pinpoint the possibility – and indeed probability – that both the more 'fundamental' institutional changes and the 'domestic developments' have influenced the 'other relevant policy developments'. This is certainly a relevant point. But a model should be as parsimonous as possible at the outset, and the issue of interplay effects will be taken up again in the final chapter.

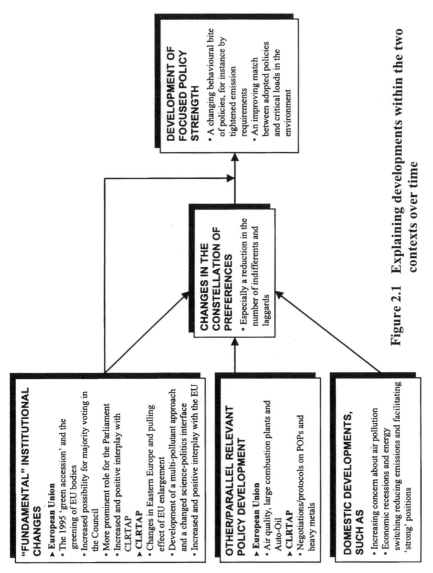

Figure 2.1   Explaining developments within the two contexts over time

In the comparison of the EU and CLRTAP, and the discussion of the background for the differing policy strength within the two contexts, the following simple model will be utilised:

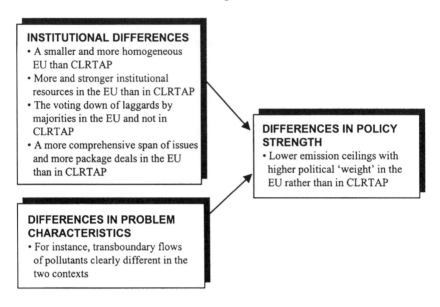

Figure 2.2   Explaining differences between the two contexts

Notes

[4]   Wetstone and Rosencrantz (1983:149).
[5]   I will take as my point of departure the regime definition suggested by Levy, Young and Zürn (1994:6): international social institutions consisting of agreed principles, norms, rules, procedures and programmes that govern the interactions of actors in specific issue-areas.
[6]   The climate change context, and especially the substantial uncertainty related to US ratification of the Kyoto Protocol, shows that subsequent ratification and entry into force cannot be taken for granted in the traditional regime context. See, for example, Agrawala and Andresen (1999).
[7]   For some recent overviews of the development and main characteristics of EU environmental policy, see Weale et al. (2000) and Chapter 11 in Wallace and Wallace (2000).
[8]   This is of course a debatable proposition. See for instance Weale (1996; 1998) for nuanced discussions.
[9]   Haigh, ed. (1992/98:2.6.). Other main forms of EU regulations are Decisions (binding in entirety upon those to whom it is addressed), Regulations (directly applicable law in the Member States), Recommendations, and Opinions.
[10] This is, of course, inspired by Pressman and Wildavsky's classic 1973 implementation study, *Implementation: How Great Expectations in Washington are Dashed in Oakland.*
[11] Note that Underdal (1999:4) also refers to a procedural component of the concept. See also Nollkaemper (1993).
[12] See, for instance, Andresen, Skjærseth and Wettestad (1994) for an initial discussion of this troika of concepts.

[13] See, for instance, Skjærseth (1998) and the interplay between the legally binding OSPARCON context and the politically binding North Sea Conferences.

[14] Despite the establishment of implementation committees in the 1990s in both the ozone-layer regime and CLRTAP. See Wettestad (1999), Chapters 4 and 5. For a discussion of the EU in comparison to international environmental regimes, see Skjærseth and Wettestad (2000) and Coffey, Jordan and Wettestad (2000).

[15] For the discussion of an EU 'implementation gap', see Jordan (1998; 1999); Knill and Lenschow (2000); and Chapter Eight in Weale et al. (2000).

[16] See Skjærseth (1998:67).

[17] Although the thinking about critical loads started in the 1980s, the concept and approach has first and foremost been developed within the context of CLRTAP in the 1990s. See for instance, Kutting (1998); Van Deveer (1998); Castells (1999), Chapter Nine; and Tuinstra, Hordijk, and Ammann (1999).

[18] See, for instance, Gehring (1994); and Wettestad (2000), Chapter Five in Andresen et al. (2000).

[19] According to Weale et al. (2000:130), 'As institutions go, the Council of Ministers is clearly in a different league from both the Commission and the Parliament. It remains the most important institution in terms of the legislative process'.

[20] The debate about the merits of 'intergovernmentalism' and 'neo-realism' versus 'supra-nationalism' and 'neo-functionalism' is of course broad. For good, recent overviews, see Introduction to Part I in Weale et al. (2000), and Chapter Three in Wallace and Wallace (2000).

[21] This is in line with Kerremans (1996) who argues for a combination of 'non-institutional' and 'neo-institutional' explanations in order to understand EU decision-making. See especially pp.234–237.

[22] As noted by Underdal (2000:32), 'institutions-as-arenas can be described by answering the question: *who* are to deal with what, *how*, when and where?' (my italics)

[23] On the Nice summit and majority voting, see ENDS Report 312, January 2001, 'Treaty reform brings little change for environment', pp.42-43.

[24] After the 1995 accession, a blocking minority requires at least 26 votes, and these six countries control 29 votes. See discussion of the Council of Ministers later in this section.

[25] For instance, Kronsell (in Andersen and Liefferink 1997:65) notes that 'acidification remains the most highly prioritised area for international co-operation'.

[26] With regard to the Council of Ministers, an interesting contribution is Holzinger (1997).

[27] See especially Wurzel (1999), but also, for instance, Edwards and Spence (1997). Skjærseth and Wettestad (2000) sum up some important contributions on the functioning of the Commission and especially DG ENV.

[28] See Wurzel (ibid:124). Hence, growth in the recent decade has been characterised as 'striking' (Weale 1996:598).)

[29] Article 157 of the EC Treaty.

[30] See Wurzel (op.cit.:125).

[31] See e.g. Haigh (1992); Earnshaw and Judge (1995, 1996); Dahl and Sverdrup (1996); Weale (1996); Wurzel (1999); and Wallace and Wallace (2000).

[32] The Greens formed their own group after the 1989 Parliamentary election, consisting of 28 members. After the 1994 elections, this group numbered 23 members. See Dahl and Sverdrup (1996:7).

[33] This is based on Pariament's web pages (http://www.europarl.eu.int/).

[34] The full name is the 'Committee on the Environment, Public Health and Consumer Policy'.

[35] See Dahl and Sverdrup (1996:8).

[36] In allocating rapporteur positions, the political party groups have introduced an informal auctioning system, according to which a number of points are allocated, depending on the strength of each party group. Trading starts as soon as dossiers emerge from the Commission and important dossiers will usually go to either the Socialist or the European People's' Party because they are the largest party groupings. See Wurzel (1999:141).

[37] For interesting general contributions on this issue, see for instance Haigh (ed.) (1992); Peters (1992); Liefferink (1996); Weale (1996); Knill (1997); and Golub (1999).

[38] ENDS Report 145, February 1987:9.

[39] Haigh (ed.), Manual of Environmental Policy, 1999 update, 2.7.

[40] Weale et al (2000:95–96) have studied the support for more stringent environmental standards in the Council between 1980 and 1995 and confirm the leader/frontrunner position of a group consisting of Denmark, Germany and the Netherlands.

[41] Holzinger lists the UK, Ireland Spain, Portugal and Greece as 'hesitants', and France, Italy, Belgium and Luxembourg as 'in-betweens' (1997:70).

[42] These exceptions included provisions primarily of a fiscal nature, policies with limited transnational effects, some aspects of water pollution control, and measures affecting Member States' choices with regard to energy supply and sources. See Haigh (ed.), *Manual of Environmental Policy* (update 2000:2.2.).

[43] However, there seems to be quite general consensus both among Parliament representatives and observers on the notion that the Parliament elected in 1999 is less green than the previous Parliaments.

[44] As pinpointed by Weale et al. (2000:125): 'The importance of qualified majority voting (QMV) in the Council is high, and *more important still is the way QMV dictates interinstitutional relations, and ultimately shapes outcomes*' (my italics).

[45] On this point, see also Earnshaw and Judge (1995).

[46] For more general discussions of the alliance-building between the Commission and the Parliament, see for instance Judge (1993); Earnshaw and Judge (1996).

[47] See here Haigh (1992); Tsebelis (1994); Weale (1999).

[48] Wurzel (1999:141).

[49] See Wettestad (1999), Ch. 4, for an elaboration of this aspect of CLRTAP as an institution.

[50] A 'critical load' is defined as 'a quantitative estimate of an exposure to one or more pollutants below which significantly harmful effects on specified sensitive elements of the environment do not occur according to present knowledge'. See e.g. Levy (1993), 'European Acid Rain: The Power of Tote Board Diplomacy', 24.

[51] See, for example, Sebenius (1990), Underdal (1990) and Wettestad (1999) for discussions of negotiation package deals and the pros and cons of comprehensiveness in this context.

[52] Central references here are Lammers (1988), Boehmer-Christiansen and Skea (1991); Boehmer-Christiansen and Weidner (1995); and Liefferink (1996).

[53] This is further discussed in Wettestad (1999), Chapter 4. According to Henrik Selin, who has studied the POPs negotiations (Selin 2000), American 'backtracking' had a significant impact upon these negotiations. Communication with Henrik Selin, October 2000.

54 This is the D3 unit within DG ENV. The part of the staff responsible for air pollution issues has not numbered much more than 10-11.

55 For a more comprehensive discussion of CLRTAP decision-making, see Wettestad (1999).

56 Except for the cases of very high level political issues, such as the introduction of the single currency.

57 See e.g. Golub (1996); Collier (1997; 1998, ed.); and Golub (1998).

58 However, as noted by Collier (1997:1, 7), both the subsidiarity principle and the deregulation 'doctrine' could *in principle* contribute to a strengthening of environmental protection in the EU, by for instance stimulating broader participation and 'bottom-up' approaches.

59 See, for instance, Boehmer-Christiansen and Skea (1991).

60 The case studies carried out in Underdal and Hanf (eds., 2000) provide numerous examples of air pollution policy advances in the 1980s and early 1990s having little or nothing to do with environmental politics as such. See for instance Boehmer-Christiansen's discussion of the crucial impact of privatisation in the UK context (Chapter Eleven). For a discussion of how economic crisis and curtailed economic production have shaped Russian air pollution policy and performance, see Kotov and Nikitina (1998).

61 In the Miles et al. project on the effectiveness of international environmental regimes, a central distinction is made between 'intellectual' and 'political' characteristics. See Underdal (2000). The book from the project is forthcoming in 2001 (Miles et al., 2001).

62 See Tuinstra, Hordijk and Ammann (1999:35-36).

Chapter 3

Background and Baseline

European Air Pollution Politics in the 1980s

Introduction

An important starting point for understanding the focused processes unfolding within CLRTAP and the EU throughout the 1990s is a good understanding of the background and the reasons for which the processes were started. Moreover, in order to study the effect of institutional change over time, an understanding of the institutional baseline is simply indispensable. However, it should be made clear that this study makes absolutely no claim to throw any new light on air pollution politics in the 1980s. Especially the EU part of this chapter simply summarises several excellent existing studies. With this caveat, let us first turn to the all-European CLRTAP context before we zoom in on air pollution politics within the setting of the European Community.

CLRTAP: The SO_2 Protocol, the Baseline NO_x Negotiations and the 1988 Protocol[63]

As indicated in Chapter One, it was acidification caused by sulphur dioxide emissions which was the initial, almost sole focus for scientific and political attention. As elaborated in Wettestad (1999), this transboundary problem must be characterised as strongly 'malign'. Scientific uncertainty was substantial. Moreover, there were very 'unfortunate' transboundary elements, with large net exporters of pollutants such as the UK experiencing little domestic air pollution damage – while net importers such as Sweden and Norway experienced considerable damage due to vulnerable soil characteristics. A main polluter in this context was the industrial sector, and especially power stations. This part of the process was crowned with its first success by the establishment of the Helsinki Protocol in 1985, calling for a 30 percent reduction of SO_2 emissions by 1993.

As the 1990s Gothenburg Protocol process analysed in the next chapter was initially branded as 're-negotiating the NO_x Protocol',[64] let us devote most attention in this section to a brief overview of some important features of the first NO_x process. The international political process to regulate NO_x was first and foremost initiated at the second session of CLRTAP's Executive Body (EB) in 1984. At this meeting, 'the need to reduce effectively the total annual national emissions of nitrogen oxides from stationary and mobile sources or their transboundary fluxes by 1995...' was recognised.[65] Compared to the more than decade-long scientific attention to SO_2, a major characteristic of the NO_x process was a weak knowledge base when the negotiations started. Hence, as opposed to the sulphur process, very much of the knowledge improvement process took place *within* the regime, parallel with the negotiating process, and over a quite short period of time.

The 1985 Helsinki meeting not only established the sulphur protocol, but also established a Working Group on Nitrogen Oxides with a mandate to focus on improving knowledge about the sources and impacts of NO_x. The Working Group on NO_x was the formal framework for the knowledge production process. A combination of work in task forces organised by a group of Lead Countries (Canada, the Nordic countries, the Federal Republic of Germany, and the United States) and subsequent assessment of conclusions in specific 'Designated Expert Groups' (comprised of government-appointed experts from all geographic areas within the ECE) led to considerable progress being made in a relatively short period of time.[66] The FRG led the legal/political drafting process, which began in Autumn 1986. At this stage, the FRG, Canada, Austria, the Netherlands and Sweden aimed for rapid and thorough reductions in NO_x emissions. It is interesting to note that already in this first NO_x negotiation process, substantial attention was given to the 'critical loads' approach, i.e. setting targets according to ecological vulnerability, not least by countries like the USSR and Canada.[67]

The Working Group meeting in September 1987 was a turning point in the negotiating process in terms of specificity.[68] A group of five countries – the FRG, Austria, Switzerland, the Netherlands and Sweden – launched a proposal for 30 percent reductions by 1995 proposal (with a 1985 baseline). Hence, they formed a sort of '30 percent NO_x club', reminiscent of the sulphur process. Other countries were less interested in reductions. The UK, Norway and Finland were only prepared to discuss a freeze of emissions. With regard to the UK, a position on the reluctant side was not so surprising. In the preceding SO_2 negotiations, the UK stood out as a central laggard. This is usually explained by the position of the UK as a major net 'exporter' of pollutants (due to wind currents), and hence not perceiving itself as much affected by acidification and air pollution. With regard to Finland and Norway, their NO_x positions were clearly different from their lead positions and role in the preceding sulphur process. This can basically be explained by differences between the sulphur and NO_x issues. Both these Nordic countries had to deal with more – and more complicated – emission sources in the NO_x than the sulphur context, and they even became aware of new and additional emissions during the negotiations. Other countries – such as the Soviet bloc, the US, Canada and Italy – were sceptical even about a freeze.[69] During the negotiations, the 30 percent NO_x club failed to gain sufficient support. By early 1988 a general consensus had emerged to stabilise emissions at 1987 levels. However, the 30 percent club (together with Denmark and Canada) argued for an early 1990 target date, while most of the others favoured 1994 as the target date.

The resulting NO_x protocol, adopted in Sofia in November 1988, called for a freeze of NO_x emissions at the 1987 baseline (or other specified baselines, on certain conditions) from 1994 onwards. Moreover, the Protocol contained general agreement to develop the concept of 'critical loads', to negotiate further reductions, and a substantial technical annex. Twenty-five countries signed the Protocol. Simultaneous to the adoption of the Protocol, but as a distinctly separate step, a group of twelve European countries signed a political Declaration calling for NO_x reductions 'in the order of 30 percent' by 1998, with a chosen baseline year between 1980 and 1986.[70]

The EU: The Central Processes on Emission from Large Combustion Plants (LCPs) and Motor Vehicles

As there are several excellent summaries of the development of EU air pollution policies in the 1970s and 1980s,[71] only main points with regard to the general development of the focused processes will be summed up, with specific attention to the effects of institutional matters and changes given specific attention in this study.

Acidification and emissions from large combustion plants: Clashing interests and intricate compromise-building

Although policy development within the European Union related to air pollution issues can be dated back to the 1970s, the main development of EU air pollution policy started in 1983/84. As described in Chapter One, the LRTAP Convention had been established in 1979 with only lukewarm support from both the UK and the FRG. Hence, it was the rapidly increasing German concern over forest damage, 'Waldsterben', in the early 1980s, and the related about-turn from policy laggard to central 'acid activist' and policy leader on the international stage which was the main impetus to stepped-up policy development, both within the EU and CLRTAP.[72] German domestic policy development with regard to the regulation of emissions from large combustion plants was a central background and model for a quite similar policy development process at the EU level.[73]

The first phase of this process was concluded by the adoption of a framework directive on combating air pollution from industrial plants in 1983. Related to an increasing saliency of the issues involved, the process on a daughter directive on emissions from large combustion plant (LCPs) started soon after. According to McCormick (1997:101),'Britain had been sure to insist that agreement on <daughter directives> would be determined by unanimity rather than by qualified majority vote, thereby allowing it to veto future proposals'. Drawing heavily on German domestic legislation, the Commission put forward a draft directive already in December 1983. This draft proposed emission limits from new plants (built after 1985) and called more specifically for national plans for at least 60 percent SO_2 reductions and 40 percent NO_x and particulates by 1995.

It soon became clear that there were differences of opinion within the Community. Germany, Denmark and the Netherlands strongly supported the proposal. The French and Belgians were largely indifferent, due to their heavy reliance on nuclear power. The UK, Italy, Greece and Ireland stood forward as clear opponents. The general background for the British reluctance has been sketched already. In addition, LCPs accounted for a comparatively high proportion (i.e. over 80 percent) of sulphur dioxide emissions in the UK and hence much was at stake. The latter two countries were concerned about possible interference with their economic development plans. When Spain and Portugal joined in 1986, the group of 'not-rich-and-not-very-green' EU states increased further. Given the unanimity requirement, it had become necessary for the Commission to introduce more flexibility and sweeteners into the proposal. Hence, in 1985 a revised proposal was designed, imposing different levels of emission reductions on the richer countries and exempting Greece, Ireland, Portugal and Luxembourg. This was clearly not enough to obtain agreement', and the initiative passed to the Member States chairing the Council.

The Dutch introduced country-specific target differentiation based on 'objective criteria', in two phases (by 1995 and 2005); the UK increased the differentiation; the Belgians introduced the idea of three phases (1993,

1998, and 2005); Denmark made further concessions to small states, before the Germans managed to get a final compromise adopted in November 1988. Notably, emissions from both existing and new plants were included in the final agreement. With regard to the former, pertaining to plants in operation before July 1987, the Directive established country-specific reduction targets to be achieved in three phases (by 1993, 1998, and 2003). By 2003, the overall EU goal for the reduction of SO_2 emissions from LCPs was 57 percent, and for NO_x the goal was a 30 percent reduction. Greece, Ireland, Portugal and Luxembourg were all included, but regarding the first three countries, the targets were only a cap on allowed increases in emissions. Regarding new plants, emission limits were specified according to the principle of 'best available technology not entailing excessive costs' (BATNEEC).

Central determining factors for this outcome pinpointed by analysts are both the forceful German presidency in the spring of 1988,[74] and a shift at this time in British policy on acidification towards a more constructive and flexible position. The latter related both to domestic electricity privatisation concerns and EU and CLRTAP diplomatic concerns.[75]

The Regulation of Vehicle Emissions: Clashing Economic Interests and Interesting Institutional Effects

As pinpointed by Vogel (1995), the regulation of vehicle emissions has been one of the most important and contentious areas of EU environmental policy, and for good reasons: 'Automobiles are among the EU's most widely traded goods, and significant automobile manufacturing takes place in seven of the Union's twelve Member States' (ibid:63).[76] In the 1970s and early 1980s, some fuel and vehicle emissions standards were adopted within the Community, modelled on ECE standards and hence 'nested' within a wider international regime.[77] The Community standards were primarily linked to the development of the single market and to prevent standards imposed by Member States from becoming barriers to trade. Also in this issue area, much of the same dynamic and rapidly increasing concern as described above 'kick-started' serious policy development within the EU.

In 1983, the FRG announced as a unilateral requirement that all cars were to be fitted with three-way catalytic converters from 1986. This position was supported by Denmark and the Netherlands, but strongly opposed by the UK, France and Italy. The standard explanation for this controversy is, first and foremost, that the car industry in the latter countries produced smaller vehicles whose competitiveness was threatened by a requirement to install expensive catalytic converters. Instead, they preferred the so-called 'lean-burn' engine. In addition, the environmental movement was comparatively weak in these countries.

On this background, the Commission in 1984 put forward two proposals for further reductions in vehicle emissions, aimed at forestalling a unilateral German move. One directive proposed the total elimination of lead from petrol; the other directive called for a further 70 percent reduction in carbon monoxide, hydrocarbons, and NO_x emissions from vehicles. The proposals were linked, since the proposed emissions standards required that all new cars would be equipped with catalytic converters and such vehicles could only use unleaded petrol. The ambition was to come up with regulations as strict as those that had recently been adopted in the US ('US 83'). Especially the emissions reductions proposal turned out to be controversial.

After complicated negotiations, and by distinguishing between requirements for 'large', 'medium' and 'small' cars on the basis of engine size, Environment Ministers managed to agree upon the 'Luxembourg compromise' in 1985.[78] Only large cars would need to have catalytic converters to achieve compliance. This outcome meant weaker EU standards than the 'US 83' standards. As a concession to environmentalists, a provision requiring the EU to adopt stricter requirements for small and medium-size vehicles as soon as 1987 was included in the Directive. Still, formal agreement to a directive was blocked by Denmark and Greece; the former seeking more stringent limits and the latter worrying that the limits were too strict, linking acceptance to greater EU financial support.

This impasse was overcome by the entry into force in July 1987 of the Single European Act (SEA) and the opening up for majority voting in measures relating to the completion of the single market. In what has been described as the first time an environmental Directive had been agreed upon by majority voting, the opponents were voted down and the Directive was formally adopted in December 1987 (Directive 88/76).

As set out in the Luxembourg compromise, the process on second stage reductions for small cars started on the heels of the process described above. Due to the entry into force of the co-operation procedure, another important institutional change introduced in the SEA, the European Parliament had a more important say in this process. Controversies and coalitions similar to the foregoing process quickly appeared. In early 1988, the Commission proposed standards which would not have made catalytic converters necessary. In its first reading, the Parliament found the Commission's proposal too lax and voted for 'US 83' standards instead. This was not accepted by the Commission, and the Council adopted the Commission's proposal in December 1988. In its second reading, the Parliament used its newly acquired powers to demand obligatory catalytic converters. This forced Environment Commissioner Ripa di Meana and the Commission to revise the proposal accordingly and then an interesting situation arose, in both institutional and political terms: Given this course of process, the Council could only go back to the previous (and less stringent) common position by unanimity. When this was unobtainable, the Council chose to accept the position put forward by the Parliament and subsequently the Commission. The new standards were made compulsory from 1992 (Directive 89/458).[79]

This agreement opened the door for a considerable further tightening of emission limits for medium and large cars. A Commission proposal requiring all new-model cars to meet standards roughly as strict as US standards at the time was adopted in the Council in December 1991 (Directive 91/441). Again, the Parliament played a certain role for the outcome, but failed in its second reading to obtain the necessary majority for further strengthening of measures.

Winding up: CLRTAP and the EU at the Brink of the 1990s

As summed up in this chapter, considerable policy development took place both within CLRTAP and the EU during the 1980s. CLRTAP was the policy forerunner. After the framework convention was established in 1979, protocols on the emission of sulphur dioxide, nitrogen oxides and volatile organic compounds were subsequently established over a period of 12 years. In terms of strength, none of these protocols can be characterised as being particularly strong. Surely, they constrained the political freedom of action a bit, but to a varying degree. Some countries had, for instance, already achieved the required reductions before signing on to the protocols.[80] Moreover, in terms of meeting environmental 'needs', the protocols were political compromises and starting points; obviously inadequate in relation to such needs.[81] However, as a development with great future significance, it should be noted that the concept of critical loads was introduced in the NO_x process.

With regard to central factors shedding light upon moderate regulatory strength, as was clearly demonstrated in the NO_x process, an important background perspective was a 'malign' problem and diverging interests. Among other things, in addition to the power stations mainly targeted in the sulphur context, the regulation of NO_x also included the 'unruly' transport sector, with a myriad of small emission sources. In terms of regime and institutional contributions, the regime was important as an arena for transnational learning and knowledge improvement. The bargaining context was fundamentally consensual, but with a certain element of flexibility. In the sulphur context, reluctant states such as the UK and Poland simply chose not to sign the 1985 Protocol.[82]

Also the EU was marked by a considerable regulatory development in the 1980s. The LCP process was fundamentally quite similar to the CLRTAP process, with inter-state bargaining and compromise-building in the Council as a central ingredient. However, there was still an important institutional difference in the need within the EU to accommodate all interests 'within' the agreement; there was no possibility for states simply to stay out of the final agreement. In terms of interests and coalitions, not so different from the CLRTAP sulphur context, the 'leader' camp consisted of Germany, Denmark and the Netherlands; while central countries in the 'laggard' camp included the UK and the Southern European states. As all such diverging interests had somehow to be accommodated, the resulting regulatory strength was not overwhelming. The adoption of the LCP Directive did not, for instance, allow the EU as such to sign on to the 1985 CLRTAP sulphur protocol.[83]

The vehicle process was somewhat differently flavoured. Single market and economic considerations were significant elements of this process. Hence, the picture in terms of factors shaping national interests, and in the end the constellation of diverging national positions, became much more complex in this context than in the LCP context. Related to the single market implications, institutional changes in the EU played a more important part here. The introduction of qualified majority voting made it possible to break the impasse over the Luxembourg compromise, and the introduction of co-operation procedure and an enhanced role for the Parliament contributed significantly to the small cars directive. However, as pinpointed by Wurzel (1999:259), the success of the Parliament in this case was partly contextually based, as the European Parliament, like national parliaments, was influenced by the general up-surge in green saliency from the mid 1980s. The resulting regulatory strength was roughly on par with US/California standards at the time.

Overall, policy-making within CLRTAP and the EU was somewhat linked in this period, but in a loose manner. The LRTAP Convention came first and acted as a stimulant for further development of air policies within the EU. CLRTAP's role as 'one step ahead' continued throughout the 1980s, with the EU unable to sign on to the first sulphur protocol and not finally adopting the 1988 NO_x Protocol until 1993.

Notes

63 This section draws heavily on Wettestad (1998).
64 At least in meeting notes produced by the Norwegian Ministry of the Environment (NME).
65 Cited in Gehring, 1994:156.
66 Stenstadvold, 1991: 91-92; Gehring, 1994:158-59.
67 Probably due to anticipated favourable effects, see Gehring (1994:165).
68 Gehring, 1994:168.
69 ENDS Report 152, September 1987, p.3.
70 Environmental Policy and Law, 18, 6, (1988):196.
71 See for instance Lammers 1988; Boehmer-Christiansen and Skea (1991); Haigh (ed.) (1992 and up-dates); Arp 1993; Liberatore (1993); Boehmer-Christiansen and Weidner 1995; Vogel 1995; Liefferink 1996; McCormick 1997; Wurzel 1999; Weale et.al 2000.
72 The 'classic' reference here is Boehmer-Christiansen and Skea (1991).
73 However, as pinpointed by Weale et al. (2000:388), domestic industrial pressure and efforts to level the European playing field are not the whole story. The Germans were also motivated by a more overriding and general concern about increasing transboundary air and water pollution.
74 According to Weale et al. (2000:390), 'Indeed, it was the German presidency, with Klaus Topfer in the chair, which used its authority to draw negotiations to a close in June 1988'.
75 See e.g. McCormick (1997:103).
76 Germany, France, and Italy are home to major car producers, while several European, American, and Japanese multinationals have production facilities in the UK, the Netherlands, Spain, and Belgium.
77 See Weale et al. (2000:399).
78 According to Wurzel (1999:265), the decision to differentiate on the basis of engine capacity was a purely political one, having nothing to do with technology or science.
79 According to Wurzel (1999:274), this directive '..was the first EU car emission directive which was mandatory rather than optional'.
80 See Underdal and Hanf (2000) for useful overviews of the countries' situation in this regard.
81 See Wettestad (2000 B).
82 For a discussion of the CLRTAP decision-making and institutional context, see Wettestad (1999).
83 See Liberatore (1993).

Chapter 4

CLRTAP's Significant Leap Forward in the 1990s

Negotiating the 1999 Gothenburg Protocol

Introduction

This chapter documents the developing strength of CLRTAP air pollution policies in the 1990s, primarily through a more detailed scrutiny of the decision-making process on the multi-pollutant and multi-effects protocol adopted in Gothenburg on November 30 1999 (hereafter: the Gothenburg Protocol). As can be recalled, the process leading up to the initial NO_x commitments in 1988 was briefly reviewed in Chapter Three. The Gothenburg Protocol process focused upon in this chapter has carried out the major revision process of CLRTAP policy requirements with regard to NO_x and VOC emissions in the 1990s. Moreover, in the process, NH_3 and SO_2 emission requirements have been put on the table as well.

In the following section an introductory overview of the process of preparing and negotiating the Gothenburg Protocol is carried out. Against the background of this overview, the third section carries out a more systematic and focused discussion on the question of the increase in regulatory strength over time. The main conclusion is that policy strength has increased considerably, although a remaining gap to environmental optimum conditions must be acknowledged. On the basis of this conclusion, main explanatory factors are then examined in section four, with the three institutional propositions developed in Chapter Two as the point of departure. Section five sums up main findings.

The Gothenburg Protocol Process 1994-99: An Introductory Overview

The Preparatory Phase: 1994-97

In a very general sense, this process was rooted in the first NO_x and VOC Protocols. In the case of the NO_x Protocol, Article 5 generally called for regular and subsequent reviews of the commitments established in 1988.[84] In the case of the VOC Protocol, the review and renegotiation requirements were more specific. Paragraph 6 under Article 2 called for a commencement of renegotiations no later than six months after the entry into force of the 1991 Protocol; explicitly calling for attention to the role of nitrogen oxides. There were also other early inputs to this discussion. For instance, in June 1992, the CLRTAP delegations of Norway, Sweden and the UK submitted a note to the Working Group on Strategies (WGS), summing up the (many) pros and (fewer) cons of broader, multi-pollutant and multi-effects approaches.[85]

Moreover, the negotiation of the second sulphur protocol in the beginning of the 1990s was clearly a milestone in terms of using the concept of critical loads and effects-based thinking in CLRTAP decision-making.[86] This process also introduced the approach of setting national emission ceilings. Together, these elements resulted in the 1994 Second Sulphur Protocol's unprecedented system of differentiated national emission ceilings within CLRTAP.

The more formal preparatory work for a multi protocol then started just after the completion of the 1994 Second Sulphur Protocol. Related to slow VOC protocol ratification progress, the work was initially branded as 'renegotiating the NO_x 1988 Protocol'.[87] However, in the work plan launched at the 1994 August meeting of the Working Group on Strategy (WGS-12), a protocol addressing both multiple effects (acidification, tropospheric ozone formation and eutrophication) and multiple pollutants (NO_x, NH_3, VOCs and SO_2) was foreseen. Various work of a scientific and technological nature was initiated.

The Task Force on Integrated Assessment Modelling (TFIAM) started working on scenarios for maximum feasible emission reductions within a multi-pollutant/multi-effects context. Several computer models were utilised with most emphasis given to the RAINS (Regional Air Pollution Information and Simulation) model. This model had been developed by the International Institute for Applied Systems Analysis (IIASA) from the late 1980s and utilised in the negotiations leading up to the 1994 Sulphur Protocol. With the aid of this model it had become possible to produce scenarios that were cost-optimised for given emission or deposition targets.[88] However, it should be noted that IIASA's work within this particular process started without a clear ECE/CLRTAP financing plan.[89]

When the WGS met in August 1995 (WGS-15), progress was generally assessed as very good, not least on the modelling side. On the background of this progress, hope was expressed that negotiations could commence in 1996.[90] At the next meeting of the WGS in February 1996 (WGS-16), TFIAM's chairman presented a progress report and indicated the presentation of cost scenarios by the end of 1996. A procedure of national review and acceptance of cost curves was agreed upon.

Moreover, a group consisting of Germany, France, the Netherlands, Austria and Switzerland presented a first proposal on central structure and elements in the coming protocol. Both national emission ceilings and Best Available Technology (BAT) requirements were envisaged in the protocol. With regard to the latter element, reluctance was expressed by a number of countries including Denmark, Finland, Russia, Canada, Ireland and Norway. Representatives of the EU presented on-going work on the Acidification Strategy and close collaboration with the CLRTAP process was anticipated.[91]

TFIAM reported back to the WGS in June 1996. Among other things it was noted that nitrogen deposition reductions of around 70 percent of the 1990 level were required in most parts of Central Europe, and the need for some further SO_2 reductions was also indicated. Based on RAINS/IIASA input, maximum technically feasible emissions reductions (from the 1990 level) were estimated to be 80-85 percent for NO_x, over 70 percent for VOCs and over 45 percent for ammonia.[92]

At the following WGS session in August 1996 (WGS-18), new inputs from both TFIAM and the Task Force on Economic Aspects of Abatement Strategies (TFEAAS) were discussed. On the background of progress witnessed with regard to the establishment of a sound scientific and technological platform for negotiations, it was concluded that such negotiations could possibly commence in March 1997 (with September as a fall-back option).[93] Basic data on the costs of abating ammonia and nitrogen oxides emissions were sent to the parties for comment in November 1996.[94] At the EB meeting in the same month, it was decided among other things to postpone the first review of sulphur dioxide commitments adopted in 1994 due to the slow progress of ratification of the 1994 Protocol.[95]

The first WGS meeting in January 1997 (WGS-19) was devoted to parallel negotiations within CLRTAP on a protocol on the emissions of persistent organic pollutants (POPs).[96] Thus, it was not until the next WGS meeting in March (WGS-20) that the multi protocol process was back on the agenda. Several pieces of the scientific and technological 'puzzle' were reviewed at this meeting. For instance: the Task Force on Emission Inventories pinpointed a number of problems related to official emissions data supplied by Parties. Moreover, a representative of the Coordination Centre for Effects (CCE) presented progress in critical load mapping and noted that current critical loads maps for acidification and eutrophication consisted of 16 national submissions. TFIAM presented various modelling progress. Overall, progress was not as good as expected.[97] Hence, for the up-coming meeting in September, TFIAM was requested to explore a number of least-cost gap closure scenarios for each of the different effects (i.e. acidification, eutrophication and ozone exposure for vegetation and human health) in order to get a better picture of trade-offs between costs and protection levels. Moreover, some 'non-optimised' scenarios, for instance related to Best Available Technology, were also requested. In addition, a clarification of the implications of possible further sulphur dioxide emissions reductions (beyond the requirements in the 1994 Protocol) in this context was called for.[98] It was explicitly pinpointed that the EU Acidification Strategy process had clarified the cost effectiveness related to such further emissions reductions.[99]

Why did things proceed more slowly at this point? First and foremost, the sheer complexity of this venture must be emphasised. It *is* a complicated matter to 'gather several pollutants and several effects under one hat'.[100] As nitrogen oxides were involved in all three effects (i.e. acidification, eutrophication and ozone formation) and ozone concentrations were complicated to calculate, it was difficult to construct reliable computer models for determining the most cost-effective measures. Add to this complexity the increasing awareness of the possibility that further sulphur dioxide emission cuts were the most cost-effective measures within the acidification context. An additional dimension was the need to coordinate with the development of the EU Acidification and Ozone Strategy.[101]

At the September WGS meeting (WGS-22), the Chairmen of both TFIAM and TFEAAS presented new reports and revised figures in response to requests raised at WGS-21. In connection with the TFIAM progress discussion, conclusions from an IIASA/RAINS workshop were presented and discussed. An important aspect in an effects-oriented strategy was the need to choose between an approach focusing on exceedances of critical loads (like the 1994 Sulphur Protocol) or a more ecosystemic approach focusing on the vulnerable areas within ecosystems (grids). Choosing one or the other would have different implications for the allocation of emissions reductions requirements. Moreover, test runs of the model had confirmed the cost effectiveness potential related to further SO_2 cuts in the acidification context. Hence, it was agreed at the meeting to ask that TFIAM include the effects of further SO_2 cuts in its further work in clarifying possible emission reduction requirements and comprehensive pollutants and effects scenarios.[102] Furthermore, a revised draft composite negotiating text for a protocol was presented at this meeting. The text was prepared by the secretariat, at the request of the WGS.[103] According to the former Head of the CLRTAP Secretariat, the secretariat played an increasingly important role in preparing draft texts for the negotiators.[104]

A central discussion item in this meeting was the best design of commitments. A group of countries including Canada, Ireland, Norway, Russia, the US and the UK supported the establishment of national emission ceilings (NECs) *only* (i.e. they wanted no other obligations than the NECs), emphasising national flexibility with regard to policy approaches and measures. The other countries supported the design of a protocol where the NECs were to be complemented by other measures, such as (binding) emissions standards. However, several of the latter countries (like Denmark, Finland, the Netherlands, Croatia, Spain, Slovakia, Slovenia and Sweden) expressed support for more flexibility with regard to existing installations rather than to new installations.[105]

The impression that the discussions were proceeding slowly at this point is supported by the marginal progress made at the Executive Body's session in December 1997. Here it was decided that the WGS was to also include SO_2 in the preparatory work for the protocol. This was quite controversial, since the 1994 Sulphur protocol had not yet entered into force – so it was in fact quite a big and important decision.[106] A second issue that was discussed was the financing of IIASA's modelling work. It was indicated earlier in this section that IIASA's modelling work started without a clear, long-term ECE/CLRTAP financing plan. The parties were not able to resolve this issue, despite a warning from the WGS Chairman that 'the lack of long-term finance for the work by IIASA could seriously threaten the review of the protocols to the Convention and might jeopardize the finalization of the multi-pollutant/multi-effect protocol'.[107]

Overall, the feeling was that the earlier plan of having the protocol ready by the end of 1998 was unrealistic and the first half of 1999 was indicated instead.[108] A representative of the European Community informed about the progress made on the Community's Acidification and Ozone Strategies. A proposal for an emissions ceilings directive covering nitrogen oxides, volatile organic compounds, ammonia and sulphur was expected to be ready in late 1998 or early 1999.[109]

The Main Negotiation Phase: 1998-99

The first WGS meeting in 1998 (WGS-26, March 16–19) was devoted to the modelling work on developing cost-effective scenarios. Progress reports on integrated assessment modelling and economic assessments of benefits were presented and discussed. Given the general skew in environmental negotiations towards having much better figures on costs than benefits, not least the results from a British study were interesting. This study carried out an *economic assessment of the benefits from reducing emissions* of the four targeted substances, seen in relation to estimated abatement costs.[110]

Two main scenarios were considered: a reference scenario (REF), based on the effects of existing and planned legislation, and a Maximum (technically) Feasible Reductions (MFR) scenario, taking into account various possibilities for reducing emissions by technical means. The extra annual cost of the change from the REF scenario to the MFR scenario was estimated to be ECU 86 billion for the year 2010. The benefits of the reductions were assessed according to the effects on health, materials, farm crops, forest productivity, natural ecosystems, and visibility. Total benefits of the order of around ECU 250 billion were indicated. Comparing costs and benefits, and although several uncertainties were acknowledged, the overall conclusion was that total benefits would exceed costs, even under a MFR scenario.[111]

In the following months, CLRTAP negotiators were occupied with the completion of the parallel heavy metals and POPs negotiations. These negotiations were concluded with protocols being signed in Aarhus in June 1998. In the ministerial declaration from the Aarhus meeting, the ministers supported 'acceleration of the negotiation of an ambitious and realistic 'multi-pollutant' protocol, with a view to finalizing it by mid-1999'.[112] With heavy metals and POPs out of the way, the negotiators were again allowed to concentrate solely on the multi protocol process. At WGS-27 (August 31-September 3), *the set of scenarios* were further clarified. Four main scenarios were indicated, all with common base and target years (1990 and 2010) These were:

- a business-as-usual scenario, which assumed full implementation of already approved legislation and agreed commitments
- full application of all the currently available options for technical abatement
- single-problem optimizations, aimed at finding the least-cost solution for attaining interim targets for one of the three environmental problems at a time, and

- joint optimizations, aimed at finding the least-cost solutions for simultaneous attainment of the interim targets for two or more environmental problems.[113]

With regard to the possible use of technical annexes, as on earlier occasions, Russia and Norway argued for annexes of a guiding nature and freedom in the choice of implementing instruments, while the other countries supported some sort of binding, technical annexes.[114] Hence, the issue was left unresolved. On the issue of sulphur emissions, as acidification was one of the targeted problems, it was agreed to include such emissions in some way. However, at this point it was unclear if this best could be done by including them in the protocol itself or revising the 1994 sulphur protocol.[115] When the Executive Body convened in December, the Working Group on Strategies informed the parties that the analysis of abatement scenarios had advanced to such a stage that the Working Group should be able to decide upon a guiding scenario for the negotiations at its next session. On the basis of four planned negotiating sessions, it was considered feasible to conclude the negotiations in 1999.[116]

The first of these concluding negotiating sessions took place at the end of January 1999. As announced at the December EB meeting, *the central discussion item was reaching agreement on a key, guiding scenario for the final negotiations.* The 'menu' to choose from included six different scenarios, combining different levels of ambitions. At the beginning of the meeting the EU Commission and a group of Northern EU countries, including Austria, Denmark, Finland, the Netherlands and Sweden, came forward with clear support for a moderately ambitious scenario called G5/2 ('median scenario'). The ambitiousness in this scenario corresponded closely with EU's separate – but closely related – Acidification and Ozone process. Running contrary to the usual North-South split within the EU on such issues, Spain and Greece also expressed support for this scenario.[117] However, a group of EU countries including Belgium, France, Ireland, Italy and Portugal favoured a lower level of ambition. This position was supported by the Czech Republic, Slovakia and Russia.

After a second round of EU internal coordination, the EU came out as a united supporter of the 'median' scenario. However, the EU Commission emphasised that this did not mean that the tentative reduction targets had been accepted. This EU clarification was the turning point in the scenario discussion. After the EU clarification, the Czech Republic announced a change in position and support for the 'median' scenario. With silent approval from the other countries, the Chairman declared the 'median' scenario accepted as the basis for the final negotiations.[118] This procedure was repeated with regard to the issue of how to deal with sulphur emissions in the new protocol. After clear support from the EU for including such emissions in the protocol, this was established as the WGS' recommendation to the Executive Body.[119]

At least two main considerations supported such inclusion. First, the 1994 sulphur protocol had come into effect in August 1998 and it was written into that protocol that this was to be reviewed and revised in the year following its entry into force. Second, analyses indicated that environmental improvements could be achieved at a much lower cost if sulphur emissions were also included in the regulatory approach.[120] With regard to the issue of technical annexes and binding BAT requirements, a group of countries consisting of Canada, Norway, and Russia did not favour such requirements and supported emissions ceilings only. Germany, Luxembourg, the Netherlands and Switzerland strongly supported such requirements, with more moderate support from other EU countries. The issue was hence deferred to the next WGS meeting.[121]

Overall, the 'median' scenario pointed towards considerable reductions of many countries' emissions (see the annexes to this chapter). Moreover, in some cases there were significant differences between the 'reference' and 'median' scenarios. As an example, with regard to NO_x emissions and the two large emitters France and Italy, the 'reference' scenario indicated reductions of respectively 46 percent and 43 percent, while the 'median' scenario pointed towards far more ambitious reductions of 63 percent (France) and 58 percent (Italy).[122]

At this stage, figures were also put on the table with regard to abatement costs, environmental improvements and related economic benefits. The total costs in 2010 for Europe under the 'median' scenario was put at 8.5 billion ECU, with the EU countries accounting for two-thirds of the costs. Total benefits were more uncertain, with a low estimate at 26.5 billion and a high estimate at 42.3 billion ECU. Still, the central point to note was that these estimates indicated *considerably higher benefits than costs*. With regard to environmental effects, significant improvements both regarding acidification, ozone and eutrophication were envisaged. For instance, IIASA estimates indicated that the 2010 ozone excess exposure for population would be respectively 78 percent ('median' scenario) and 43 percent ('reference' scenario) less than in 1990.[123]

Only moderate progress was made when negotiations resumed at WGS-29 in March. The central but difficult matter of national emission ceilings was carefully avoided.[124] Instead, this meeting concentrated on the issue of *technical annexes and BAT requirements*. Agreements prior to the 1994 sulphur protocol contained technical annexes of a guiding nature. The

1994 protocol combined emission ceilings, mandatory emission standards (limit values) for new, stationary plants, and guiding BAT requirements. The majority of the countries regarded this approach as a good one overall, also for the Gothenburg Protocol. However, there was still clear disagreement as to whether the limit values in the annexes were to be mandatory or cast in the form of recommendations. Most of the countries supported mandatory requirements for new plants (with regard to SO_2, NO_x and VOC emissions), with more nuances on the issue of requirements for existing plants. Norway was the only country opposing mandatory requirements on principal grounds.[125]

At WGS-30 in early June, the key issue of emission ceilings was back at the top of the agenda. In a tour-de-table, it soon became clear that *almost all of the countries backed away on some points from the tentative emission ceilings derived from the 'median' scenario* adopted as a guiding approach in January.[126] With regard to sulphur emissions, for instance Poland put forward a proposed ceiling 80-90 percent higher than suggested in the 'median' scenario. But also the UK, France and Italy proposed ceilings considerably above 'median' levels. Overall, the June sulphur proposals pointed towards 2010 SO_2 emissions 23 percent above 'median' levels.

Turning to NO_x, VOC and NH_3 emissions, the overall gaps to 'median' levels were lower (8 percent NO_x, 10 percent VOC, 9 percent NH_3). France proposed NO_x and NH_3 ceilings considerably above 'median' levels; Denmark, Finland and several Eastern European countries proposed NO_x and VOC ceilings considerably over 'median' levels (see annexes for an overview of proposed emission ceilings). Several contingent positions were put forward, linking their own positions and flexibility to other provisions in the protocol, like especially the limit values, or linking positions to the willingness and flexibility of other parties.[127] Delegations were given an instructive overview of the sub-optimal environmental implications of their proposed emissions ceilings by Markus Amann of IIASA, who had developed a scenario based on the proposals at the time.

With regard to the other key negotiating issue – the role of BAT requirements and limit values – little progress was made. A clear majority of the countries supported binding limit values for new, large combustion plants and mandatory BAT requirements for stationary and mobile sources. With regard to limit values for existing plants, a group consisting of Austria, Germany, France, Switzerland and the Netherlands strongly supported binding values. As other countries such as Russia and several Eastern European countries opposed such values, the issue had to be deferred to the final meeting in September. Finally, on the basis of a

Russian proposal, and resembling the approach adopted in the 1991 VOC Protocol, it was opened up for countries designing specific 'Pollutants Emissions Management Areas' (PEMAs), in which the forthcoming protocol would apply. In other areas within such countries (for instance Russia and the US) not contributing to long range transboundary air pollution, the protocol would not apply.

The Concluding Session: Strange – or Sophisticated – Behaviour?

The key, concluding negotiating session took place in the end of August and beginning of September. Given the principal decision in January to base the protocol on the 'median' scenario, a central challenge here was to move countries' positions closer to those implied by this scenario. This happened in a few, notable cases. For instance, in the case of sulphur emissions, Denmark moved from 60 (thousands of tonnes per year) in June to 55 in September. The UK moved from 700 in June to 625 in September.[128] Similarly, in the case of NO_x, Denmark and Finland moved considerably; Denmark from 162 in June to 127 in September. Conversely, there were countries that ended up with *higher* NO_x ceilings than proposed in June. Portugal and the Netherlands are the most notable examples here. With regard to VOCs, it can be noted that the UK again moved to a lower ceiling, while the 'NO_x progressives' Denmark and Finland moved to higher ceilings than proposed in June. However, most countries stuck to their June proposals overall (see annexes for complete, September emission ceilings).

Hence, the distance and gap to the principally guiding 'median' scenario largely remained in the protocol adopted in September. This spurred critical comments in journals like *ENDS Report* and *Acid News*. *ENDS Report* stated that 'at Geneva, most countries took a highly unambitious approach'.[129] *Acid News* reported 'strange behaviour' in Geneva, and how deplorable it was that 'most of countries "were" unwilling to take the necessary steps to cut down emissions even to the extent required to meet the modest targets for which they themselves had voted barely half a year ago'.[130] The countries were given a last chance to improve their bids by October.

With regard to the other central issue of BAT and limit values, some final compromises were struck. Mandatory limit values for new LCPs were decided upon. With regard to existing LCPs, limit values were to become mandatory by the end of 2007 at the latest, or eight years later for economies in transition. As an additional element of flexibility, states could apply emissions reduction strategies which achieved 'equivalent overall emission levels for all source categories together'.[131] Overall, CLRTAP Secretary Lars Nordberg put forward quite a different perspective on the protocol than the views expressed in ENDS Report and Acid News. As noted in Chapter One, according to Nordberg the agreement was 'the most sophisticated environmental agreement ever negotiated and will yield great benefits, for both our environment and health'.[132]

The Protocol was formally adopted in Gothenburg on November 30. Emission ceilings were almost identical to those put forward in September, except by Sweden and Belgium, who lowered their ceilings somewhat.[133] At the same time, six guidance documents on control techniques and economic instruments to the protocol were adopted. This was a new feature of the agreements under CLRTAP.

The Development of Policy Strength: A Substantial Improvement, but Far from 'Enough'

As these negotiations started out as 'NO$_x$ renegotiations', it is reasonable to give specific attention to the development of the NO$_x$ targets over time. However, given the fundamental multi-pollutant approach, it does not make sense to focus *exclusively* on the development of NO$_x$ commitments.

Turning first to the more specific NO$_x$ regulatory development in relation to the 1988 baseline as summed up in Chapter Three, the 1988 Protocol cannot be characterised as very ambitious, with its 'stabilisation by 1994' requirement. Although an explicit business-as-usual 'reference' scenario was not developed in that process, it is quite likely that the stabilisation requirement was quite close to such a scenario for most of the countries. As twelve countries signed the independently prepared 30 percent reduction Declaration, the stabilisation target may even have been more moderate than business-as-usual for several of the countries.

Hence, as the main perspective, in a broad comparison, the 1999 Protocol is clearly a significantly stronger international instrument. As can be recalled, this Protocol aims at a reduction of NO$_x$ emissions of 41 percent by 2010 with a 1990 baseline. Moreover, the development of country-specific emission ceilings means a considerable increase in regulatory specificity and sophistication. However, as pinpointed by several observers, the NO$_x$ commitments adopted were 10 percent weaker overall than those calculated in the 'median' scenario.[134] Only Germany, Greece, the Netherlands, the UK, Sweden and some East European countries ended up with 'median' level NO$_x$ emissions ceilings. Moreover, as can be recalled, even the 'median' scenario failed to close the critical loads gap, both in terms of acidification and ozone.

Inclusion of the other substances does not alter this picture. The agreed emission cuts of SO_2 and VOCs are considerably more ambitious than earlier CLRTAP commitments. Moreover, including ammonia means that an important first step has been taken within CLRTAP in closing what has been referred to as a regulatory gap in European air pollution policy.[135] However, as in the case of NO_x, the fully-fledged regulatory strengthening picture is not only rosy. Negotiators have described the outcome as 'patchy'.[136] Further, the other final emissions ceilings ended up above 'median' levels. In fact, the sulphur ceilings ended up 34 percent higher than 'median' levels. For VOCs and NH_3, the gap was similar to the case of NO_x; i.e. 10 percent above 'median' levels.[137]

With regard to the dimensions of bindingness and specificity, no change has occurred in terms of the former. However, specificity has increased considerably. This especially applies to emissions of NO_x and VOCs (and NH_3 emissions of course, which were not previously regulated). In comparison with the basically flat rate reductions in the NO_x and (to a somewhat less degree) VOC Protocols, the NO_x and VOC emission ceilings in the NEC Directive are different for all the Member States. This means, at least in principle, that policies have become much more 'tailor-made' to fit the specific circumstances of each country than what was previously the case. With regard to the new sulphur dioxide commitments, they can be seen more as a refinement of the differentiation process which was started in the 1994 Protocol.

Summing up, there has been a substantial improvement of policy strength, but still far from 'enough' in relation to critical loads. How, then, did this come about?

Shedding Light on the Increase in Policy Strength: A Case of Better-functioning Institutions?

Let us first turn to the specifically focused institutional aspects.

A Better-functioning Institutional Setting?

A rough comparison with CLRTAP as an institution during the NO_x negotiations a decade earlier uncovers both similarities and differences. On the one hand, the basic functioning of the institution was quite similar. Both processes functioned on the basis of a consensus principle, and both processes developed on the basis of a close science-politics dialogue. On the other hand, Chapter Two drew attention to three potentially important institutional developments: First, in terms of membership, the break-up of the old Soviet bloc and the changes in Eastern Europe were focused. It was suggested that these changes have made CLRTAP parties more homogenous and led to more East-West coalition building. Combined with the 'pulling-effect' of the EU accession process, this may have led to more constructive CLRTAP decision-making and possibly contributed to increasing CLRTAP policy strength.

With regard to changes in decision-making procedures and approaches, the development of a multi-pollutant and multi-effects approach in the 1990s was focused. This development could mean an increasing ability to address several pollutants together and develop broader, integrative policy packages thereby generally improving decision-making capacity and possibly contributing to increasing CLRTAP policy strength. In addition, the possible positive 'spill-over' effects from the parallel EU Acidification Strategy and NEC Directive process were pinpointed.

Let us first turn to the membership issue and the possibility of more constructive CLRTAP decision-making related to more homogenous post-Cold War CLRTAP parties, more East-West coalition building, and a 'pulling-effect' of the EU accession process. With regard to the first element here, there seems to be widespread consensus on the notion that the general decision-making atmosphere has certainly become more open and relaxed than in the old Cold war days. In this context, it should be noted that in order to facilitate full involvement in the negotiations of countries with economies in transition, a Trust Fund for Assistance to Countries in Transition (TFACT) had been established by the Executive Body in 1994.[138] Donor countries, mainly from western Europe, deposited money into TFACT, the Executive Body decided on its use, and the secretariat was authorised to offer funding to one government-designated expert from each qualified country. This arrangement contributed to wide participation in the negotiations.[139]

However, as will be further elaborated later, these generally positive developments seem to have had very little effect on the main positions adopted in the negotiations. Moreover, given the enlargement process within the EU, one might have expected greater negotiation flexibility and more progressive positions in primary EU candidates such as Poland and Hungary. At least with regard to Poland, this does not seem to hold true.[140] All in all, although the general development of the East-West negotiation atmosphere seems to have been captured well by this proposition, the anticipated effects on positions did not follow suit.

Let us then move on to changes in decision-making procedures and approaches and the development of a multi-pollutant and multi-effects approach. Although the NO_x process in the 1980s was also heavily science-driven, the multi-pollutant process was marked by a unique and close interplay between scientific and technological bodies and institutions and negotiating bodies.[141] As one element in this, for the first time in CLRTAP negotiating history, there was an explicit scrutiny of abatement costs.[142] Moreover, the multi-pollutant and multi-effects approach driving the negotiations gave, of course, the negotiations a different institutional flavour from the process in the 1980s. Experienced analysts emphasise here the fact that the new approach was effects-based (or 'effects-driven'); in other words, it was possible to quantify the damage and compare to the ultimate target of no exceedance.

This comprehensive approach was – apart from making the whole package more rational and cost-effective – also an important key for encompassing (geographically) varying interests. The main driving forces in terms of impacts in Scandinavia and the Netherlands have been acidification and eutrophication; in many Central European countries (such as Germany, France, Belgium, and also the UK) it is increasingly air quality and public health, the latter also being the case to some extent in Southern Europe. Thus, by linking several effect-areas virtually everyone would be able to find some benefits that suited their interests.[143] Hence, this logic may help us understand why a number of countries proposed and ended up with somewhat more ambitious ceilings than in the business-as-usual scenario; providing some support for the second institutional proposition put forward. However, the fact that final ceilings *overall* ended up closer to the business-as-usual scenario than what was in principle the guiding, 'median' scenario, indicates that the short-term policy-driving effects of the multi-pollutant approach should not be exaggerated either.[144]

So what about the third institutional proposition put forward; drawing attention to a changing institutional environment, specifically in the form of possible, positive 'spill-over' effects from the parallel EU acidification/NEC process? As described in Chapter Three, the CLRTAP NO_x negotiations in the 1980s were also accompanied by related policy development within the EU. The motor vehicles negotiations had clear implications for NO_x emissions and the LCP negotiations circled around both SO_2 and NO_x emission limits. However, the EU and CLRTAP processes developed mainly according to their own, separate logic. The relationship between the two institutions grew far closer from the mid 1990s. First, both institutions relied heavily on modelling and scientific input produced at IIASA. Moreover, from the moment the EU's work on acidification and ozone strategies began to be specified by the development of a directive on National Emission Ceilings, i.e. in the autumn of 1996, the similarity between the processes became striking.

What did this similarity mean, then, in practice? As noted in the discussion above on comprehensiveness and package deals, links between processes may, in principle, mean both an integrative potential and a deadlock and impeding potential. From the CLRTAP point of view, the EU's financing of IIASA's modelling work after 1996 was a clear, positive interplay effect. Without the EU financial contribution to IIASA's work, the progress of the CLRTAP process could have been seriously slowed down. Moreover, CLRTAP discussions on technical annexes etc. could benefit from existing policies and guidelines within the EU context.

Did CLRTAP then benefit, more particularly, from parallel, stronger policies and positions developed within the less comprehensive and more homogenous EU context? Seemingly not very much. To some extent, this had to do with an unfortunate timing of events. There is little doubt that 'progressive' EU/CLRTAP actors hoped to be able to reach political agreement within the EU context *prior to* the final negotiation phase within CLRTAP.[145] In this way, anticipated more ambitious EU NEC ceilings and positions could have been 'transposed' into the CLRTAP context and contributed new political energy into this context. However, the EU process did not proceed as quickly as hoped for, and the resignation of the Santer Commission on March 16 1999, the day before the NEC Directive was to be launched, meant an additional delay. Hence, instead of what some had hoped for, the CLRTAP process got ahead of the EU process. Moreover, although the NEC Directive *was* put forward by the Commission in June, and pointed towards relatively ambitious ceilings for countries such as France, Germany, and the UK,[146] the EU countries did not enter the final CLRTAP meetings on the background of ceilings politically rubber-stamped in the EU Council of Ministers. There is, however, little evidence to suggest that EU policy dynamics in any way impeded CLRTAP progress. Hence, although the EU influenced CLRTAP policy-making in a positive way, and probably more strongly than ever, the 'EU effect' must be characterised as moderate.

Are there, then, other important institutional issues not highlighted by the propositions developed in Chapter Two? One such factor could be the role of the secretariat. Both participants in the negotiation process and observers pinpoint the policy-enhancing effects of a more active secretariat, providing strong formal and informal support during and in between all meetings.[147]

Tentatively summing up, although the basic functioning of CLRTAP as an institution was quite similar at the end of the 1990s to what it was at the end of the 1980s, several influential institutional differences can be noted. Most significantly, there was a unique, close interplay between scientific and political bodies and the multi-pollutants/effects approach which facilitated negotiations in several ways: The effects-based approach made possible quantification of damage and 'distance' to ultimate environmental objectives; the multi-effects approach provided 'benefit incentives' to all involved countries; and the multi-pollutant/multi-effects approach resulted in a higher level of demonstrable cost-effectiveness. Moreover, as a more moderately important development, parallel policy development within the EU and related EU financing of shared modelling work carried out at IIASA contributed positively to CLRTAP progress. However, in order to assess the more precise importance of these developments, other explanatory perspectives need to be taken into consideration.

Helpful Related Policy-making Within CLRTAP?

Within both the EU and CLRTAP contexts, *other policy developments* have taken place which have potentially influenced the focused processes. In Chapter Two, it was noted that such spill-over could take the form of policy goals being adopted in one context (for instance air quality goals) logically pointing to the need for stricter emissions reduction goals. But it could also take the form of specific 'integrative' package deals being formed with progress in the field of emissions reduction policies becoming possible due to linkages to other processes.

As mentioned, two other potentially significant processes have unfolded within CLRTAP during the period in question, resulting in protocols on heavy metals and persistent organic pollutants (POPs) being established in 1998. However, apart from the fact that the focus on the heavy metals and POPs processes in the Spring of 1998 provided a useful break in the complex process of juggling with multi-pollutants and multi-effects, neither of these other processes had any noticeable effect upon the Gothenburg Protocol negotiations. So attention can quickly be shifted to a limited opening up of the 'black box' of domestic politics.

A More Benign Constellation of Positions Due to Domestic Developments?

As noted in Chapter Two, an in-depth opening up of the 'black box' of domestic politics is beyond the scope of this study. Hence, it was suggested that prime attention be given to the background for the movement of previously indifferent parties and especially key laggards in a more green and constructive direction.

Let us then first sum up the central developments in terms of national positions. As can be recalled from Chapter Three, in the NO_x process in the 1980s the impression is clearly that the FRG exerted clear leadership, backed especially by Austria, the Netherlands, Switzerland and Sweden. Moreover, these five countries formed a NO_x '30 percent club' in 1987. The Nordic coalition, which played a quite important role in the sulphur negotiations, broke down in the NO_x context, with Finland and Norway moving towards more moderate and laggard positions. In the Gothenburg Protocol process, although the overall impression is that Germany played an important role in this process too, it was less forceful and clear-cut than in the NO_x negotiations in the 1980s.[148] But given the emerging strong focus on various, complex scientific inputs, the role of systemic actors may have become more important in keeping track of such inputs, not least the relationship between scientifically derived emission ceilings and the related political bids from the parties. Here, the well-functioning and more active secretariat may have provided enhanced 'systemic' leadership.

Moreover, the impression is also that the somewhat more low-key position of Germany was more than outweighed by an overall more pro-environmental and benign constellation of positions. For instance, Nordic collaboration was quite good in the concluding one and a half years of the negotiations.[149] Furthermore, most of the 'progressive' countries back in the 1980s adopted relatively 'progressive' positions in this follow-up process. For instance, in the process of deciding upon a guiding scenario for the final negotiations, central members of the '30 percent club' in the first NO_x negotiations such as Austria, Denmark, the Netherlands, and Sweden, supported the relatively ambitious G5/2 scenario. These countries also followed up by putting forward tentative emission ceilings quite in line with this scenario, although, in general, almost all of the countries backed away on some points from the emission ceilings derived from the guiding scenario.[150]

But the role of the 'Eastern' countries, including Russia, was not much more constructive in the Gothenburg Protocol process than in the earlier NO_x negotiations.[151] These countries did, for instance, back a guiding scenario with lower ambitiousness than the G5/2 scenario, and they were slow in the process of putting forward proposed emission ceilings. However, in terms of final ceilings these countries ended up pretty average – with some ceilings above those derived from the guiding scenario and some ceilings in line with this scenario.[152]

However, a particularly important and interesting 'Western' change took place in the 1990s process. The big emitter and earlier laggard, the UK, moved closer towards the 'progressive' camp. Especially in the con-cluding rounds of the negotiations, the UK was one of the countries which showed greatest negotiation flexibility.[153] As will be further documented in Chapter Five, in the 1990s the evidence of increasing rural and urban problems related to air pollution became stronger, and public concern especially about the urban element started to grow. Much of the local air quality problems in the (southern) UK relate to fine particles and ozone, and – not least important – it was demonstrated that *about half of the ozone in the UK is actually imported from Europe*. Hence, it was realised that a central key to improvements in the UK was the strengthening of international policies. Judging by the Scandinavian experience from the 1970s, the perception of a domestic problem growing due to 'acid import' from abroad is a powerful triggering mechanism for governmental interest in strong(er) international action.

Summing Up

Although regime-induced knowledge development was important in the first NO_x negotiations in the 1980s, this aspect was considerably developed in the Gothenburg Protocol process a decade later. The multi-pollutants/-effects approach clarified the 'distance' to environmental objectives; broadened the range of benefit incentives; and improved general cost-effectiveness. So in terms of the three institutional propositions put forward, the proposition highlighting the possible beneficial effects of the multi-pollutant approach pinpointed changes and effects clearly important for the outcome.

As a more moderately important development, parallel policy development within the EU and related EU financing of shared modelling work carried out at IIASA contributed positively to CLRTAP progress.

With regard to the third proposition, pinpointing the possibility of more constructive CLRTAP decision-making related to several changes in the East-West relationship, although the general development of the East-West negotiation atmosphere was captured well by this proposition, the anticipated effects on positions did not receive much support from the evidence scrutinised.

So what about other explanatory factors and perspectives? In terms of positive spill-over from other relevant policy development within CLRTAP, although two other protocol negotiation processes were concluded during the negotiations on the Gothenburg Protocol, neither of these had any noticeable effect upon the process given prime attention in this context. So attention could quickly be shifted to the development of national positions and a limited opening up of the 'black box' of domestic politics.

The overall picture here was not radically different from the process in the 1980s. True, the passing of a decade meant that various types of learning had taken place, both about the nature of the air pollution problems and ways of dealing with them. Probably the most important change in the course of the negotiation process was a more constructive and progressive role played by the UK, partly related to increasing domestic concern over air pollution and the growing perception of being polluted from abroad.

Finally, in terms of institutional dynamics, it is easy to ignore a simple and central factor, namely the need for review and renegotiation established in earlier protocols. It should here be recalled that an important foundation for the CLRTAP Gothenburg Protocol was the review clauses established in earlier protocols, and especially the 1988 NO_x Protocol. All in all, the single most important factor accounting for the strengthening of CLRTAP policy which stands out is the regime-induced knowledge improvement and the development of the multi-pollutant and multi-effects approach. As this development is the fruit of activities dating back to the 1980s, there is hence clear merit in seeing the Gothenburg Protocol as the jewel in the crown for CLRTAP as a dynamic regime.

Annex 4.1 Emission ceilings for sulphur – guiding scenarios, political bids and Gothenburg outcome
(thousands of tonnes of SO_2 per year)

Party	Emissions				Bids		Gothenburg Protocol
	1980	1990	G5/2r	REF	June 99	Sept. 99	% change
Armenia	141	73	-	-	72	-	73	0%
Austria	400	91	35	40	-	39	39	-57%
Belarus	740	637	494	494	-	480	480	-25%
Belgium	828	372	76	193	127.5	121	106	-72%
Bulgaria	2050	2008	378	846	896	856	856	-57%
Canada	4643	3236	-	-	-	-	-	-
Croatia	150	180	23	70	70	70	70	-61%
Czech Rep.	2257	1876	283	366	283	283	283	-85%
Denmark	450	182	60	90	60	55	55	-70%
Finland	584	260	116	116	116	116	116	-55%
France	3208	1269	219	448	400	400	400	-68%
Germany	7514	5313	463	581	550	550	550	-90%
Greece	400	509	546	546	-	546	546	7%
Hungary	1633	1010	296	546	550	550	550	-46%
Ireland	222	178	36	66	42	42	42	-76%
Italy	3757	1651	290	566	500	500	500	-70%
Latvia	-	119	104	104	-	107	107	-10%
Liechtenstein	0.39	0.15	-	-	-	-	0.11	-27%
Lithuania	311	222	107	107	-	145	145	-35%
Luxembourg	24	15	3	4	4	4	4	-73%
Netherlands	490	202	50	73	50	50	50	-75%
Norway	137	53	18	32	22	22	22	-58%
Poland	4100	3210	722	1397	(1100-1400)	1397	1397	-56%
Portugal	266	362	141	141	(165)	170	170	-53%
Republic of Moldova	308	265	38	117	-	135	135	-49%
Romania	1055	1311	148	594	-	918	918	-30%
Russian Federation*	7161	4460	2186	2344	-	(2352)	-	-
PEMA	1062	1133	-	-	-	635	635	-44%
PEMA (SOMA)	3135	1873	-	-	-	-	-	-
Slovakia	780	543	92	137	110	110	110	-80%
Slovenia	235	194	14	71	(30)	27	27	-86%
Spain	2959	2182	747	774	-	774	774	-65%
Sweden	491	119	67	67	67	67	67	-44%
Switzerland	116	43	23	26	26	26	26	-40%
Ukraine	3849	2782	1457	1488	1457	1457	1457	-48%
UK	4863	3731	499	980	700	625	625	-83%
USA	-	-	-	-	-	-	-	-
EC	26456	16436	3348	4685	-	4059	4059	-75%

* Figures apply to the European part within EMEP

Annex 4.2 Emission ceilings for nitrogen oxides – guiding scenarios, political bids and Gothenburg outcome
(thousands of tonnes of NO_2 per year)

Party	Emissions				Bids		Gothenburg Protocol
	1987	1990	G5/2r	REF	June 99	Sept. 99	% change
Armenia	52	46	-	-	46	-	46	0%
Austria	213	194	91	103	-	107	107	-45%
Belarus	263	285	290	316	-	255	255	-11%
Belgium	338	339	127	191	180.5	184	181	-47%
Bulgaria	416	361	266	297	266	266	266	-26%
Canada	2131	2104	-	-	-	-	-	-
Croatia	-	87	87	90	87	87	87	0%
Czech Rep.	816	742	188	296	235	286	286	-61%
Denmark	312	282	113	128	113-162	127	127	-55%
Finland	288	300	152	152	152-190	170	170	-43%
France	1630	1882	704	858	900	860	860	-54%
Germany	3177	2693	1081	1184	1100	1081	1081	-60%
Greece	-	343	344	344	-	344	344	0%
Hungary	265	238	137	198	198	198	198	-17%
Ireland	115	115	55	70	65	65	65	-43%
Italy	1811	1938	902	1130	1000	1000	1000	-48%
Latvia	-	93	118	118	-	84	84	-10%
Liechtenstein	0.65	0.63	-	-	-	-	0.37	-41%
Lithuania	171	158	134	138	-	110	110	-30%
Luxembourg	-	23	8	10	-	11	11	-52%
Netherlands	599	580	266	280	238	266	266	-54%
Norway	229	218	142	178	156	156	156	-28%
Poland	1530	1280	654	879	(800-879)	879	879	-31%
Portugal	-	348	144	177	220	260	260	-25%
Republic of Moldova	71	100	64	66	-	90	90	-10%
Romania	580	546	328	458	-	437	437	-20%
Russian Fed.[a]	2653[b]	3600	2653	2653	-	(2653)	-	-
PEMA	-	360	-	-	-	265	265	-26%
Slovakia	197	225	115	132	130	130	130	-42%
Slovenia	57	62	34	36	(45)	45	45	-27%
Spain	892	1113	726	847	-	847	847	-24%
Sweden	437	338	159	190	175	168	148	-56%
Switzerland	174	166	76	79	84	79	79	-52%
Ukraine	1094	1888	1222	1433	(1222)	1222	1222	-35%
UK	2618	2673	1181	1186	1181	1181	1181	-56%
USA	20689	21584	-	-	-	-	-	-
EC	-	13161	6053	6850	-	6671	6671	-49%

[a] Figures apply to the European part within EMEP.   [b] Not including all sources

Clearing the Air

Annex 4.3 Emission ceilings for volatile organic compounds – guiding scenarios, political bids and Gothenburg outcome
(thousands of tonnes of VOC per year)

Party	Emissions			Bids		Gothenburg Protocol	
	1990	G5/2r	REF	June 99	Sept. 99		% change
Armenia	81	-	-	81	-	81	0%
Austria	351	142	205	-	159	159	-55%
Belarus	533	-	-	-	-	309	-42%
Belgium	324	103	193	147	144	144	-56%
Bulgaria	217	185	190	188	185	185	-15%
Canada	2880	-	-	-	-	-	-
Croatia	105	86	111	90	90	90	-14%
Czech Rep.	435	156	305	220	220	220	-49%
Denmark	178	85	85	85-111	85	85	-52%
Finland	209	110	110	110-150	130	130	-38%
France	2957	989	1223	1100	1100	1100	-63%
Germany	3195	995	1137	995	995	995	-69%
Greece	373	261	267	-	261	261	-30%
Hungary	205	137	160	(137)	137	137	-33%
Ireland	197	55	55	55	55	55	-72%
Italy	2213	1030	1159	1159	1159	1159	-48%
Latvia	152	56	56	-	136	136	-11%
Liechtenstein	1.56	-	-	-	-	0.86	-45%
Lithuania	103	105	105	-	92	92	-11%
Luxembourg	20	7	7	-	9	9	-55%
Netherlands	502	157	233	191	191	191	-62%
Norway	310	195	195	195	195	195	-37%
Poland	831	475	807	(800)	800	800	-4%
Portugal	640	102	144	-	202	202	-68%
Republic of Moldova	157	42	42	-	100	100	-36%
Romania	616	500	504	-	523	523	-15%
Russian Federation	3566	2723	2786	-	(2786)	-	-
PEMA	203	-	-	-	165	165	-19%
Slovakia	149	140	140	140	140	140	-6%
Slovenia	42	40	40	(40)	40	40	-5%
Spain*	1094	648	669	-	669	669	-39%
Sweden	526	241	290	241	241	241	-54%
Switzerland	292	144	144	144	144	144	-51%
Ukraine	1369	770	851	(797)	797	797	-42%
UK	2555	1101	1351	1351	1200	1200	-53%
European Community	15353	6026	7128	-	6600	6600	-57%

* Figures apply to the European part within the EMEP area.

Annex 4.4 Emission ceilings for ammonia – guiding scenarios, political bids and Gothenburg outcome
(thousands of tonnes of NH_3 per year)

Party	Emis-sions	Bids				Gothenburg Protocol
	1990	G5/2r	REF	June 99	Sept. 99	% change
Armenia	25	-	-	0.06	-	25	0%
Austria	81	66	67	(66)	66	66	-19%
Belarus	219	140	163	-	158	158	-28%
Belgium	107	60	96	74.5	74	74	-31%
Bulgaria	144	105	126	108	108	108	-25%
Croatia	37	29	37	30	30	30	-19%
Czech Rep.	156	101	108	101	101	101	-35%
Denmark	122	69	72	69	69	69	-43%
Finland	35	31	31	31	31	31	-11%
France	814	642	777	780	780	780	-4%
Germany	764	413	571	550	550	550	-28%
Greece	80	73	74	-	73	73	-9%
Hungary	124	77	137	90	90	90	-27%
Ireland	126	116	126	116	116	116	-8%
Italy	466	356	432	419	419	419	-10%
Latvia	44	35	35	-	44	44	0%
Liechtenstein	0.15	-	-	-	-	0.15	0%
Lithuania	84	72	81	-	84	84	0%
Luxembourg	7	7	7	7	7	7	0%
Netherlands	226	104	136	105	128	128	-43%
Norway	23	21	21	23	23	23	0%
Poland	508	468	541	(468)	468	468	-8%
Portugal	98	65	67	-	108	108	10%
Republic of Moldova	49	41	48	-	42	42	-14%
Romania	300	227	304	-	210	210	-30%
Russian Federation*	1191	894	894	-	(894)	-	-
PEMA	61	-	-	-	49	49	-20%
Slovakia	62	39	47	39	39	39	-37%
Slovenia	24	16	21	(20)	20	20	-17%
Spain*	351	353	353	-	353	353	1%
Sweden	61	48	48	58	58	57	-7%
Switzerland	72	63	66	63	63	63	-13%
Ukraine	729	588	649	(592)	592	592	-19%
United Kingdom	333	264	297	297	297	297	-11%
United States of America	264	-	-	-	-	-	-
European Community	3671	2667	3154	-	3129	3129	-15%

* Figures apply to the European part within the EMEP area.

Notes

[84] See Article 5, 'Review process'.

[85] See EB.AIR/WG.5/R.32, June 11, 1992, Second generation abatement strategies for SO_2, NOx, NH_3 and VOC, note submitted by the delegations of Norway, Sweden and United Kingdom.

[86] Thanks to Andrew Farmer for pinpointing the importance of the Second Sulphur Protocol for the Gothenburg Protocol process.

[87] At least in meeting notes produced by the Norwegian Ministry of Environment.

[88] Acid News 2, April 1996, pp. 5-6.

[89] As noted later, this issue was raised, but not resolved, at the EB meeting in December 1997.

[90] NME Note, March 9, 1995, WGS meeting summary.

[91] NME Note, February 22, 1996, WGS meeting summary.

[92] EB.AIR/WG.5/R.64, 17 June 1996, WGS, 'Integrated assessment of abatement strategies for nitrogen and volatile organic compounds', Status report by the Chairman of the Task Force on Integrated Assessment Modeling.

[93] NME note, August 29, 1996.

[94] ECE/EB.AIR/49, 10 December 1996, Report of the fourteenth session of the Executive Body, p. 7. These data were based on inputs from IIASA, Imperial College (London) and the Stockholm Environment Institute (SEI).

[95] ECE/EB.AIR/49, 10 December 1996, op. cit.

[96] For a good overview and analysis of the POPs process, see Selin (2000).

[97] This is one of the main conclusions in NME's meeting summary, dated March 24, 1997.

[98] EB.AIR/WG.5/42, WGS-20 summary, pp. 5-6.

[99] This is pinpointed in the NME meeting summary, March 25, 1997, p. 2.

[100] Acid News 2, June 1997, p. 6.

[101] Ibid.

[102] NME meeting summary, dated September 30, 1997.

[103] EB.AIR/WG.5/R.80, 30 May 1997, Draft composite negotiating text for a protocol on nitrogen oxides and related substances.

[104] Communication with Lars Nordberg, former Head of the CLRTAP Secretariat, October 16, 2000.

[105] NME meeting summary, dated September 30, 1997; op. cit.

[106] Pinpointed by Christer Ågren; communication with Ågren, October, 2000.

[107] ECE/EB.AIR/53, 7 January 1998, Report of the fifteenth session of the Executive Body, p. 6. See also NME meeting summary, dated January 1, 1998.

[108] Acid News 1, March 1998, p. 11.

[109] ECE/EB.AIR/53, op. cit., p. 7.

[110] According to Christer Ågren, this type of work was actually initiated by the EU DG ENV when preparing the Acidification Strategy in the autumn of 1996. It was later 'carried over' to the CLRTAP process. The study in question was carried out by M. Holland et al., AEA Technology, in Oxfordshire; commissioned by the DETR. See EB.AIR/WG.5/R.97, 21 January 1998 ('Economic assessment of benefits'); Acid News 2, June 1998, 'Benefits of reduction assessed', pp. 16-18.

[111] Acid News, op. cit., p. 18. According to Christer Ågren, health effects were to a very large part dominating the benefits analysis. Materials included only modern materials, and natural ecosystems were in practice set at zero monetary value. This means that in fact only small parts of the benefits were quantified and included.

[112] International Environment Reporter, July 8, 1998, 'Environment ministers sign protocols on heavy metals, organic pollutants', p. 663.

[113] Bjørkbom (1998:3).

[114] NME meeting summary, dated Sept.15, 1998, p. 4.

[115] Acid News 3, October 1998, p. 4.

[116] EB.AIR/CRP. 19/Add.1, 8 December 1998, p. 2.

[117] The position was also supported by Croatia, Hungary, Latvia, Poland, and Slovenia. Norway also came out as a supporter, in the wake of the EU clarification. Switzerland was the only country supporting a higher level of ambition. See NME WGS-28 meeting note, dated February 3, 1999.

[118] Ibid.

[119] Ibid.

[120] Acid News 1, March 1999, p. 1.

[121] NME WGS-28 meeting note, dated February 3, 1999, p. 3.

[122] Acid News 1, March 1999, p. 4.

[123] Ibid., p. 5.

[124] Acid News 2, June 1999, p. 5.

[125] NME WGS-29 meeting note, dated April 7, 1999.

[126] This section draws heavily on NME WGS-30 meeting note dated June 8, 1999. It also draws upon EB.AIR/WG.5/62, dated 16 June, 1999.

[127] EB.AIR/WG.5/62, op. cit., p. 2.

[128] These figures refer to 'thousands of tonnes of SO2' or other substances. For an overview of September positions, see Acid News 3, October 1999, p. 4.

[129] ENDS Report 296, September 1999, p. 44.

[130] Acid News 3, October 1999, p. 2.

[131] ENDS Report 296, op. cit., p. 45.

[132] UN/ECE Press Release ECE/ENV/99/11, 24 November 1999.

[133] See Acid News 4, December 1999, p. 5.

[134] Acid News 3, October 1999, p. 4.

[135] See Liefferink (1996), Chapter 8.

[136] Interviews, Autumn 1999.

[137] Ibid.

[138] See Selin (2000:137).

[139] Communication with Lars Nordberg, former Head of the CLRTAP Secretariat, October 16 and November 30, 2000.

[140] Interviews with Swedish CLRTAP negotiators, Autumn 1999.

[141] This uniqueness was emphasised by several participants in the process, interviewed during the autumn of 1999.

[142] According to one interviewee, this did not matter very much for the outcome of the negotiations.

[143] Thanks to Christer Ågren for clarifying these aspects.

[144] However, in a more long-term perspective, the development and adoption of a multi-pollutant approach may stand out as a real turning-point in terms of air pollution policy development.

[145] Interviews with EU an CLRTAP negotiators, autumn 1999. Communication with Christer Ågren, February and November 2000.

[146] See comparative table in ENDS Report 296, September 1999, p. 44.

[147] Communication with Henrik Selin and Lars Nordberg, autumn 2000. See also Selin (2000).

[148] Interview with Matthew Ferguson, IEEP, November 1999.

[149] Ibid.

[150] As noted in section 5.2.1, Denmark for instance put forward both NOx and VOC ceilings well above the ceilings in the guiding scenario. See Annex 4.2 and 4.3 to this chapter.

[151] Interviews with CLRTAP negotiators, Autumn 1999.

[152] For instance, Poland ended up with both SO_2, NOx and VOC ceilings considerably above ceilings in the guiding scenario, while a country such as Lithuania ended up with both NOx and VOC ceilings somewhat below those in the guiding scenario, and SO_2 and NH_3 ceilings slightly above those derived from this scenario. See Annexes to this chapter.

[153] Interviews, Autumn 1999.

Chapter 5

How the EU Took Up the Challenge of Acidification and Smog in the 1990s
The Acidification Strategy and NEC Directive

Introduction

In the previous chapter we saw how the Convention on Long-Range Trans-boundary Air Pollution (CLRTAP) took a significant step forward in terms of policy-making with the development and adoption of the Gothenburg Protocol. We can now investigate further the interesting and quite parallel policy development within the EU. In this chapter we will examine how the EU took up the challenge of acidification and smog in the 1990s by the development first of the Acidification and Ozone Strategies, and then by a directive setting national ceilings for the emission of the most important pollutants. The National Emission Ceilings (NEC) Directive was developed in conjunction with a further strengthening of policies addressing emissions from combustion plants and vehicles, and the improvement of air quality. This interplay is documented and discussed below. Moreover, given the central place of the 'science for policy' tool of critical loads and the subsequent policy tool of setting national emission ceilings also within the EU context, CLRTAP and EU policy-making have become increasingly intertwined. This interesting development is also documented and discussed in the chapter.

With regard to the more specific structuring of the chapter, the following section carries out a first overview and 'thick description' of the initiation and development of both the Acidification Strategy and NEC Directive process and the main related air pollution policy processes within the EU context. On this basis, section three contains a brief discussion of the question of the increase in policy strength over time, concluding that the EU development in this particular case is even more similar to the development within CLRTAP than anticipated. Hence, policy strength has indeed increased considerably also within the EU context, but far from enough to ensure optimal environmental conditions. In section four considerable space is devoted to discussing how well the various explanatory propositions developed in Chapter Two can throw light upon the EU policy developments. Hence, the impact of 'deeper' EU institutional changes, the interplay with other relevant EU policy-making, and various domestic developments are discussed. Section five sums up main findings.

Developing the EU Acidification/Ozone Strategies and a NEC Directive: An Introductory Overview

How It All Started

The process has roots going back at least to the year 1992. In February of that year it was reported that the Commission was considering new emissions reductions targets for SO_2 and NO_x. This was based on a set of emissions projections which was produced in connection with the drafting of the EU Fifth Environment Action Programme. These projections indicated that, under a business-as-usual energy price scenario, critical loads for sulphur and nitrogen inputs would be exceeded over a large area of the EU by 2010. Hence, emissions reductions by 2010 in the order of 35 percent (SO_2) and 30 percent (NO_x) were indicated as necessary.[154]

These targets were then adopted in the 1993 Fifth Action Programme.[155] Following this, EU policy-making attention turned towards the development of air quality standards, with work being conducted on a new framework directive on air quality standards.[156] As an important external event, within CLRTAP, negotiations on the Second Sulphur Protocol were concluded with the adoption of the 1994 Oslo Protocol. In this Protocol, the EU as an entity took on the commitment to reduce sulphur emissions by 62 percent within 2000.[157] Adding important political energy to the EU process early in 1995, the then EU new-comer, Sweden, began to press for the development of a more comprehensive EU Acidification Strategy with the 1994 Oslo Protocol as an important point of reference.[158] This really set the ball in motion.

Developing the Acidification and Ozone Strategies: 1995-97

The Swedish initiative led the Council of Environment Ministers in March 1995 to call upon the Commission to develop an integrated program for tackling acidification.[159] DG ENV took on the task, and a Commission Staff Working Paper was presented to the Council of Ministers in December 1995. A central conclusion in this Paper was that although existing and forthcoming EU legislation would reduce acidifying emissions, even within a 'strict' reduction scenario, depositions would exceed critical loads in significant parts of Europe. Moreover, comprehensive and cost-effective solutions were called for.[160] On the basis of this Paper, the Council instructed the Commission to 'identify additional measures [which] will be needed in order to complete the existing policy into a more coherent acidification strategy, able to reach the goal of no exceedance of critical loads' as soon as possible, and at the latest by mid-1997.[161]

So the DG ENV started working on a more full-fledged strategy document. As an intermediate step in this process, a Commission working paper was presented to the Member Countries at the end of October in 1996. Aided by the RAINS model developed at IIASA (see Chapter Four), the working paper laid out a reference scenario, two scenarios showing maximum technically feasible reductions (MFR), three least-cost scenarios (with 45, 50 and 55 percent gap closure), and three scenarios for sensitivity analysis.[162] Due to the high costs related to the more ambitious MFR options, DG ENV ended up by tentatively recommending the medium least-cost scenario, which would mean a 50 percent reduction of the area within the Union in which critical loads for acidification would be exceeded by 2010. The estimated annual cost for the target year 2010 in this scenario was 8.4 billion ecu.[163]

A more elaborate draft strategy was then circulated to Member States in January 1997. The centrepiece of this draft strategy was the setting of *national emission ceilings* for SO_2, NO_x and ammonia. As a major surprising element, it turned out that the biggest cuts would be required in terms of SO_2, a previously much-regulated substance.[164] With regard to the proposed sulphur ceilings, particularly large reductions would be required by Italy, Belgium, Spain, Ireland, France and the UK.[165] Moreover, work on a parallel *ground-level ozone strategy* was announced, also targeting NO_x and in addition, VOCs. Hence, a need for close coordination of these processes was emphasised.[166] As work had started on the development of a subsidiary directive on ground-level ozone in the wake of the 1996 adoption of the framework directive on air quality, there were at this point at least three related processes in progress.[167]

Despite some critical comments from Member Countries, the Commission decided to formally launch its Acidification Strategy on March 12, 1997.[168] The Strategy included several elements, with the establishment of national emissions ceilings for each pollutant and each member state, coordinated with the parallel development of the Ozone Strategy as a major building block. Other important elements included the revision of the Large Combustion Plant Directive (cf. Chapter Three); the designation of Baltic and North Sea sulphur dioxide control areas, the proposed ratification of the 1994 CLRTAP Sulphur Protocol, and, not least, a draft Directive limiting the permissible sulphur content of heavy fuel oil to 1 percent by January 1, 2000. As indicated in the earlier draft, the Commission aimed for a 50 percent gap closure, meaning in this context a 50 percent reduction by 2010 of the area within the Union in which critical loads for acidification were exceeded.[169]

Soon it became clear that revising the LCP Directive would re-activate the main conflict issues of the 1980s. In May, the Commission received heated reactions from a number of Member States to a circulated draft of a revised Directive. The Draft outlined new and much tighter sectoral ceilings for emissions from existing plants by 2010, as well as stricter emission limit values (ELVs) for the emissions of SO_2 and NO_x from new LCPs. The UK Environment Minister feared a close-down of all but two coal-fired power plants. Moreover, France expressed fears that such limits would hinder plans to diversify its energy supply, while Sweden, the Netherlands, Greece and Spain questioned the need for *sectoral* emissions ceilings – with *national* ceilings in development under the Acidification Strategy.[170]

The first debate in the Council of Ministers on the Commission's March Acidification Strategy took place on October 16. It turned out that a number of Member States regarded the Strategy as demanding excessively costly reductions in sulphur dioxide emissions for too small an environmental gain. This included most of all the Southern countries, and especially Italy. The UK and Ireland were more undecided, while the Northern countries were more positive. On the basis of the overall quite critical response to the further work on the Strategy, the Council emphasised the need to identify more low-cost options.[171] The issue was further debated in the Council of Ministers in mid-December. Similar to the October session, a North-South split clearly emerged. Several means were used by the proponents of the draft Strategy in an effort to narrow this gap in positions. First, it was emphasised that any Community Strategy in this area should fully take into account that the problem of acidification affects some countries and regions more than others, due to greater ecosystem vulnerability, prevailing winds and locations of emissions. Moreover, it was acknowledged by the Commission that although national emissions ceilings could be useful, the strictness of such ceilings could impose an unacceptable burden on certain Member States, and more in-depth discussion was needed on this point.[172]

Overall, the Council conclusions can be characterised as somewhat ambivalent. While at the same time the Council asked the Commission to refine its analysis, the long-term target of 'no exceedance of critical loads' was re-iterated; the establishment of interim targets was supported; it was noted that 'national emission ceilings can constitute an effective as well as flexible approach'; the foreseen ozone strategy was welcomed; and a list of 'technical refinements' was annexed. Although not explicitly spelled out, this refinement was to be made when the NEC proposal was further developed and based on both ozone and acidification targets.[173]

Refining the Acidification Strategy: 1998 - Spring 1999

Although the Acidification Strategy was a strategy, and not a draft directive, the Parliament was expected to give its opinion. So the Strategy moved on to the Parliament's institutions during the spring. As a first step, on April 23 1998 the Environment Committee unanimously adopted a report on the Communication from the Commission. In addition to supporting the main elements in the package put forward by the Commission, the Committee suggested several strengthening elements. These included setting a target date for 2015, at which point acidification in all areas should be below critical levels. Moreover, the Committee called for the strengthening of current legislation on emissions from large installations such as power stations and wider use of financial incentives in reducing sulphur and nitrogen emissions.[174]

This input was followed up by the Parliament in plenary on May 13. In addition to a general support for the Strategy's main points, the Parliament adopted the Environment Committee's call for a 2015 target (at which point acidification areas should not exceed critical levels in any area). Moreover, as suggested by the Environment Committee, several additional policy elements were called for: A strengthening of current legislation on emissions from large installations; the full application of the precautionary principle; the increased use of financial instruments in order to reduce emissions; and the need to establish rules applicable to ships using EU ports. All this added up to 28 proposed amendments.[175]

Meanwhile, the Commission pondered upon the May input from the Parliament and the various amendments suggested there. In the beginning of July, the Commission made two important moves in this context. First, in relation to the 28 amendments tabled by the EP in May, the Commission signalled that it could accept 'entirely or partially' 16 of these amendments, these mainly being related to marine areas and shipping.[176] Second, the Commission came forward with a formal proposal for a revised Large Combustion Plant Directive. This proposal would only apply to *new plants* coming into operation after January 1, 2000, and suggested twice as strict emission limit values with regard to SO_2, NO_x and dust emissions as the existing limit values at the time. Gas turbines were now included. The suggested new limit values were accompanied by a general up-dating of the Directive, taking into account the technical progress achieved in the LCP sector over the years. With regard to the controversial issue of requirements to existing plants, it was announced that a revised proposal including national ceilings was on the drawing board.[177]

In the course of the autumn of 1998, the Commission received several LCP inputs of a critical nature. First, in a report to the Commission, the International Institute for Applied Systems Analysis (IIASA) concluded that by concentrating on new plants, the Commission's proposal would have little environmental effect. According to IIASA's estimates, by 2010 85 percent of SO_2 emissions and 66 percent of NO_x emissions would still stem from plants built before 1987.[178] Moreover, three environmental NGOs called upon the Commission to include existing plants in the LCP revision process, with emission limits coming into force from January 2004, and to tighten further the proposed emission limits for new plants. According to the NGOs, the proposed limits failed to match the best available techniques.[179] The Commission itself launched a discussion paper proposing a further integration and coordination of EU air pollution policy, possibly into a single, umbrella clean air strategy. This would enhance the development of cost-effective solutions. Such a strategy should be reconsidered and revised at regular intervals, for instance every five years.[180]

But it was not until the beginning of March 1999 that the LCP Proposal was again debated in a number of EU institutions. With regard to the Environment Council (meeting on March 11), the earlier North-South split reappeared. Although the general aim of the proposal was welcomed by all the Ministers, the Northern countries basically argued for stricter limits and the inclusion of existing plants in the legislation, while southerners such as Spain and Greece were worried that this legislation would require disproportionate efforts from countries not affected by the acidification problems.[181] Spain was especially critical, and argued that the directive would affect Member States' energy policies and should hence be based on Article 130s (2). Given that this article requires unanimity, this would in practice provide Spain with veto power in the further process.[182]

Moreover, as part of the European Parliament's first reading process, on March 17 the Parliament's Environment Committee adopted a call for strengthened regulations with an 'overwhelming' majority. This call included stricter emissions limits, not least an inclusion of all existing LCPs in the regulatory scope, an inclusion of offshore gas turbines, and improved

Member State emissions information to the public.[183] This was followed up by the Parliament's first reading meeting in plenary on April 14. Although a majority was obtained for strengthening elements proposed by the Environment Committee, the opposition was considerable. In consequence, the Environment Committee's recommendations were adopted with 283 votes in favour, but 233 against, and 10 abstentions. MEPs from both Spain and the UK maintained that the adoption of rules which were too strict could easily lead to resistance and non-compliance.[184]

Launching and Adjusting the NEC Directive: Spring 1999-2001

The Commission was scheduled to adopt and present its proposal for a new national emission ceilings directive on March 17. However, cutting a fascinating side-story short, the Santer Commission was forced to resign on March 16, and all policy initiatives were put on hold. According to *International Environment Reporter*, it was Finland (ready to assume EU presidency in July and anxious to get things moving) along with environmental lobby groups, who urged the Commission to come forward with proposals and not to wait until a new Commission took office sometime in the fall.[185]

On June 9 the caretaker Commission managed to put forward the NEC draft directive in effect merging the Acidification Strategy and Ozone Strategy processes (Directive COM (1999) 125 final).[186] The draft Directive set for the first time, individual limits for each Member State's total emissions by 2010 of four pollutants: SO_2, NO_x, VOCs and ammonia (NH_3). Moreover, in line with the Acidification Strategy's emphasis on cost-effectiveness, estimated costs and benefits were presented. On the cost side, a total figure of 7.5 billion euros as annual cost for the target year 2010 was indicated. Moreover, estimated costs for each country were presented. Five countries stood out as high cost implementers: Belgium, France, Germany, the Netherlands and the UK. In terms of benefits, a benefit range from euro 17 billion to 32 billion was indicated. Hence, based on these figures, benefits clearly exceeded costs. In addition, several review and reporting procedures were suggested, including annual emissions reports and the drawing up of inventories and emissions projections up to the year 2010.

The NEC directive proposal was complemented by an air quality directive proposal for ozone in ambient air (COM (1999) 125). This was the third proposal for a daughter directive under the Air Quality Framework Directive adopted in September 1996. The daughter directive proposed aspirational, non-binding target values for ozone by 2010; targets 'widely seen as ambitious', according to *Environment Watch*.[187] To protect human health, the proposal took its lead from the relevant WHO guideline, which calls for a limit on ambient ozone concentrations of 120 micrograms per cubic metre (μ/m3). It was suggested that this limit could be breached up to 20 days per calendar year.[188] Fulfilling these targets, health-related ozone exposure would be reduced by 35 percent, and vegetation-related ozone exposure would be down by 20 percent. In addition, requirements were included to monitor ozone concentrations in ambient air, and to subsequently report to the public on the findings of that monitoring.

Within the environmental NGO camp, these proposals were received with satisfaction. The NGOs emphasised that the proposals should be treated as an integrated package. Moreover, they pinpointed that the cost figures were overestimates, while the monetary estimates of the benefits were underestimates.[189] However, central actors within the industry camp remained unhappy.[190] European employers federation UNICE pointed out that the reference scenario in itself implied costs close to 60 billion euro, and argued that any environmental improvements would be 'small' and 'based on modelling estimates which are known to be unreliable'.[191]

Within the CLRTAP context, a multi-pollutant protocol agreement was reached in September 1999 (see Chapter Four). Compared with the ceilings proposed by the EU Commission in the June draft directive, EU Member States generally committed themselves to less ambitious ceilings within the ECE/CLRTAP context. Neither the new environment commissioner, Margot Wallström, nor environmental watchdogs such as the European Environment Bureau, were satisfied. Wallström told *International Environment Reporter* 'I don't agree with the position the Member States took in Geneva and I will do everything I can do to get them to adopt the Commission standards proposed earlier this year'.[192]

The first major opportunity to discuss national positions on NECs and ozone standards arose at the Environment Council meeting in mid-October.[193] Exploiting the 'window of opportunity' of this Council meeting, the Commission published its annual report on ozone pollution on the day of the meeting. Among other things, this report pinpointed that the existing health protection threshold for ozone was exceeded on 20–60 days in the Mediterranean countries, with most critical conditions in Italy, Greece, France and Spain. However, the report seemingly failed to influence positions in the Council. Ministers from eight countries – the four Mediterranean states plus France, Ireland, Finland and the UK – made it clear that they preferred to stick to the ceilings agreed to within the CLRTAP context. Austria, Germany, Luxembourg, the Netherlands and Sweden signalled a willingness to go further than the protocol, but not as far as the Commission's proposal. The latter group of countries was also favourable to including existing plants in the LCP revision process. With regard to the proposed ozone targets, it was again the Mediterranean countries which objected most strongly, arguing that their climatic conditions are more favourable to ozone formation than in Northern Europe. The Council, however, came out in support of the Commission's proposal for an interim guideline for ozone, with a review in 2004.

Furthering the LCP revision process, the Commission tabled an amended proposal on November 25, accepting most of the Parliament's suggested amendments, but with some crucial exceptions. It did not accept proposals for stricter limits, nor inclusion of existing LCPs in the legislation.[194] When the CLRTAP Protocol was adopted at the beginning of December, Environment Commissioner Wallström refused to sign the Protocol on behalf of the EU – claiming that to do so would jeopardise the prospects for more demanding limits under the NEC Directive.[195]

Moreover, at the Environment Council meeting in mid-December, no progress was made on the central issue of whether or not to include existing installations in the revised LCP directive. The Council President, Finland's Environment Minister Satu Hassi, produced several compromise proposals, but all were reportedly rejected by a group of countries led by Germany, including Austria, Denmark and Sweden. These countries were strong supporters of including of existing installations. The UK, along with Greece, Italy and Spain, took a strong opposite view, and argued for dealing with existing plants within the NEC context.[196]

The Parliament picked up on the NEC and ozone processes at the end of February 2000. With regard to NECs, the Environment Committee suggested deleting some sea and air transport exceptions allowed by the Commission and, not least, spelling out more clearly the demand for review and revision of the Directive. Within the ozone context, the need for a specific 2020 target date was pinpointed, in contrast to the Commission's more open suggested formulation 'within a foreseeable time period'.[197] In the Parliament's plenary meeting on March 14, the Environment Committee's positions both on NECs and ozone targets were adopted.

However, members of the Parliament's Industry Committee voiced critical concerns. These concerns included an insistence that NECs should be set jointly by the EU and national governments, and criticism of the Commission's proposed methodology for calculating emissions. With regard to the ozone targets, Industry Committee spokesman John Purvis warned of 'the serious implications for our industries and our competitiveness...if the Commission's proposal wins through'. As a comment upon the positions taken by the Industry Committee, the Parliament's rapporteur on the ozone directive, Chris Davies (UK), pinpointed that if these positions had been adopted by the EU, they would have left the EU 'in a much weaker position than the USA'.[198]

When the Environment Council met at the end of March, some progress was claimed. As a response to questions put to the Member states by the Portuguese Presidency, a reportedly large majority of the delegations said they were willing to accept more ambitious targets than agreed to in the CLRTAP context. Moreover, states such as the UK explicitly linked the NEC and LCP contexts as a key to further progress.[199]

Building upon this limited progress, reaching a further consensus on NECs and revised LCP targets emerged as key issues at the up-coming Environment Council meeting in June. Expectations in advance were mixed. Both the Commission and the Portuguese Presidency had high hopes for reaching a political agreement, while key players in the EP were more sceptical.[200] With regard to NECs, positive signals had been received from the UK, France and Portugal. Moreover, the Presidency had worked out a possible LCP compromise, basically adding a flexibility element to the inclusion of existing plants. On one hand, these plants would be granted a 'residual life' and an additional service period for two to three years. On the other hand, in accordance with the IPPC Directive the installations would be required to meet some type of 'Best Available Technology' (BAT) requirements by 2007.[201] This double-edged approach would leave operators to decide whether they would make the necessary investments or close obsolete installations.[202]

In the end, the Council meeting on June 22 turned out to be quite successful. The suggested LCP compromise on existing plants was accepted.[203] Equally important, a compromise NEC agreement was also reached.[204] On the one hand, countries such as Greece, Spain, the UK and Belgium moved sufficiently to ensure an overall somewhat more ambitious emission reductions profile than had been achieved within the CLRTAP context. For instance, in terms of achieved protection, the EU ceilings were between 0.6 percent (NH_3) to 5 percent (SO_2) stricter than the CLRTAP ceilings (see Chapter Six). On the other hand, there was still a considerable gap in relation to the initial ceilings proposed by the Commission. For instance, in terms of sulphur, the UK was assigned a ceiling of 497 kilotonnes (kt) by the Commission, but ended up with the considerably higher 585 kt ceiling. Germany was assigned 463 kt by the Commission, but ended up with 520 kt. Similarly, France was assigned 218 kt, but ended up with a 375 kt ceiling. Overall, the Council ceilings were 5 percent to 17 percent higher than those proposed by the Commission.[205]

With regard to reporting and reviews, each member country was to draw up an emission reductions program and report this to the Commission at the latest by October 2002. In addition, states should report yearly on their emission levels and provide forecasts for 2010. The Commission was then to report to the Parliament and Council of Ministers in 2004 and 2008 on progress being made.[206] Commenting upon the outcome, the Environment Commissioner, Wallström, expressed some degree of satisfaction stating that 'this will mean a significant contribution to tackle the kind of air pollution that really affects human health'.[207]

Progress on the related ozone issue followed in the fall. The October 10 Environment Council adopted the ground-level ozone directive. As expected, the basic 120 micrograms per cubic metre limit was adopted as a voluntary target value, and allowed to be breached up to 25 times a year from 2010. The latter element was a compromise brokered by the French Presidency; with Greece, Spain, Portugal and Italy pushing for a '40 breaches per year' limit, and the Commission and the green EU states supporting a '20 breaches per year' limit.[208] The voluntary, guiding nature of the target values set the Council and the Commission on a collision course with the Parliament, which in its first reading had demanded mandatory target values.[209]

Further bolstering the Council's common position on NECs and LCPs obtained in June and formally adopted in November, the Commission came out in basic support of this common position in mid-November; although pinpointing that the common positions were not the most cost-effective way of cutting emissions. The Commission 'recognised' that Member States had made considerable efforts since the Gothenburg Protocol, and that there were important uncertainties related to the implementation of the Kyoto commitments and the enlargement process which strengthened the case for accepting the ceilings on the table.[210]

The common position of the Council and the Commission raised the stakes for the Parliament in its second reading phase in the spring 2001. However, at the March 13–14 session, where both NECs and LCPs were debated, the Parliament ended up reaffirming its earlier call for stricter regulations. As heralded in *Europe Environment*: 'MEPs Get Tough on Large Combustion Plants and National Emission Ceilings'.[211] In the NEC context, the Parliament called for lower emission ceilings for three of the four targeted substances (i.e. SO_2, NO_x and VOCs) than those adopted by the Council in June 2000. In the case of VOCs, the suggested ceilings were identical with those initially proposed by the Commission in June 1999. With regard to SO_2 and NO_x, the suggested ceilings were in fact a little lower than the initial Commission proposals.[212]

In addition, the Parliament re-tabled the setting of a specific, final date when the ultimate goal of the legislation – no exceeding of critical loads – should be achieved. The goal, was 'in principle' to be met by 2015, with an absolute deadline of 2020. Moreover, the Parliament again suggested deleting some sea and air transport exceptions initially allowed by the Commission. On the issue of LCPs, the Parliament basically called for a certain tightening up of the compromise adopted by the Council in June 2000; i.e. cutting down on the exemptions for existing plants and a tightening up of the emission limits for both old and new plants. In terms of closing loopholes, it was for instance suggested to end the '20,000 hours after 2008' derogation for existing plants in 2012.[213]

Not unexpectedly, the stage was now set for a final round of the NEC and LCP processes within the context of a Conciliation Committee. Informal 'trialogue' meetings between the representatives of the Council, the Parliament and the Commission were held on April 27 and May 29. It was reported from these meetings that the Member States had 'little room for manoeuvre' regarding almost all the key NEC and LCP amendments put forward by the Parliament in its second reading. In the context of NECs, several delegations had 'stalled' on the call for further SO_2 and NO_x emission reductions.[214]

Hence, the nature of the Conciliation Committee compromise finally brokered on June 25 did not come as very big surprise.[215] In essence, although the Parliament achieved certain concessions, the outcome was not radically different from the common position adopted in the Council a year earlier. Hence, the NECs adopted in June 2000 will apply at least up to the first review in 2004. Moreover, the reviews in 2004 and 2008 will assess the extent to which the long-term objective of not exceeding critical loads can be met by 2020, and 'if appropriate', be accompanied by proposals for modified emission ceilings.

With regard to LCPs, the final outcome is a quite complicated compromise between the Council's common position and the Parliament's demands put forward in the second reading. A good illustration is the '20,000 hours after 2008' derogation for existing plants agreed to in the Council's common position. The Parliament suggested ending this derogation in 2012 – and the final outcome was an ending date of 2015.[216] However, according to the European Environmental Bureau, the compromises were disappointing from an environmental viewpoint and overall were far closer to the positions of the Council than the Parliament.[217] The two directives were then finally and formally adopted by EU internal market ministers on September 27, 2001.

The NEC and LCP agreement left only one element unresolved in this round of air pollution policy-making, namely the ground-level ozone directive. In March 2001, the Commission came out generally in favour of the Council's common position adopted last October. As the Commission saw it, the Council had taken aboard most of the amendments the Parliament tabled in the first reading and which had been incorporated in the Commission's amended proposal.[218] However, it soon became clear that the Parliament was far from satisfied with concessions made by the Council.

In the second reading process in June 2001, the rapporteur Chris Davies condemned the Council for 'watering down the Commission's – already weak – proposal' and regretted 'that the Council <had> only accepted ten of the 19 amendments adopted by the Parliament at first reading' (*Europe Environment*, June 12, 2001, p.17). It was no surprise then that the Parliament on June 15 ended up re-stating its earlier calls for a '20 breaches per year' limit (instead of the 25 breaches limit adopted by the Council and backed by the Commission), and making 2010 a binding deadline for achieving the target values 'save where this is physically impossible' (instead of the more open and guiding 'as far as possible' nature of the target values adopted by the Council). Similarly, the Parliament called for a legally binding long-term objective of full compliance with WHO guidelines by 2020 (instead of the Council's more open 'in principle' acceptance of this long-term target).[219] As the council could not accept these amendments, conciliation talks started in the beginning of October 2001.

The Development of Policy Strength: Considerably Stronger – but not 'Strong Enough'?

'The Leap Forward': A Clear Strengthening of Behavioural Bite

Piecing together a CLRTAP-derived baseline. In order to measure the strengthening of policy more precisely, it is of course necessary to establish as clear a baseline as possible. As concluded in Chapter Three, the adoption of the Large Combustion Plant Directive in 1988 furnished the EU with a significant building block in its developing acidification and air pollution policy. Although LCPs figured centrally in the 'emissions profile' of important EU polluters, the LCP requirements did not allow the EU as an entity to sign up to the 1985 CLRTAP sulphur protocol. Hence, at the start of the 1990s, in terms of national, comprehensive EU emission ceilings similar to those adopted in the summer of 2000, none were primarily adopted within the EU context.

However, CLRTAP developments in the late 1980s and early 1990s provide us with a sort of 'fall-back' baseline. As further discussed in Chapters Three and Four, the 1988 NO_x Protocol called for emissions stabilisation by 1994. Hence, it implicitly established a basic 'no increase' national emission ceiling for all the CLRTAP parties, including of course the EU countries. The EU commitment in this context was further bolstered by the fact that the European Community as an entity signed on to the Protocol.[220] Moreover, in the same vein as the NO_x Protocol, the 1991 VOC Protocol established a basic 30 percent national emission ceiling for all the CLRTAP parties, including the EU countries. Also in this context the EU commitment was further bolstered by the Community signing the Protocol as an entity.[221] Furthermore, the 1994 CLRTAP Sulphur Protocol formally introduced the concept of differentiated, national emission ceilings. Moreover, somewhat similar to the LCP Directive, the Protocol also differentiated targets between the countries over time. Hence, the Protocol set out individual and varying national reduction targets for the year 2000 for half of the countries, and additional 2005 and 2010 targets for the other half (with 1980 as base year). For instance in the case of the UK, emissions were to be reduced 50 percent by 2000; 70 percent by 2005; and 80 percent by 2010. The Community also signed on to the Protocol as an entity.[222]

In addition to the 'CLRTAP-derived' EU ceilings, the Environmental Action Programmes contain interesting policy benchmarks of some relevance in this context. For instance, the Fifth EAP called for a 30 percent reduction of both NO_x and VOC emissions within the EU by the year 2000, with a 1990 baseline. Moreover, as indicated in section 5.2, the Programme set up the general target in the acidification context of 'no exceeding ever of critical loads and levels', but with no time frame specified. [223] However, these targets were not binding.

All in all, due to the lack of comparable national emission ceilings adopted by the EU in the 1980s and early 1990s, this section has compiled an EU national emission ceilings baseline, primarily based on the commitments made by the EU countries and the EU as an entity within the CLRTAP context. This means that there is no such baseline for ammonia emissions, as these emissions were not targeted in the CLRTAP context before the 1999 Gothenburg Protocol. 'Armed' with this baseline, let us then try to pin down progress made by the quite recent adoption of the NEC Directive.

NECs and policy strengthening a decade later

As indicated above, the establishment of *national* emission ceilings is a regulatory innovation in the field of EU air pollution control. In terms of the dimension of bindingness, in relation to the baseline argued for in this specific context, noticeable changes have taken place. The adoption of the EU NECs means that the earlier, more implicit EU national emission ceilings have now been formally codified in the EU context. Hence, the weight of such commitments for EU members has increased considerably. Moreover, quite similar to the CLRTAP development discussed in the previous chapter, it can also be argued that specificity has increased substantially. This especially applies to emissions of NO_x and VOCs (and NH_3 emissions of course, which were not previously regulated). In comparison with the basically flat rate reductions in the CLRTAP NO_x and (to a somewhat less degree) VOC Protocols, the NO_x and VOC emission ceilings in the NEC Directive are different for all the Member States. This means, at least in principle, that policies have become much more 'tailor-made' to fit the specific circumstances of each country than was previously the case.

Turning then to the central dimension of ambitiousness, it is clear that noticeable changes have taken place also in this respect. First, the inclusion of additional substances in the emission ceilings system means that regulatory scope has been increased. This pertains first and foremost to the inclusion also of ammonia (NH_3) emissions in this context. In terms of 'behavioural bite', quite similar to the discussion carried out in Chapter Four, the overall picture is one of a substantial strengthening. A direct and very precise comparison is complicated by the fact that baselines and timetables differ between the CLRTAP/EU commitments in the late 1980s and early 1990s - and the baseline and timetable in the NEC Directive.

However, in some cases the picture is crystal-clear. It is obvious that reducing NO_x emissions in the EU by 51 percent within 2010 is a much more ambitious target than the mere 'stabilisation by 1994' commitment of the 1988 CLRTAP Protocol. This is not only related to the difference in figures. It also has to do with the fact that achieving such sizeable reductions becomes increasingly expensive for many countries when the initial and relatively cheap abatement options are no longer sufficient. In terms of SO_2, as noted in the previous chapter, the existence of the 2010 NECs in the 1994 Sulphur Protocol means that a more direct and precise assessment of the increase in policy strength can, in principle, be carried out. For instance, the UK's EU SO_2 NEC is 585 kilotonnes (kt) in comparison with the 980 kt ceiling in the 1994 Protocol – indicating a 40 percent strengthening of policy.[224] Hence, in terms of SO_2 emissions, the strengthening of policy can be pinpointed very clearly.

However, there are two sides to every story. Let us take a further look at the gap between policy requirements and environmental needs and the possibility of 'missed opportunities' to bridge this gap.

The Gap between Policies and Critical Loads: A Reduction, but not Elimination

As noted in Chapter Two, although the 'behavioural bite' of regulations may increase considerably, this does not automatically imply a match – or even improving match – between environmental and health needs and policy responses. This depends upon the nature of these needs and their development. In order to assess the developing match between needs and responses in this case, as in the previous section, we need some sort of baseline. Is it then possible to say something brief yet still meaningful about the state of this match in the early 1990s? With regard to the acidification context, development of the critical loads modelling tool allows us to estimate that these levels were being exceeded in around 32.5 million hectares of ecosystem area in 1990.[225] As to the urban air quality situation, one central indicator is the extent to which ground-level ozone exceeded World Health Organization limits in 1990. According to the EU Commission and IIASA, these limits were exceeded about 50–60 days in the worst affected areas of the EU (i.e. Italy, Northern France, Germany and Belgium) in 1990.[226] These scattered data can, of course, be interpreted in a number of ways. Nevertheless, they offer a clear indication that established national and international policies – including EU policies – were not in step with environmental needs.

Recently adopted EU policies mean that the gap to critical loads will be substantially reduced by 2010 – on the condition, of course, that these policies are faithfully implemented. With regard to acidification, the area where acid depositions exceed critical loads will be reduced considerably. A NEC Directive as proposed by the Commission in June 1999 would have reduced this area down to around 5 million hectares, or about 3.5 percent of the ecosystem area. The watering-down of the Directive automatically implies that a somewhat smaller reduction of the area where acid depositions exceed critical loads will take place. Moreover, breaches of the World Health Organization's guideline for protecting human health can be expected to fall to around 20 days per year in the most affected parts of Europe. The impact on human health of particulates like PM10 will also be reduced.[227]

However, the other side of the coin is that significant gaps and shortcomings will still remain. As pinpointed by the EU Commission itself, even if the Acidification Strategy was to be implemented in full, including a NEC Directive as proposed by the Commission in June 1999, acid depositions would still be causing substantial damage to the most sensitive areas in 2010. Moreover, with regard to ozone, the threshold for protecting vegetation will still be exceeded almost everywhere. In addition, despite tightened EU air quality standards, particulates like PM10 are likely to cause a 'substantial impact' on human health in 2010.[228]

Summing up: Considerably Stronger – but not 'Strong Enough'

Even a rather crude comparative venture like the one carried out in this context reveals that EU policy strength has increased substantially within the air pollution field – in terms of both bindingness and specificity, but most importantly and conspicuously in terms of ambitiousness and 'behavioural bite'. National emission ceilings for EU countries codified within the CLRTAP context have been replaced by ceilings codified within the EU institutional structure. Flat rate reductions have been replaced by a complex net of differentiated commitments. New substances such as ammonia have been drawn into the regulatory picture, and emission targets have generally been tightened.

The implication of this development is that the gap between adopted policies and 'environment-friendly' emission levels has been substantially reduced. However, current policies even faithfully implemented will still leave a significant gap in 2010. Hence, an overall score in terms of the development of policy strength such as 'considerably stronger, but still not strong enough' lies close at hand. Against this background, let us turn to the interesting question of how this development has come about.

How did 'Considerably Stronger' Policies Come About?

Introduction

In order to shed light upon this considerable strengthening of policy, Chapter Two concluded with three main explanatory perspectives. First, changes in the institutional set-up and functioning of the EU were focused upon, pertaining to membership, decision-making procedures and interplay with other institutions. In terms of membership changes, the possible 'greening' effect of the 1995 enlargement was given specific attention.

With regard to changes in decision-making procedures, the effects of in-creased room for majority voting in the Council and a more prominent role for the European Parliament in the decision-making process were focused upon. In terms of changes in the interplay with other institutions, the possible greening effect of a closer relationship with CLRTAP was pinpointed.

As a second explanatory perspective, and also pertaining to the EU level, the possible positive 'spill-over' effect of changes in related EU environmental policies was focused upon. Within the specific air pollution context, as briefly touched upon earlier in this chapter, recent years have witnessed an interesting further development both of fuel and vehicle emissions requirements, air quality legislation and requirements pertaining to Large Combustion Plants.

Finally, as the third and main alternative explanatory perspective to the two foregoing EU level perspectives, the greening effect of crucial domestic developments was pinpointed. Fully opening up the 'black box' of domestic politics is beyond the scope of this study, but the background for the movement of earlier indifferents and especially key laggards in a more 'green' and constructive direction will be given special attention.

Let us first turn to the interesting institutional changes.

The Changes in EU Membership, Decision-making Procedures and Interplay with Other Institutions Focused Upon in this Study

Greening effects of the 1995 enlargement?[229] As discussed in Chapter Two, the accession of Austria, Finland, and Sweden in 1995 generally meant a strengthening of the 'rich and green' group within the EU. Together with the traditional EU environmental 'pioneers', Germany, the Netherlands and Denmark, these six countries acting together can form a blocking minority in the Council. Moreover, it is reasonable to assume that this accession of new Member States has influenced the composition, staffing and function-ing of all the major EU institutions. The discussion of these developments in Chapter Two ended up in the formulation of the following proposition for further scrutiny: the 1995 accession of a group of 'rich and green' new Member States, specifically concerned about air pollution, has greened the staffing of both the Environment Directorate and other Directorates within the Commission, and also the composition of the Parliament and the Council – subsequently and together leading to a more benign constellation of preferences in the Council and ultimately increasing EU air pollution regulatory strength.

In terms of the role of the Commission and the 'parachuting in' of new staff after the 1995 enlargement, 'gasping for cleaner air' so to speak, the processes focused on in this context surely contain interesting elements. As noted earlier, at the Council meeting in March 1995, Sweden asked for a report by the Commission in which an assessment should be made of the impact on acidification of current and proposed EU legislation, and as a follow-up to that report, for the Commission to develop an Acidification Strategy for the EU. The Commission responded that it would undertake such an assessment. At a later stage (in April–May), the DG ENV/D3 Head of Unit, Perera, asked Sweden for expert assistance to make the assessment. Sweden agreed, and Leif Bernegård (from the Swedish EPA) was placed temporarily at D3 from July–December 1995. In November 1995, the report (i.e. Commission Staff Working Paper on Acidification) – which had been produced with the help of IIASA and also a British consultant – was presented. In the meantime, during the summer and autumn of 1995, Sweden had contacts with several Member States in order to prepare for the adoption of Council conclusions in December 1995, the aim being that the Council Conclusions should request the Commission to develop an EU Acidification Strategy.

After this had been successfully achieved, DG ENV again asked Sweden (and also other Member States) for expert assistance to prepare the strategy. Sweden again agreed, and preparatory meetings started in the spring of 1996. A new Swedish national expert, i.e. Christer Ågren, joined DG ENV formally in June 1996. He had long experience with the twists and turns of acid politics, as he had started working in the Swedish NGO Secretariat on Acid Rain back in 1982. Being very familiar with both the science and politics of international and national air pollution control, Ågren had good contacts with IIASA and was hence instrumental in bringing the institute into the EU decision-making process. Up to this point in time, key personnel in the Commission and the Environment Directorate had favoured a 'Best Available Technology' (BAT) approach. Due both to coincidences and new staffing related to the enlarged membership within the Union, by mid-1996 there was an increased flexibility in terms of regulatory approaches and ways of making progress.[230]

Nordic personnel continued to figure centrally in the Environment Directorate's further work on the Strategy and the NEC Directive. When Ågren left in 1997, he was succeeded by a Norwegian, Mari Sæther. When she left by the end of 1998, she was again followed by a Swede, Katja Löfgren from the Ministry of Environment, who stayed until the summer of 1999. In addition to this, a Dane (Jens Gammeltoft) has figured centrally in DG ENV's final work on the NEC Directive. Hence, although there surely are some coincidences involved, this process can to some extent be interpreted as a successful Nordic and particularly Swedish 'parachuting in of national servants to strategic positions within the Commission'.[231]

However, in addition to the important role of new, dedicated staff in DG ENV, process insiders pinpoint several other factors which contributed to relatively smooth sailing for the Acidification Strategy and the NEC Directive within the often rough internal Commission seas (confer for instance the Auto-Oil I process further described later in this chapter).[232] First, other Directorates (as well as many Member States) did not really pay that much attention. This, in turn, was a result of the fact that DG ENV worked quickly and efficiently. Time-tables were kept, in spite of the fact that they were very demanding. Transparency was very good (very different from Auto-Oil I!) and nearly all papers were sent out to experts several weeks in advance of expert meetings. Most of the preparatory work was done by consultants in a way that was totally new to the Commission – and at the same time very familiar to the Member State experts (as it was largely following the routines of CLRTAP).

Of the opposing Member States it was virtually only the UK (and later also Italy) that mobilised opposition, and so sent their 'signals' to other DGs. Other opposing States did not really 'wake up' until after March 1997. Moreover, while the opposition from industry (primarily oil, coal, and electricity) was crystal clear, it was at the same time quite weak, i.e. they did not mobilise sufficiently to produce good, strong arguments. Strong industry opposition did not really get going until February 1997, i.e. only three–four weeks before the scheduled adoption of the Acidification Strategy by the Commission. Finally, but not less important, proponents of the Acidification Strategy could point to a principal agreement in the fifth Environmental Action Program on the objective of 'no exceeding ever of critical loads and levels'.[233]

Let us then move on from the Commission to the European Parliament. As noted in Chapter Two, in terms of strategic positions within the Parliament it is generally acknowledged that the positions of Committee Chairs and Rapporteur (for specific policy-making processes and directives) are the most important. Moreover, given that the Chairs do not change that often, the position of Rapporteur is more within reach for policy entrepreneurs. Surely related to the general priority given to the acidification and air quality issues by the Nordic countries, no less than three Rapporteurs in this context have had Nordic background: Anneli Hulthen of Sweden functioned first in this position in connection with the Acidification Strategy. For the NEC directive, she was succeeded by Riita Muller of Finland. It can also be noted that in connection with the related

Directive on the sulphur contents of liquid fuels, Heidi Hautala of Finland has functioned as the Rapporteur.

However, the Nordic and particularly Swedish/Finnish dominance in these matters has not been total. For the LCP directive, the Rapporteur has been Rita Oomen-Ruijten of the Netherlands, and for the Ozone directive, the Rapporteur has been Chris Davies of the UK. Interviews with Nordic Parliament representatives confirm the impression that priority has been given to the acquirement of these positions – as part of a coordinated effort to move these issues successfully through the EU system. However, it was also acknowledged in these interviews that the impression of a 'Nordic green mafia' could backfire and there is hence a balancing act to be performed.[234]

Let us then finally move on to the Council of Ministers. Recall here for instance Holzinger's (1997:80) interesting claim that '..in the eyes of the three original frontrunner states...the <1995> newcomers must be very welcome to the EU. With respect to environmental decision making, their accession greatly improves the situation in the Council of Ministers. Therefore it can be presumed that the environmental policy of the EU will become more progressive in the future than in the past'. In terms of the Acidification Strategy, as has been noted, this came about as a direct offspring of the influx of new members. Although some relevant policy developments took place in the early 1990s, the more specific Acidification Strategy process started with a call from the Council of Environmental Ministers for a report assessing the acidification situation in March 1995; following pressure from the Swedes. This was followed in December 1995 by a call from the Council again, this time for the Commission to develop an EU Acidification Strategy.

In the next couple of years, the Council of Ministers was not formally involved. However, much political footwork took place. The Swedes paid visits to Italy and Greece among others in order to reduce Southern reluctance to policy initiatives in this issue area, and they also held several meetings with the British.[235] The next main formal involvement of the Council took place at several meetings in the fall of 1997; in the wake of the Commission's launching of the Acidification Strategy. These meetings clearly showed that there was quite compact Southern reluctance and opposition, and there were also several Northern intermediates, including the UK and Ireland. In addition to Sweden, the main proponents at this stage included Austria, Denmark, Finland, and the Netherlands. Germany was no principal supporter of the NEC approach and gave priority to the related LCP revision process and the BAT approach pursued here.[236]

This basic constellation of positions was repeated at the relevant Council meetings during 1998 and 1999.

We have now come to the crucially important Council meeting in June 2000, where the final hammering out of a common position upon the NEC Directive took place. With regard to the dynamics of this meeting, as often is the case with the Council meetings, only scattered information has leaked out. Should the outcome of the meeting be interpreted as a defeat or victory for the enlarged green frontrunners? Given the noticeable watering down of the Commission's initial proposal and its ambitiousness, the outcome cannot be counted as an unfettered victory for the green frontrunners.

On the other hand, given the wide-spread pessimistic expectations beforehand on the possibilities of achieving a common position, the outcome must in some sense be considered as a success. Moreover, in a somewhat longer comparative time-span than just going back to the Commission's 1999 proposal, the considerable strengthening of policy inherent in the Council outcome emerges as quite striking. However, as will be elaborated in following sections, obtaining support for the NEC outcome from the central green frontrunner, Germany, was in no way unproblematic. And there are also other factors, such as a softening of the British stance, that need to be taken into account in order to get a more comprehensive and satisfactory understanding of the outcome (this will be further discussed later).

In summary, there are very interesting pieces to the puzzle regarding the extent to which the work on the Acidification Strategy and NEC Directive was stimulated by the 1995 enlargement to be found within the Commission, Parliament and Council. Particularly interesting and influential developments seem to have taken place within the Commission and the DG ENV, but the Nordic dominance in terms of relevant Rapporteur positions acquired in the Parliament is also striking, and the strengthening of the green frontrunner coalition in the Council has also been positive (but hard to document and measure precisely!). An assessment of the relative importance of all this for the outcome of the processes must wait until more pieces in the explanatory puzzle have been identified and discussed. Suffice to conclude at this stage that this particular perspective surely deserves some weight in the final 'verdict'.

Greening effects of more majority-voting in the Council and an increased influence for the Parliament? Turning then to the issue of changes in decision-making procedures, as further elaborated in Chapter Two, majority-voting in the Council takes away the single laggard's veto power and changes the decision-making logic. Moreover, under certain circumstances, such as an increase in the group of green front-runners in the Council, increased majority-voting can be envisaged as contributing to a greening effect upon Council outcomes. In addition, and parallel to the issue of majority-voting, the involvement of the European Parliament has been changing over time. Given the Parliament's developing green profile compared to other EU bodies in the 1980s and 1990s, this is interesting in the environmental policy context. The changing of paragraphs and bases for legislation have increased both the room for majority-voting and the involvement of the Parliament. The increasingly common co-decision procedure opens up for several rounds and readings by the Council and the Parliament, and the possible final negotiation round between these bodies in a Conciliation Committee. Taken together, it is not unthinkable that these procedural developments have also influenced the course of the specific air pollution policy process focused upon in this context.

Against this background, it was first proposed that the 1995 accession cannot by itself explain a strengthening of policy. An increased possibility for majority-voting in the Council has to be brought into the picture. Majority-voting has meant a more 'powerful' aggregation of preferences and has given the 1995 enlargement a more decisive effect in the Council proceedings, ultimately leading to increasing policy strength. The third proposition zoomed in on the increasing role for the comparatively green Parliament in EU decision-making: Other procedural changes are the ultimate cause of policy changes. A more prominent role for the Parliament in decision-making and the related added weight of EP amendments have more generally contributed to a greening of preferences in the Council, and especially the final round of conciliation has forced the Council to move in a policy strengthening direction.

In order to review these propositions, let us first focus on and go through the Parliament's involvement in this process in more detail. As regards the Acidification Strategy itself and the draft directive on sulphur in fuels, the first main involvement of the Parliament took place in April/May 1998, when the Environment Committee, and subsequently the Parliament in plenary, debated the Acidification Strategy Communication and the draft sulphur in fuels directive from the Commission. In the plenary, a general support for the main points of the Strategy was expressed in a resolution. As regards the draft sulphur in fuels directive, a total of 28 strengthening amendments were adopted; in this first round unanimously. In the resolution on the Acidification Strategy, as the very first point, in addition to a basic support for the emission ceilings in the Commission's proposal, it was suggested to develop 'a new, ambitious target for 2015', whereby in principle the critical loads should not be exceeded in any part of the area.

Moreover, several suggestions for stricter regulation of the emissions from shipping were put forward.[237]

However, it can be noted that this unified posture did not apply to all elements of the Acidification Strategy. When a year later the Parliament debated a central element of the Acidification Strategy package, namely revised LCP requirements, a North-South split became apparent in the Environment Committee's debate. Still, the Committee's ultimate strengthening recommendations were allegedly adopted by 'an overwhelming majority'.[238] The North-South split reappeared in the plenary debate however, with the South being joined by countries such as the UK. The final round of voting brought the split clearly into the open, when only a narrow majority was obtained for the strengthening proposals (i.e. 283 for; 233 against; 10 abstentions).

With regard to the NEC Directive process, the Directive was intended to have been launched in March 1999. However, due to the unexpected resignation of the Commission, the Directive was not formally launched until June. In the meantime, an important procedural change had taken place. From May 1 1999, legislative processes under 130s were 'moved' into the co-decision procedure as a result of the entry into force of the Amsterdam treaty. This meant that the NEC-proposal would follow co-decision, and it also meant that the closely related revision process of the LCP-directive changed procedure; revised LCP requirements also to be decided upon according to co-decision. When the Commission then formally launched the draft NEC Directive in June 1999, some of the Parliaments's suggestions in the resolution on the Acidification Strategy had been incorporated. For instance, most of the Parliament's suggested design of a reporting system had been incorporated in the Draft Directive. However, perhaps the most conspicuous element of the Parliament's suggested amendments, namely the call for a 2015 target of no exceeding of critical loads, had not been included.[239]

In the Environment Committee and Parliament's first reading discussions on the draft NEC Directive in February and March 2000 with Riita Myller from Finland as Rapporteur, the basic support for the NECs as proposed by the Commission was restated. But several suggested amendments were (re-)adopted. However, none of them can be characterised as very dramatic in relation to the Commission proposal. For instance, in relation to the Commission's suggested intermediate reviews in 2004 and 2008, the Parliament suggested moving these forward one year to 2003 and 2007 respectively, with a specific focus on accession countries and transport emissions. Moreover, it was suggested making the intermediate review requirements much more clear and specific by both placing them as a separate article, and spelling out clearly what they should include. In addition, it was suggested deleting some sea and air transport exceptions allowed by the Commission, and furthermore placing the interim environmental objectives (i.e. 2010 NECs) more centrally (from being part of the annexes, into the body of articles). Finally, the call for setting a specific 2015 long-term objective was repeated, 'whereby in principle the critical loads must not be exceeded in any part of the Community with the final target of no exceedance of critical levels and loads in the year 2020 and the effective protection of all people against recognised health risks from air pollution'.[240] The resolution was adopted in the plenary by 484 to 46 votes.[241]

Overall, these suggestions did not win through in the compromise adopted in the Council in June. The main limited victory for the Parliament which can be noted was that the Council agreed to move the interim environmental objectives from the annexes into the body of the articles (i.e. Article 5), hence adding to their political 'weight'.[242] Furthermore, with regard to the dynamics of this key meeting, can our reasoning and proposition developed in connection with the role of majority voting throw further light on the outcome of the meeting? Was the formation of a qualified majority and the quick voting down of laggards *the* keys to 'getting to yes' at this meeting? Seemingly not. As indicated in the previous section, the outcome of the meeting must primarily be understood as a complex compromise and package deal. As a result of the building of this compromise, earlier reluctants and potential 'blockers' in this process such as Spain and Greece, chose to move to greener positions more acceptable to the majority, instead of being voted down. However, this does not rule out the more indirect impact of majority voting as a sort of 'hidden stick' and a stimulant to the building of an overall acceptable compromise.

The ball was then kicked back to the Parliament for a second reading. As indicated in section 5.2, the common position of the Council and the Commission raised the stakes for the Parliament.[243] Early reports from the process indicated that the Parliament was prepared to go along with the Council's figures, acknowledging that they, 'even though modest', were 'an acceptable and balanced compromise for the time being'. It was pinpointed that possible modification of the NECs would require a new and more elaborate scientific assessment in order to be equitable.[244] In the Parliament discussion in March 2001, British Deputy Chris Davies pinpointed that the whole process was based on a 'fiendishly complicated' Commission model, and he could not see 'how we, as legislators – not technical experts – can propose more ambitious targets for individual countries unless we pull figures out of the air, which seems an amateurish way of making law' (*International Environment Reporter*, March 28, 2001, p.248). However, when the second reading finally took place in June 2001, the position of the Parliament had changed on this matter and revised and stricter NECs were suggested for SO_2, NO_x and VOCs. It is reasonable to believe that the considerable lobbying by environmental NGOs which took place during the winter and spring of 2001, played a significant role in bringing about this change.[245]

However, the Parliament's impact on the NEC conciliation outcome finalised in the beginning of July 2001 strikes one as being on the moderate side. Although the reviews in 2004 and 2008 have been given added emphasis, it is still the NECs adopted in the Council's common position from June 2000 which will be the ones guiding the Member States. The pressure of the Parliament has probably increased the chances of the 2004 review resulting in tightened NECs, but there is absolutely no guarantee that an enlarged Union will choose this course in due time. Some of the background for limited impact for the Parliament's demands so far is found in the firm opposition from some countries in the Council to a further tightening of the SO_2 and NO_x emission ceilings.[246] But the moderate impact also has something to do with the 'technicalisation' of the decision-making process, as hinted at by Chris Davies above. Basing policy so firmly on science and modelling surely has its advantages in terms of rationality, but inevitably raises the threshold in terms of underpinning proposals for policy revisions.

In summary, as suggested in the proposition guiding this part of the analysis, the Parliament has clearly placed itself in the camp within the EU system pushing for the most ambitious strengthening of EU policy in this area. Basically, it has supported the targets and ambitiousness expressed in the Commission's various inputs to this process, not least the NEC Directive proposal put forward in June 1999. Hence, it has surely contributed to the strengthening of policy which has taken place. However, it cannot be counted as a crucially important driving force in this process. This is partly due to the simple fact that the Commission and the Parliament have been in basic agreement in most of this process, and the room for pressure and drama has hence been limited – compared for instance to the Auto-Oil I process. In addition, the Parliament has overall not succeeded with its suggested policy inputs in respect to the Commission nor the Council.

Given the high degree of consensus within the Parliament on the content of these inputs, the reasons for lack of success in terms of imprint on the process must be sought elsewhere. One central factor here has to do with the framing of the issue. Basing the NECs on a 'fiendishly complicated' model was in many ways a good thing, but the resulting complex web of commitments introduced a certain inflexibility and exclusiveness to the process and robbed campaigners of simple and easily communicated focal points. With regard to the other procedural development focused on in this context, i.e. the increased room for majority-voting, this general development seems to shed only limited additional light on the outcome of this particular process. Although 'hidden stick' effects cannot be ruled out, the outcome of the crucial June 2000 Council meeting comes out as a classic EU compromise.

Greening effects due to a changing organisational environment? The CLRTAP effect.[247] In dealing with (transboundary) air pollution, Chapter Two noted that the EU certainly does not operate in an organisational vacuum. From its establishment in 1979, policy development within the LRTAP Convention has stimulated air pollution policy-making in the EU, forming a benchmark to which EU policy entrepreneurs have been able to link on to. As was documented in Chapter Four, there is no doubt that CLRTAP regulatory development in the 1990s has been formidable, culminating in the adoption of the Gothenburg Protocol.

Hence, it was suggested as very well possible that the development of EU regulatory strength in the 1990s had been positively influenced by partly parallel development of policies within CLRTAP – with EU policy entrepreneurs using policy development and knowledge improvement within CLRTAP as regulatory benchmarks and stimulants within the EU context. So it was proposed that the substantial knowledge improvement and policy development in the 1990s within the CLRTAP context has functioned as a regulatory inspiration and stimulant; strengthening the position of EU policy entrepreneurs in the field of air pollution and leading to a more benign constellation of preferences and ultimately increasing regulatory strength.

As a natural starting point for such a discussion, let us first establish the decision to use IIASA as a central scientific consultant also in the EU context as a crucial one. Hence, this fundamental 'parallelism', where the EU generally benefited both from scientific and technological advances and policy clarifications taking place within CLRTAP started as early as mid-1995. However, looking more closely at the timing of events, it is tempting to conclude that for several years the EU was a little ahead of CLRTAP in terms of policy development. For instance, at the time when the Acidification Strategy and the first, tentative EU emission ceilings were presented in March 1997, CLRTAP negotiators on their behalf were partly occupied with other and parallel CLRTAP processes (i.e. heavy metals and POPs negotiation processes), and in the multi-pollutant context they were occupied with the more general discussion of different reduction scenarios (see Chapter Four).

According to policy-makers involved in the process, the intention was clearly also that the EU process should be finished ahead of the CLRTAP process.[248] This was related to a general anticipation that it would be possible to achieve stronger reduction commitments within the EU context than in the broader CLRTAP context. The plan developed in connection with the preparation of the Acidification Strategy was to first prepare the Ozone Strategy, then – based on both the Acidification and Ozone Strategies – to develop the NEC proposal smoothly and quickly. In such a scenario the EU could become a helpful, contributing force in the efforts to increase policy ambitiousness in the concluding phase of CLRTAP negotiations on a multi-pollutant and multi-effects protocol. However, things took a different turn.

One of the main problems was the slowing down of work within DG ENV. In fact a draft NEC proposal was ready within DG ENV already by the autumn of 1998. For various bureaucratic reasons, it was decided to have it re-written in a different format, i.e. as one consolidated document, together with the ozone strategy. This was also at the time when staff workload as well as turnover was very high in unit D3 of DG ENV. So this by itself probably delayed the proposal two to three months. Instead of being adopted by the Commission in November or December of 1998 as scheduled, it was placed on the agenda for adoption on 17 March 1999.

Then the Commission was forced to resign on 16 March. Although the caretaker Commission managed to present the draft NEC Directive in June 1999, the CLRTAP Protocol was in fact ready only a few months later. This meant that the CLRTAP emission ceilings became an important point of reference in the final phase of the EU decision-making process, instead of the other way around as intended. Although this surely did not increase the flexibility and willingness of several EU countries to accept ambitious reduction commitments, its negative impact should not be over-stated. Reluctant countries would have been reluctant in any event, and most of the countries still adjusted their positions somewhat in the spring of 2000. But the impression of an unfortunate timing of events remains.

Despite this chain of events, it is not at all reasonable to conclude that CLRTAP policy development has not influenced the course and shape of this EU process. First, it is important to realise that that CLRTAP experience and expertise had a major impact on the Acidification and Ozone Strategies, which in themselves introduced a new way of working and thinking within the Commission. The process of producing these strategies also paved the way for the revision of the sulphur-in-fuels and the

LCP directives. Moreover, the idea of setting national emission ceilings emanated from the 1994 Sulphur Protocol, and the very multi-pollutant and multi-effects approach emanated from within the CLRTAP system. The role of IIASA here is, of course, central and the shared use of IIASA's services over time proved beneficial to all parties involved.

Thus, in conclusion, despite an unfortunate timing of events in the final phases of the processes within the two contexts, the CLRTAP influence on the shape of the EU process should be seen as significant. Furthermore, although both general CLRTAP system influences and more specific spill-over effects from the Gothenburg Protocol process could in principle be envisaged, a closer scrutiny shows it to be most correct to put emphasis on the more general *CLRTAP system* influence.

Challenging the 'Institutional Changes' Perspective I:
The Development of Related EU Policies

Introduction. As noted in Chapter Two, there has been an interesting further development in recent years of various other air pollution policy processes of potential relevance for understanding the development and outcome of the Acidification Strategy and NEC Directive process. This relates both to the fuel quality and vehicle emissions issue and issues of air quality and strengthened requirements to Large Combustion Plants. Positive and policy-enhancing spill-over from these processes to the Acidification Strategy and NEC Directive process was not seen as unlikely. Such spill-over could take the form of policy goals being adopted in one context (for instance air quality goals) logically pointing to the need for stricter emissions reduction goals. But it could also take the form of specific integrative package deals being formed; with progress in the field of emissions reduction policies becoming possible due to linkages to other processes. Hence, the first rival proposition drew attention to the possibility that other relevant policy developments within the EU have had positive spill-over effects upon the focused policy processes, leading to more benign constellations of preferences and ultimately increasing regulatory strength.

With this as a backdrop, let us first turn to the Auto-Oil I programme and developments within the fuel quality and vehicle emissions context.

The moderate relevance of fuel quality and vehicle emissions: Auto-Oil I. It is difficult to write about the development of EU air pollution policy in the 1990s without at least providing a short description of the Auto-Oil I programme.[249] The Auto-Oil process was initiated by the Commission in 1992. The general backdrop for the initiation of this process was multifarious. The adoption of the strengthened 1990 US Clean Air Act, the then recently formulated WHO air quality targets, and growing frustration in industry circles over a policy-making approach paying too little attention to costs in relation to benefits, have all been indicated.[250] There was thus an interest in finding more cost-effective solutions.[251] As a response to these various concerns, a symposium on vehicle emission standards for the year 2000 was organised and attended by a wide range of actors including Commission and government officials, industry and NGO representatives, and Members of the European Parliament.[252] A central theme of this Symposium was the development of cost-effective measures based on ambient air quality standards.

The Commissioners for Environment, Industry and Energy then invited the European Automotive Manufacturers Association (ACEA) and the European Petroleum Industry Association (EUROPIA) decided to collaborate in the realisation of a technical research programme. It was decided to launch three independent but interrelated, projects:

- Urban ambient air quality studies. The aim here was to predict the air quality of seven European cities and ground level ozone across the EU for the year 2010, and on this basis derive emission reduction targets
- A 'European Programme on Emissions, Fuels and Engine Technologies', jointly carried out by ACEA and EUROPIA and focusing on the effect on emissions of vehicle technology and fuel characteristics, and
- A cost-effectiveness study, calculating the costs and emissions impact for different emission reduction measures.

At the outset, it was envisaged to have legislation proposals ready by the end of 1994, but things got delayed.[253] Hence, it was not until June 18, 1996 that the Commission formally put forward the first two proposals for directives to take effect in the year 2000. Central components in this initial package of proposals consisted of tighter emission standards for passenger cars and fuel specifications for fuel and diesel.[254] Together, these measures were designed to reduce vehicle emissions of carbon monoxide, volatile organic compounds and urban particulates to 30 percent of the 1995 level by 2010.[255] An overall annual cost estimate of 5.5 billion euros was indicated. According to then Environment Commissioner Ritt Bjerregaard, the proposals were 'extremely ambitious'. The measures were to be followed by an Auto-Oil II phase, specifying requirements for the year 2005. Together with already adopted proposals, emissions of NO_x from road traffic were envisaged to drop by 65 percent by 2010 from 1995 levels, and those of VOCs, carbon monoxide and urban particulate matter by 70 percent. Between a third and a half of these reductions would be attributable to the Auto-Oil programme.[256] The June 1996 package set the ball rolling for the second and more openly political part of this process.

In its first reading in April 1997, the Parliament was quite critical to the Commission proposals. The Parliament called for both stricter fuel standards and lower emission limits than those proposed by the Commission, and also mandatory 2005 requirement instead of the indicative limits proposed by the Commission.[257]

When the Environment Council of Ministers met in June, the critical Auto-Oil inputs from the Parliament served as the main backdrop. Described as 'a rare decision where the European Union's Council of Ministers strengthened an environmental legislative proposal from the European Commission', the Ministers unanimously adopted stricter fuel standards than those proposed by the Commission – but not as strict as those proposed by the Parliament. The Council ended up supporting the Commission in terms of emission limits.

Then, in its second reading, the Parliament ended up giving only a qualified backing for the Council's common position on the Auto-Oil directives. The Parliament emphasised mandatory 2005 limits, somewhat tougher fuel specifications, and restated roughly the same call for stricter emission limits as submitted in the first reading. The stage was then set for the final rounds in a Conciliation Committee, during the Spring of 1998.

These were crowned with success by the end of June – described as a 'last-gasp success for the UK Presidency'.[258] With regard to the hotly-debated 2005 requirements, the Parliament's call for mandatory standards generally won through. Regarding the issue of fuel quality, standards for the years 2000 and 2005 were identical to those agreed by the Council of Ministers; i.e. by January 2000, sulphur levels in petrol and diesel were to be reduced to 150 ppm and 350 ppm respectively (with limited derogations until 2003). Finally, the indicative 2005 vehicle emissions requirements agreed to by Ministers in June 1997 were now made mandatory. However, the content of the standards was in line with what had been adopted earlier by the Council.

This is of course a very superficial account of a process which is interesting from several perspectives. The first, technical phase of the process has been criticised for being far too exclusive and shutting out the viewpoints and expertise of Member States and environmental NGOs. Furthermore, the process is clearly an example of how the Parliament has developed into a co-legislator with clout. Although the Parliament did not at all manage to gain support for all of its suggested policy amendments, it had an important impact both in terms of contributing to a strengthening of the standards with regard to the sulphur content of fuel oils and not least in terms of making 2005 limits mandatory. According to well-informed observers, these are 'radical changes'.[259]

However, in this context, we are especially interested in the interplay with and possible effect upon the Acidification/Ozone Strategies and NEC Directive process. Overall, the 'objective' interplay and relatedness of the Auto-Oil and Acidification/NEC processes is clearly there.[260] The follow-up of Auto-Oil I legislation will contribute to a reduction of the Member States' emissions of both sulphur dioxide (through the strengthened fuel standards) and NO_x /VOCs (through the stricter vehicle emission limits). In IIASA's modelling work underpinning the NEC Directive proposal, the Auto-Oil I requirements were included in the 'reference' scenario. This contributed to a lowering of figures within this scenario and, probably more important, to lower incremental costs related to the NECs proposed by the Commission than what would have been the case without the Auto-Oil legislation.[261]

But apart from such more general links, there is little to indicate that the development of the Auto-Oil I process made very much of an impact upon the Member States' positions in the Acidification/NEC context. Hence, although the outcome of Auto-Oil I is a significant event in the development of EU air pollution policy, this specific interplay cannot be reckoned as a central intake to understand the NEC outcome.

Air Quality Considerations: Important in Preparing the NEC Directive. As indicated in Chapter Three, a few air quality directives were adopted in the first part of the 1980s. Work on considerably more comprehensive and stronger EU air quality legislation started in the very early 1990s. By the spring of 1993, early drafts of a framework directive on air quality were discussed in meetings between the Commission and national officials.[262] More than 20 substances were targeted[263] and a system consisting of different types of quality objectives was envisaged. 'Alert thresholds' were related to the top three pollutants; 'guide values' recommended by international expert groups such as the WHO were to be established for all the pollutants; and 'limit values' were to be set for the pollutants in stages.[264]

The Commission then formally put forward a proposal for an air quality framework directive in the beginning of July 1994.[265] Important goals of the legislation were to put pressure on Member states to achieve continuous improvements in air quality and to move closer towards harmonisation of national air quality measurement programmes. Furthermore, it was declared important to make information on air quality available to the public. Focus was explicitly on air quality in cities, and where Brussels, Athens and London were mentioned as examples of 'problem cities'.[266]

However, the more *specific* air quality limit values and alert thresholds were to be developed in several following daughter directives. For pollutants already subject to EU air quality legislation (such as sulphur dioxide and nitrogen oxide) the Commission intended to put forward daughter directives by the end of 1996.[267] A specific proposal on ozone was to follow by early 1998, and proposals related to the eight new substances in the EU system (such as carbon monoxide and cadmium) would be put forward by the end of 1999.[268] A common position on the framework directive was obtained in June 1995 and the directive was formally adopted in September 1996.[269] A key ingredient in the directive was a requirement for all EU countries to adopt a measuring system in accordance with a common standard, and to report the results regularly to the Commission.[270]

As the next step, several groups of experts, consisting of representatives from the Commission, the European Environment Agency, the World Health Organization, Member States, industry, and ENGOs, came up with proposals for daughter directives; the first one for standards for sulphur dioxide, nitrogen dioxide, particulate matter and lead (DAUGHTER I). When this directive was formally launched by the Commission in October 1997, it was pinpointed that the proposed limit values would require a further 10 percent reduction of SO_2 and NO_x emissions than what would be achieved from existing and pending legislation.[271]

Moreover, the ozone issue was put forward and given a boost by work being started on a specific Ozone Strategy in the beginning of 1997. Among the elements of this Strategy was a daughter directive for ozone as a follow up of the 1996 framework directive, but the Strategy also called for the setting of 'interim objectives' and national emission ceilings for NO_x and VOCs. In June 1998, a joint position was obtained on DAUGHTER I, signalling a distinct, overall tightening of standards, but also with standards for particulates and NO_x 'significantly diluted' from those originally proposed by the Commission.[272] This directive was then formally adopted in April 1999.[273]

In the meantime, the second daughter directive was put forward by the Commission in December 1998 on benzene and carbon monoxide (DAUGHTER II).

Then, complementing the NEC directive proposal put forward by the Commission in June 1999, a proposal for a directive on ozone in ambient air was presented (DAUGHTER III). On the first page of the Commission's explanatory memorandum, the relationship between the elements is described as follows: 'While the ceilings should ensure that ozone is tackled effectively at the regional and transboundary scale, the target values establish a minimum level of protection at the local scale'.[274] As further elaborated in section 5.2, partly incorporating central Parliament amendments, DAUGHTER III was adopted by the Council in October 2000, and the second reading in the Parliament is now pending.

With regard to the relationship to the Acidification Strategy and NEC Directive process, as was the case with Auto-Oil and vehicle requirements, there are clearly 'objective' links. The process of strengthening EU air quality legislation was well into gear when the work on the Acidification Strategy started in 1995 and policy-makers were well aware that a central prerequisite for obtaining stronger air quality objectives was a strengthening of various types of emission limits. With the linking of the Acidification and Ozone strategies in 1998, the formal relationship grew even tighter. Hence, acknowledging the air quality considerations are essential elements in order to understand the background for the setting of the NO_x and VOC NECs in the Commission proposal put forward in June 1999.[275]

However, these considerations glide somewhat into the background in the following political debacles involving the Parliament and the Council, and are thus less important clues as an aid to understanding these most recent developments.

The Renegotiation of the Large Combustion Plants Directive: Good Contacts Getting Very Intimate. The 1988 Large Combustion Plant Directive (see Chapter Three) stated that an evaluation of its effects and a proposal for a tightening of the requirements were to be presented before July 1995. However, by June 1995, informed observers pointed out that no proposal was in sight.[276] Soon after, it was reported that the Commission was considering replacing the LCP Directive with a 'daughter' of the emerging directive on integrated pollution prevention and control (IPPC).[277]

This latter idea met with opposition from several Member States and instead the further renegotiation process was moved into the context of developing a comprehensive Acidification Strategy. It can here be noted that the background analyses carried out in connection with the Acidification Strategy pointed to the need for lowered emissions from the LCPs and DG ENV used these analyses to inject political energy and urgency into the slowly-progressing revision process.[278] The main milestones in the development of the LCP process have been covered earlier, so let us here repeat only the main points of conflict.

First and foremost, the way of including existing plants in the revised directive was a major stumbling block. Several Member States, with the UK as a central and vocal front-runner, feared costly re-fitting measures. For instance, in May 1997, an upset UK Environment Minister claimed that the limits suggested by the Commission – particularly for NO_x – could close down all but two coal-fired plants.[279] Hence, it should, for instance, be recalled that requirements to existing plants were *not* included in the Commission's draft directive launched in July 1998. Second, the very stringency of the limits pertaining to new plants was, of course, heatedly debated. Here there was both a divide between Northern 'frontrunners' and Southern 'laggards', but there was also some disagreement within the Northern group.

As to the more specific effects on the NEC process, the relationship between these processes did not become really intimate before the spring of 1999. Prior to that, the LCP renegotiation was more generally linked to the development of the Acidification Strategy, as one of several elements. Moreover, as in the case of Auto-Oil, revised LCP requirements were included in IIASA's modelling work underpinning the NEC Directive proposal and contributing to lower incremental costs related to the NECs proposed by the Commission than what would have been the case without stricter LCP legislation in the pipeline.[280]

However, from the spring of 1999, Member States increasingly emphasised the need to see NECs and revised LCP requirements as a package.[281] As a good example, in the March 2000 Environment Council, the UK announced a willingness to accept stricter NEC targets if, in exchange, existing installations could be excluded from the revised LCP Directive.[282] In order to understand how it was possible to obtain a NEC common position at the crucial June 2000 Environment Council – against the expectations of many insiders and observers – the package perspective is highly relevant. Furthermore, it cannot be excluded that some countries' acceptance in this final phase of somewhat lower NECs had something to do with the final wording of the LCP compromise. Here, it is natural to think especially about the UK. Although it did not succeed in holding existing plants out of the revised Directive, a considerable flexibility was obtained. According to *Acid News*, 'the compromise will, at worst, make it possible to go on operating plants that are only used 25–40 percent of the time (which is becoming ever more usual, for instance in the case of coal-fired power plants in Britain) for almost twenty years more'.[283]

As has been described earlier, this flexibility was a little constrained in the final conciliation outcome, but Member States such as the UK had once again been favoured, according to environmental NGOs.[284] It is clear that the Parliament's second reading and the following conciliation talks mark a high point in terms of explicit linking of the NEC and LCP processes. However, as the changes made to the NEC Directive were quite moderate, the further closeness of the two processes has had only limited effect in this final phase.

Challenging the 'Institutional Changes' Perspective II: Opening the 'Black Box' of Domestic Developments

As noted in Chapter Two, the logical main alternative perspective to the internationally focused institutional and policy factors discussed so far is a perspective pinpointing various *domestic developments*, highlighting the possibility that a more benign constellation of preferences and increasing regulatory strength have been caused by domestic developments having little or nothing to do with the activities of the international institutions. Furthermore, it was realised in Chapter Two that an in-depth opening up of the 'black box' of domestic politics is beyond the scope of this study.

Hence, it was suggested that prime attention be given to the background for the movement of earlier indifferent parties and especially key laggards in a more green and constructive direction. Increasing public concern about air pollution is a central – and relatively easily measurable – possible driving force in this context. But there are numerous other possibilities, including economic recessions and energy switching having absolutely nothing to do with environmental politics as such. As a focal point in this connection, the following proposition was formulated: A domestically induced greening of laggards and indifferents have lead to a more benign constellation of preferences and subsequently higher policy strength.

Within the environmental policy context, three main groups of EU countries could be identified at the beginning of the 1990s: the 'rich and green' (Denmark, Germany, and the Netherlands); the 'rich but less green' (Belgium, France, Italy, Luxembourg, and the UK); and finally the four cohesion countries (Greece, Ireland, Portugal and Spain). Given the reasoning above, it is the latter two groups that interest us most in this context. Turning first to the three key states within the 'rich but less green' group, i.e. France, Italy and the UK, the *French* situation was for a long time one of stable, quite low concern. France has never experienced a 'Waldsterben' uproar and the impression is that concern over air pollution (effects) has never been really high on the French agenda.[285] Moreover, in the 1999 Euro-barometer, the French express least urgency of all in terms of the need to fight pollution.[286]

Still, experienced observers point out that that urban air quality has been afforded steadily increasing attention in France over the last 2–3 years, also at the national, government level. While not as prominent in the public debate as in the UK (see below), it is clearly noticeable in French media and public debate.[287] Hence, there are certain indications of a somewhat growing societal demand for stronger air pollution policies in France in the most recent years.

With regard to *Italy*, the prevailing alkaline character of soils and geographic position of the Italian peninsula (making Italy a net exporter of air pollution) have reduced acidification problems and the related concern about air pollution problems hitherto.[288] However, several recent reports point to Italy as one of several Southern European problem nations with a steadily increasing urban pollution and related ozone problems. Moreover, according to the 1999 Euro-barometer, Italians are among those who are generally most concerned about environmental issues (along with Greece, Portugal, and Spain).[289] Hence, there are reasons to expect that the societal demand for stronger (EU) air pollution policies would be on the increase in Italy.

However, such a development does not seem to have taken place so far, and according to the Swedish NGO Secretariat on Acid Rain, Italy has been among those countries 'most energetically opposing EU directives for reducing emissions of transboundary, ozone-forming pollutants'.[290] Moreover, according to Christer Ågren of the Acid Rain Secretariat, the impression is that, in both France and Italy, the concerned public and the governments expect that local air quality problems should be dealt with by local actors – not by EU or international action.[291]

The *British* development is interesting indeed. As described in Chapter Three, the UK in the 1980s was one of the main laggards in international air pollution politics. Wind currents transported considerable British sulphur emissions far from Britain, and domestic concern about acidification and air pollution was low. Hence, strong international measures and costly power station abatement measures were not looked upon favourably by the British government. In the first part of the 1990s, several changes took place. First, economically motivated energy switching from coal to gas brought down British sulphur emissions 'for free'.[292] Moreover, the evidence of increasing both rural and urban problems related to air pollution became stronger, and public concern especially about the urban element started to grow. Much of the local air quality problems in the (southern) UK relate to particulate matter and ozone, and – not least important – it was demonstrated that about half of the ozone in the UK is actually imported from Europe.

On this background, and as formally required by the 1995 Environment Act, the government started developing a national Air Quality Strategy. It is very interesting to note that the UK organised a ministerial meeting comprising ministers from eight Northern European countries to discuss the ozone problem in May 1996.[293] This meeting concluded with a call for urgent action at EU level to reduce emissions of ozone precursors by over 60 percent from existing levels, and to eliminate ozone episodes in the region by 2005.[294] Soon after, leaks from the developing UK Strategy indicated among other things more ambitious ozone targets than those agreed upon at the ministerial meeting.[295] The Strategy was formally launched in March 1997. When the Labour party acceded soon after, it promised to implement the Strategy 'as a matter of urgency', but started also immediately on a review and revision process.[296]

When the review of the Strategy was published in January 1999, it included plans to tighten five of the eight air quality targets in the initial Strategy.[297] Nevertheless, an element given substantial attention was a 'substantial watering down' of the earlier target in terms of fine particles, despite strong opposition from local authorities and environmental groups. An important reason given for this watering down was the transboundary nature of such pollutants and the futility of much stronger standards in the UK than at the European level.[298] Hence, a central key to improvements in the UK was the strengthening of EU and international standards. As fine particles are formed by the oxidation of sulphur and NO_x emissions, the NEC Directive was the most relevant EU policy in development. According to *ENDS Report*, Environment Minister Meacher stated an intention to press for concerted EU action on PM10 at up-coming EU meetings.[299] The final Strategy, with a watered down PM10 target, was then published in January 2000.[300]

In summary, this brief overview indicates that there are several domestic developments which may contribute to shedding light on less defensive and more flexible UK positions on air pollution issues adopted in the recent years. Moreover, judging by the Scandinavian experience from the 1970s, the perception of a domestic problem growing due to 'acid import' from abroad is a powerful triggering mechanism for governmental interest in strong(er) international action. In addition, as pinpointed by for instance Knill (1997), there has been a shift away from the German technological approach in EU clean air policy in the 1990s towards more flexible approaches, such as air quality standards and national emission ceilings. It can be assumed that this increasing match between EU and UK regulatory approaches also contributed to making the British more positive to EU and international action in this issue area.

Finally, some interesting developments can also be witnessed in the three southern cohesion countries, *Greece*, *Portugal* and *Spain* – traditionally EU environmental laggards. In terms of ozone concentrations and urban pollution, the message from monitoring stations and scientific studies in the recent years is clear: EU threshold values have been exceeded frequently and widely.[301] This is somehow reflected in the 1999 Euro-barometer, where 70 percent are more worried about air pollution than in 1995, and the Greeks and Portuguese express the most alarmist concern.[302] However, this trend has not so far resulted in significant changes within the sphere of party politics, and only very vague echoes seem to have found their way to Brussels. Still, it cannot be ruled out that this increasing concern has contributed to the somewhat more refined and flexible positions expressed by the cohesion countries in the more recent concluding phases of EU air pollution policy-making processes.

Summing Up

The adoption of the NEC Directive means that EU policy strength has increased substantially within the air pollution field – in terms of both bindingness and specificity, but most importantly and conspicuously in terms of ambitiousness and 'behavioural bite'. National emission ceilings for EU countries codified within the CLRTAP context have been replaced by ceilings codified within the EU institutional structure. Flat rate reductions have been replaced by a complex net of differentiated commitments. New substances such as ammonia have been drawn into the regulatory picture, and emission targets have generally been tightened. Hence, the gap between adopted policies and 'acceptable' emission levels has been substantially reduced. Although current policies, even faithfully implemented, will still leave a significant gap in 2010, an overall 'considerably stronger, but still not strong enough' policy development score was formulated.

How then, can we account for this considerable strengthening of policy? Within the 'fundamental institutional changes' perspective developed in Chapter Two, the first proposed explanation centred around how the 1995 accession of a group of 'rich and green' new Member States specifically concerned about air pollution, greened the staffing of both the Environment Directorate and other Directorates within the Commission, and also the composition of the Parliament and the Council – subsequently and together leading to a more benign constellation of preferences in the Council and ultimately increasing EU air pollution regulatory strength. This proposition made a lot of sense in this specific context. Particularly interesting and influential developments seemed to have taken place within the Commission and the DG ENV, with several influential Scandinavian experts succeeding each other. But the Nordic dominance in terms of relevant Rapporteur positions acquired in the Parliament is also striking, and the strengthening of the green frontrunner coalition in the Council – although hard to document and measure precisely – can also be assumed to have mattered.

The next institutional propositions suggested looking beyond the 1995 accession and focusing on the effects of other institutional changes. First, an increased possibility for majority-voting in the Council has led to a more powerful aggregation of preferences and can have given the 1995 enlargement a more decisive effect in the Council proceedings; ultimately leading to increasing policy strength. As a second development, a more prominent role for the Parliament in decision-making and the added weight of Parliament amendments can have contributed to a greening of preferences in the Council, and the final round of conciliation in particular can have forced the Council to move in a policy-strengthening direction.

Neither of these propositions seemed to hit the nail on the head in this context. Although the functioning of the Council in specific processes is shrouded in secrecy, and 'hidden stick' effects of majority-voting can never be ruled out, the outcome of the crucial June 2000 Council meeting stands out as a classic EU compromise – with concessions to all camps and clear winners hard to identify.

With regard to the Parliament, it clearly placed itself in the camp within the EU system pushing for the most ambitious strengthening of EU policy in this area. Up until the Parliament's second reading and the very last decision-making phase, it has supported the targets and ambitiousness expressed in the Commission's various inputs to this process. Hence, although the Parliament has surely contributed to the strengthening of policy having taken place, it cannot be counted as a crucially important driving force in this process. This is partly due to the simple fact that the Commission and the Parliament have been in basic agreement in most of this process, and the room for pressure and drama has thus been limited. In addition, the very complexity of NEC modelling and decision-making has complicated the task of justifying calls for tighter emission ceilings. Hence, the Parliament has overall not succeeded neither in respect of the Commission nor the Council with its suggested policy inputs.

As the final institutional element, the greening effect due to a changing organisational environment was pointed out with developments within CLRTAP specifically focused upon. The substantial knowledge improvement and policy development in the 1990s within the CLRTAP context may have functioned as a regulatory inspiration and stimulant, strengthening the position of EU policy entrepreneurs in the field of air pollution and leading to a more benign constellation of preferences and ultimately increasing policy strength. This proposition clearly highlighted important aspects. CLRTAP experience and expertise had a major impact on the Acidification and Ozone Strategies, which in themselves introduced a new way of working and thinking within the Commission. Moreover, the idea of setting National Emission Ceilings emanated from the 1994 Sulphur Protocol; the very multi-pollutant/multi-effects approach emanated from within the CLRTAP system; and the over time, shared use of IIASA's services proved beneficial to all parties involved. Hence, despite a some-what unfortunate timing of events in the final phases of the processes within the two contexts, the more general *CLRTAP system* influence on the shape of the EU process should be seen as significant.

The 'institutional change' perspective was then mildly challenged by two perspectives laid out initially in Chapter Two as essentially rival and independent. The first of these perspectives pinpointed parallel, relevant policy development in the EU, with attention primarily given to the pos-sibility of positive and policy-enhancing spill-over from the development of several other air pollution policy processes. This relates both to the fuel quality and vehicle emissions issue, and issues of air quality and strength-ened requirements to Large Combustion Plants. Such spill-over could take the form of policy goals being adopted in one context logically pointing to the need for stricter emissions reduction goals. However, it could also take the form of specific integrative package deals being formed.

Of the three processes discussed in this context, the Auto-Oil I fuel quality and vehicle emissions process had only very general links to the Acidification Strategy and NEC Directive process.

The air quality considerations were certainly important in the preparatory phases. With the linking of the Acidification and Ozone strategies in 1998/99, the formal relationship grew even tighter. Hence, acknowledging the air quality considerations are essential elements in order to understand the background for setting the NO_x and VOC NECs in the Commission proposal put forward in June 1999, but these considerations seem to glide more into the background in the following political debacles.

The renegotiation of the LCP Directive was in the pipeline before work started on the Acidification Strategy, but picked up speed after the renegotiation was moved into the broader Acidification Strategy context. Still, the relationship between these processes did not become really inti-mate before the spring of 1999. After that, Member States increasingly emphasised the need to see NECs and revised LCP requirements as a package. Hence, in order to understand how it was possible to obtain a NEC common position at the crucial June 2000 Environment Council – against the expectations of many insiders and observers – the package perspective is highly relevant. Furthermore, it cannot be excluded that some countries' acceptance in this final phase of somewhat lower NECs – such as the UK – had something to do with the final wording of the LCP compromise.

In sum, it is hard to understand the development and outcome of the Acidification Strategy and NEC Directive process without acknowledging the links especially to the air quality and LCP renegotiation processes. However, although air quality improvements in a general sense presuppose reduced emissions, the very establishment of the Acidification Strategy process did not come about due to these other processes.

Finally, a limited opening up of the 'black box' of domestic politics was put forward as the main logical alternative perspective to the internationally focused institutional and policy perspectives discussed above. More specifically, it was suggested that a domestically induced greening of laggards and the indifferent nations could have led to a more benign constellation of preferences and subsequently higher policy strength. With regard to France, Italy, Greece, Portugal and Spain, they have all experienced a disturbing situation, particularly in terms of ozone concentration and urban pollution, and public concern has been on the increase in these countries in recent years. However, this has had limited effects hitherto in terms of strengthened policies and positions, and several of these countries do not favour stronger *EU* policies as a response to these problems.

With regard to the earlier 'dirty man of Europe', the UK, an interesting greening of positions was noted. Both energy switching from coal to gas and reduced British sulphur emissions 'for free', and increasing concern over both rural and urban problems related to air pollution must be taken into account in this context. Not least important, it was realised during the first part of the 1990s that at least half of the UK's problems were 'imported' from abroad; providing a powerful incentive to adopt a more positive attitude towards the strengthening of European policies in this field. Hence, such a domestic perspective stands out as simply essential in order to understand the more flexible and progressive positions taken by the UK on these issues in the recent years.

Winding up, as pointed out in Chapter Two, given the complexity of the institutions and policy problems under scrutiny, there are quite surely factors and linkages which have received only superficial attention in this study. For one thing, the EU system is so rich and complex in terms of institutions and policies that the risk of overlooking influential factors and interplay is very high. Moreover, the fascinating and comprehensive 'black box' of domestic politics has been opened just a crack. Finally, getting a solid grip on the intricate interconnectedness of EU and domestic policy-making is a tough challenge in all studies of this sort. The interplay in practice between the three perspectives, here initially set out as largely independent factors, has turned out to be considerable – and one theme among several worthy of follow-up and closer scrutiny.[303]

Notes

[154] The SO_2 baseline was 1985, and the NOx baseline was 1990. See ENDS Report 205, February 1992, p. 35.

[155] See Commission of the European Community (1993), 'Towards sustainability', p. 81.

[156] ENDS Report 219, April 1993, pp. 38-39.

[157] This commitment was ratified by the EU on April 24, 1998. See UN/ECE CLRTAP web site.

[158] According to the ENDS Report, acidification strategy was 'designed to underpin the pan-European SO_2 targets agreed under a recently revised UN Economic Commission for Europe protocol' (ENDS 246, July 1995, p. 34).

[159] Acid News 3, June 1995, p. 2.

[160] EU Commission Staff Working Paper on Acidification, November 27, 1995. SEC(95) 2057.

[161] EU Council conclusions, Acidification, 20 December 1995, 13006/95.

[162] According to Tuinstra et al. (1999:39), RAINS was the only model used by the Commission, in contrast to the use of several models within the CLRTAP context.

[163] Acid News 5, December 1996, p. 1-4. Communication with Christer Ågren, October, 2000.

[164] ENDS Report 264 January 1997, p. 37.

[165] Ibid.

[166] Ibid., p. 38.

[167] See Amann and Lutz (2000).

[168] EU Commission Communication IP/97/205, March 12, 1997. See comments in ENDS Report 264, January 1997, p. 37.

[169] EU Commission Communication IP/97/205; Europe Environment, March 25, 1997, pp. 1-3; ENDS Report 266, March 1997, p. 40. Strictly speaking, the modelling aimed at 'at least 50 percent gap closure in each EMEP grid cell' (Communication with Christer Ågren, October, 2000).

[170] ENDS Report 268, May 1997, pp. 40-41; 282, July 1998, p. 49.

[171] ENDS Report 273, October 1997, p. 37; Europe Environment, October 28, 1997, pp. 12-13; Acid News 3, October 1997, p. 7.

[172] EU Council conclusions on a Community strategy to combat acidification, December 19, 1997, 13622/97. See also Acid News 3, October 1997, p. 7.

[173] Communication with Christer Ågren, October, 2000.

[174] Europe Environment, May 12, 1998, p. 4.

[175] Europe Environment May 12, 1998, p. 4; Europe Environment May 26, 1998, p. 3.

[176] Europe Environment, July 21, 1998, p. 18.

[177] ENDS Report 282, July 1998, pp. 49–50; Europe Environment, July 21, 1998, pp. 1–4.

[178] Acid News 4, December 1998, pp. 8-9.

Clearing the Air

[179] These NGOs were the European Environmental Bureau, The European Federation for Transport and the Environment, and the Swedish NGO Secretariat on Acid Rain. Ibid., pp. 9-10.

[180] ENDS Report 288, January 1999, pp. 46-47; Acid News 1, March 1999, p. 6.

[181] Europe Environment, March 16, 1999, pp. 14-15.

[182] Environment Watch, February 19, 1999, p. 6.

[183] Europe Environment, March 30, 1999, p. 9.

[184] Europe Environment, April 27, 1999, p. 19.

[185] International Environment Reporter, June 23, 1999, p. 521.

[186] See comments in Europe Environment, June 15, 1999, p. 11 and ENDS Report 293, June 1999, pp. 45-46.

[187] Environment Watch, June 18, 1999, p. 7.

[188] Ibid., p. 9.

[189] Europe Environment, June 15, 1999, p. 13. These organizations were the European Consumers Organization, the European Environmental Bureau, the European Public Health Alliance, the International Society of Doctors for the Environment, Stop Acid Rain, and the European Federation for Transport and Environment.

[190] ENDS Report 293, op. cit., p. 45.

[191] Ibid.

[192] International Environment Reporter, September 29, 1999, p. 785.

[193] The following account draws upon ENDS Report 297, October 1999, p. 53; Environment Watch, October 15, 1999, pp. 1–3; and Europe Environment, October 19, 1999, pp. 24–25.

[194] Europe Environment, December 14, 1999, p. 13.

[195] ENDS Report 299, December 1999, p. 41.

[196] Environment Watch, November 12, 1999, pp. 1–2; ENDS Report 299, December 1999, p. 43; Europe Environment, January 7, 2000, p. 3.

[197] Europe Environment, March 7, 2000, p. 2.

[198] International Environment Reporter, March 29, 2000, p. 269; Environment Watch, May 26, 2000, pp. 9–10.

[199] Europe Environment, April 4, 2000, p. 4.

[200] This is based on interviews in the Commission and the Parliament in the beginning of May 2000. See also Europe Environment, 20 June, 2000, p. 30.

[201] The Integrated Pollution Prevention and Control (IPPC) Directive was adopted in October 1996. The purpose of the directive is to see measures to reduce emissions to air, water and land in relation to each other; in order to attain 'a high level of protection of the environment taken as a whole'. See Haigh (ed.), Manual Of Environmental Policy (update 1999:6.18-1).

[202] Europe Environment, op. cit., p. 31.

[203] The agreements set January 1 2008 as the date when emission limits for SO2, NOx and dust will apply to all plants with a thermal input over 50 megawatts, including existing plants licensed before July 1 1987. Moreover, the oldest, most polluting plants were allowed to operate 20,000 hours beyond this date before they have to be shut down. See Environment Watch, July 7, 2000, p. 6.

[204] See comments in Environment Watch, ibid.; Europe Environment, 4 July, 2000, pp. 3–5.

[205] EU Press release June 22, 2000, 'EU Commission welcomes agreement to curb air pollution', IP/00/657; communication with Christer Ågren, October, 2000.

[206] Acid News 3, October 2000, pp. 6-7.

[207] Reuters/Planetark, 'EU states agree to cut smog and acid rain', June 23, 2000.

208 ENDS Environment Daily, October 5, 2000, 'Clash looms over watered down plan to curb ozone' ; Europe Environment, October 17, 2000, p. 3.

209 International Environment Reporter, October 11, 2000, p. 779.

210 Europe Environment, November 28, 2000, p. 14.

211 See Europe Environment, March 20, 2001, pp.13-14. See also Acid News 2, June 2001, pp.1, 3-5; ENDS Report 315, April 2001, p.55; International Environment Reporter, March 28, pp.236-237 and p.248.

212 For instance, in the case of SO$_2$, the Commission initially proposed a 3634 kt ceiling. The Council then agreed upon a 3850 kt ceiling in June 2000. The Parliament's second reading proposal was a 3491 kt ceiling.

213 With regard to emission limits, these were tightened for SO$_2$ emissions from smaller plants and for NOx emissions in most categories. A total of 18 amendments were proposed in the LCP context. See articles referred to in footnote 207.

214 See Europe Environment, June 12, 2001, p.18, and May 23, 2001, p.10.

215 The compromise was accepted by the Council on June 27 and then by the delegation of the Parliament on July 3, 2001. See EU Press Release, July 3, 2001, 'Large Combustion Plants' and National Emission Ceilings Directives/ Agreement'; and ENDS Report 319, August 2001, p.52.

216 In terms of emission limits and NOx, a two-stage approach was introduced. In the first stage, up to 2016, the limit for the largest existing plants was a little bit strengthened compared with the common position, i.e. from 650 to 500 mg/Nm3. This was far less than called for by the Parliament, i.e. 200 mg/Nm3. However, it was agreed to introduce the 200 mg/Nm3 limit from 2016 on. See Europe Environment, July 10, 2001, p.15.

217 See EEB Press Release, July 4, 2001.

218 See Europe Environment, March 20, 2001, p.12.

219 See Environment Update/Euractiv, June 15, 2001; Europe Environment, June 12, 2001, pp.17-18; Europe Environment June 26, 2001, p.30; and International Environment Reporter, June 20, 2001, p.512.

220 The EU ratified the NOx Protocol in December 1993.

221 However, by November 2000, the EU had still not ratified the VOC Protocol.

222 The EU ratified the 1994 Sulphur Protocol in April 1998.

223 EU Commission, 'Towards Sustainability – A European Community programme of policy and action in relation to the environment and sustainable development' (1993:81).

224 However, these commitments are still not 100 percent comparable, as the 1994 Protocol had a 1980 baseline and the NEC Directive has a 1990 baseline.

225 See the presentation of IIASA's assessments in the Commission's Communication on 'A European strategy to combat acidification', reprinted as a supplement to Europe Environment, no. 497, April 8, 1997.

226 See Acid News 4, December 1998, pp. 1–5.

227 See ENDS Report 288, January 1999, pp. 46–47. See also various trend data summed up in Acid News 1, April 1997, p. 6 and Acid News 3, October 1997, p. 11.

228 ENDS Report 288, ibid.

229 This section has benefited tremendously from invaluable inputs from Christer Ågren!

230 Interviews, Fall 1999 and Spring 2000.

231 Cf. Wurzel (1999), p. 126.

232 This section draws heavily on communication with Christer Ågren, October, 2000.

233 My interpretation, based on a number of interviews, Fall 1999 and Spring 2000. With regard to the reference to the Fifth EAP, see EU Commission (1993),'Towards sustainability', p. 81.
234 Interviews in Brussels, May 2000.
235 Interviews in Stockholm, Fall 1999.
236 Interviews, Fall 1999 and Spring 2000.
237 See Parliament Resolution A4-0162/1998.
238 Europe Environment, March 30, 1999, p. 9.
239 See for instance Europe Environment, June 15, 1999, p. 11. According to EU insiders interviewed in Brussels in May 2000, this proposal was something of a stray proposal anyway.
240 EP Document A5-0063/2000, suggested amendments by the Parliament. See also Environment Watch, March 31, 2000, pp. 2-3.
241 Ibid.
242 On this point, see Environment Watch, July 7, 2000, p. 5.
243 Parliament Draft Recommendation for second reading, December 8, 2000.
244 Ibid.
245 Communication with Christer Ågren, March 5, 2001.
246 See Europe Environment, June 12, 2001, p.18.
247 The discussion in this section has benefited considerably from various comments and inputs from Christer Ågren (October, 2000).
248 Ibid.
249 For more in-going and comprehensive analysis, see e.g. Wurzel (1999); Friedrich et al (2000); Weale et al (2000), Chapter Eleven; and Young and Wallace (2000), Chapter 2.
250 See Weale et al. (ibid.) and Haigh (1992/1998:6.8-8).
251 Interview with Matthew Ferguson, IEEP, November 1999.
252 Friedrich et al. (1998:105).
253 According to ENDS Report 257, June 1996, p. 41.
254 More specifically, the following proposals were put forward: first, a proposal on the reformulation of petrol and diesel fuels. A key 2000 target here was petrol with 200 parts per million (ppm) of sulphur (down from the estimated market average of 300 ppm); and diesel with 350 ppm of sulphur (down from the estimated market average of 450 ppm). Second, a proposal to strengthen the existing emission limits for passenger cars (these being based on Directive 70/220 on Motor Vehicle Air Pollution Control, last amended by Directive 94/12). Targeted substances included were carbon monoxide (CO), hydrocarbons (HC), nitrogen oxides (NOx) and, only for diesel cars, particulates. Emission limits for 2000 were proposed, but 'indicative' lower limits for 2005 were also included.
255 ENDS 257, op. cit.
256 Acid News, October 1996, p. 1.
257 With regard to *emission limit values*, in relation to the Commission's proposals, lower limit values were suggested with regard to NOx emissions and particles from diesel-driven vehicles. Moreover, *binding* limit values for the year 2005 instead of indicative limits were proposed for NOx, carbon monoxides, ozone and sulphur emissions. With regard to *fuel quality*, a lower allowable sulphur content of diesel was suggested.
258 ENDS Report 281, June 1998, p. 48.
259 Communication with Christer Ågren, October, 2000.
260 The Auto-Oil I Directives are for instance briefly mentioned in point 4.4, 'Consistency with other Community policies', in the Commission's NEC Directive proposal (see

Proposal for a Directive of the European Parliament and of the Council on national emission ceilings for certain atmospheric pollutants, COM (1999) 125 final).

[261] Communication with Christer Ågren, February, 2001.

[262] See ENDS Report 219, April 1993, p. 38.

[263] The top 14 were sulphur dioxide; nitrogen oxides; ozone; particulates; black smoke; lead; carbon monoxide; cadmium; acid deposition; toluene; benzene; benzo-a-pyrene; formaldehyde; and PAN. Ibid.

[264] Ibid.

[265] See International Environment Reporter, July 13, 1994, pp. 589–590, and ENDS Report 234, July 1994, pp. 41-42.

[266] International Environment Reporter, July 13, op. cit., p. 589.

[267] The complete list here included sulphur dioxide, nitrogen oxide, black smoke, suspended particulates and lead.

[268] The complete list here included carbon monoxide, cadmium, acid deposition, benzene, polyaromatic hydrocarbons, arsenic, fluoride, and nickel.

[269] Directive on ambient air quality assessment and management, 96/62/EU.

[270] Acid News 2, June 1997, p. 7.

[271] See International Environment Reporter, October 15, 1997, p. 953.

[272] See Acid News 3, October 1998, p. 7 and ENDS Report 281, June 1998, p. 47. As pinpointed by ENDS Report, exceedance of the particulate matter value would be permitted on 35 occasions in 2005 – compared to the 25 occasions suggested by the Commission. NOx limits could be breached up to 18 times – compared to the eight breaches suggested by the Commission.

[273] Directive 1999/30/EU.

[274] Proposal for a Directive of the European Parliament and of the Council on national emission ceilings for certain atmospheric pollutants; Proposal for a Directive of the European Parliament and of the Council relating to ozone in ambient air, COM (1999) 125 final, p. 2.

[275] Cf. Acid News: 'There is a close connection between the air-quality directive for ozone and that for national ceilings on emissions. It was under the assumption that its proposal for ceilings on the emissions of nitrogen oxides and volatile organic compounds, the substances that give rise to the formation of ozone, would be accepted by the member countries that the Commission reckoned its limit for ozone concentrations would be realized' (Acid News 4, December 2000, p. 12).

[276] See Acid News 3, June 1995, p. 2.

[277] This directive was adopted in 1996. See Haigh (ed.), Manual of Environmental Policy (update 1999, 6.18.1). The possible replacing of the LCP Directive was announced in ENDS Report 246, July 1995, p. 33-34.

[278] Communication with Christer Ågren, February 2001.

[279] ENDS Report 268, May 1997,

[280] Communication with Christer Ågren, February, 2001.

[281] For instance, according to Environment Watch, May 7, 1999: 'In the Council of Minister...current president Germany has dropped the <LCP> dossier from its agenda in deference to the view of many delegations that the LCP revision and the forthcoming national emission ceilings (NECs) directive should be dealt with *as a package*' (p. 11; my italics).

[282] See Europe Environment, April 4, 2000, p. 4.

[283] Acid News 3, October 2000, pp. 8-9.

[284] See EEB Press Release, July 4, 2001.

[285] See for instance Skea and Du Monteuil, in Underdal and Hanf (2000).

[286] See 'What do Europeans think about the environment?', European Commission, 1999:13.

[287] Communication with Christer Ågren, October 2000.

[288] See Lewanski, in Underdal and Hanf (eds., 2000).

[289] Ibid., 15.

[290] 'Ground-level ozone - High levels ignored further south', Acid News no.1, March 2000:15.

[291] Communication with Christer Ågren, October 2000.

[292] See here Boehmer-Christiansen in Underdal and Hanf (2000:279-313); Collier (1997).

[293] The participating states were Germany, France, the Netherlands, Belgium, Ireland, Denmark, Luxembourg and the UK. See ENDS Report 256, May 1996, p. 43.

[294] Ibid.

[295] See e.g. ENDS Report 257, June 1996, pp. 15-18.

[296] See ENDS Report 270, July 1997, p. 34.

[297] ENDS Report 288, January 1999, p. 17.

[298] Ibid.

[299] Ibid., p. 19.

[300] DETR (2000). See comments in ENDS Report 300, January 2000, pp. 37–38.

[301] See various 1999 EU studies: the EEA Report and also reports from the EU Commission on the concentration levels of tropospheric ozone in 1998 and 1999.

[302] European Commission, 'What do Europeans think..', op. cit.:15.

[303] The author will, in colloboration with Andrew Farmer, pursue the interplay between EU air pollution policies further in an EU-financed project on 'Institutional Interaction'.

Chapter 6

Comparing the EU and CLRTAP

Explaining Policy Differences –
and Why They are So Small

Introduction

Building upon the mainly separate histories and case studies carried out in the two previous chapters, this chapter addresses the relationship between CLRTAP and EU policy-making in a more systematic manner. As noted in Chapter Two, although there are considerable differences between CLR-TAP and EU policy-making, it is still meaningful to compare CLRTAP protocols and EU directives in terms of policy strength. The earlier chapters hinted at a difference in the favour of the EU NEC Directive in relation to the CLRTAP Gothenburg Protocol. This difference will be further substantiated and discussed in this chapter.

The remaining part of the chapter will discuss possible explanations for differing policy strength in this particular context. As the problems addressed are fairly similar, could it be that the difference in policy strength stems from substantially differing institutional contexts? There is little doubt that in principle the EU is a stronger decision-making body than a classic inter-governmental regime such as CLRTAP. However, the crucial question is the extent to which the EU can take advantage of such principle strengths *in practice*. Finally, in addition to exploring the institutional issues in more depth, the notion of these institutions addressing 'fairly similar problems' will be re-examined more critically. Probing this superficial similarity in more depth, do more underlying and hidden differences then come to the forefront?

'Changing Places?' Have EU Air Pollution Policies become Clearly Stronger than CLRTAP Policies?

As hinted at in earlier chapters, the relationship between CLRTAP and the EU in terms of policy leadership has gradually been changing. A development of the relationship between CLRTAP and the EU may be envisaged in several stages. In the mid 1980s, CLRTAP was the clear policy leader. Recall, for instance, that when the negotiations on the first Sulphur Protocol were concluded in Helsinki in 1985, the EU as an entity was not able to sign the agreement. The EU Commission did not sign on to the Protocol at a later stage either, as it apparently did not feel secure that the then existing EU policies would add up to compliance with the 1995 30 percent reduction target.

A decade later, the relationship was becoming much more balanced. For instance, by the time the negotiations on the second sulphur protocol came to an end in Oslo in 1994, policy development within the EU, partly in the form of the LCP Directive, made it possible for the EU to sign and later ratify this protocol as an entity. The intriguing question then becomes whether, at the end of the century, the EU has taken over as the leader in terms of policy strength? Judging at least by the case of the NEC Directive and the Gothenburg Protocol, the answer is a qualified yes. But such a claim needs to be substantiated in more detail.

As discussed in Chapter Two, the notion of policy strength – and hence discussion of differences in such strength – includes several dimensions. The central dimension of 'ambitiousness' refers primarily to the level of standards and the degree of behavioural change required. But there are also more procedural and legal aspects related to the 'bindingness' and 'specificity' of the policies adopted. For instance, with regard to the issue of bindingness, there are clearly formal differences between EU directives and CLRTAP protocols, stemming from the quite different fundamental nature of these institutions. But before we delve deeper into such questions, let us first sum up the simple differences in ambitiousness expressed by the differing figures in the EU NEC Directive (common position) and CLRTAP Gothenburg Protocol. The following table juxtaposes directly the emissions ceilings in the June 2000 NEC Directive common position with the emissions ceilings in the December 1999 Gothenburg Protocol.

Table 6.1 Emission ceilings in the EU NEC Directive and the CLRTAP Gothenburg Protocol (kilotonnes)

	SO_2 EU	SO_2 CLR-TAP	NO_x EU	NO_x CLR-TAP	VOC EU	VOC CLR-TAP	NH_3 EU	NH_3 CLR-TAP
Austria	39	39	103	107	159	159	66	66
Belgium	99	106	176	181	139	144	74	74
Denmark	55	55	127	127	85	85	69	69
Finland	110	116	170	170	130	130	31	31
France	375	400	810	860	1050	1100	780	780
Germany	520	550	1051	1081	995	995	550	550
Greece	523	546	344	344	261	261	73	73
Ireland	42	42	65	65	55	55	116	116
Italy	475	500	990	1000	1159	1159	419	419
Luxembourg	4	4	11	11	9	9	7	7
Netherlands	50	50	260	266	185	191	128	128
Portugal	160	170	250	260	180	202	90	108
Spain	746	774	847	847	662	669	353	353
Sweden	67	67	148	148	241	241	57	57
UK	585	625	1167	1181	1200	1200	297	297

Overall, in terms of achieved protection, the difference between the EU and CLRTAP ceilings is most striking in terms of sulphur dioxide. In this respect, there is a 5 percent difference in favour of the EU. With regard to the other substances, the differences are even smaller. In terms of NO_x, there is a 2 percent difference, and in terms of VOCs, the difference is 1.4 percent in favour of the EU. Finally, in terms of ammonia, there is hardly any difference at all – just 0.6 percent.[304] Taken together, the EU NECs are hence around 3 percent more ambitious than the CLRTAP Gothenburg ceilings. This difference is clearly much more moderate than that which was in the pipeline when the Commission presented its draft NEC Directive in June 1999, and also what one easily would expect on the basis of the EU 'simply being a far more significant institution than CLRTAP'.

But, as noted above, this rather moderate difference in numbers is not the whole story. There is clearly also a dimension of bindingness and political 'weight' to be kept in mind. As was noted in Chapter Two, convincing arguments can be put forward for seeing EU directives as politically far stronger legal instruments than regime protocols. This is primarily due to the fact that EU directives are directly enforceable on the Member states once they are adopted, and there is also the existence of the European Court of Justice as an EU institutional 'stick' and enforcer, with no direct counterpart in international regimes. Certainly, there is an 'implementation gap' pertaining to EU environmental policies (Jordan 1998). But there is certainly an 'implementation gap' pertaining to the CLRTAP context also, for instance witnessed in many countries' quite lacklustre follow-up of the 1991 VOC Protocol.[305]

It is interesting to note that this perspective on the differing political 'weight' of the institutions was given empirical support in Underdal and Hanf's (2000:378) study on air pollution policy-making in nine European countries: 'Several of the country studies report that EU directives and regulations have had considerable more 'teeth' and therefore greater impact on domestic policies than ECE protocols. The combination of its greater institutional weight and its ability to reward and support as well as to punish gave the EU a major advantage in terms of inducing real changes in the domestic policies and behaviour of member countries – particularly the laggards'. Based on similar reasoning, *Acid News* subsequently found a clear reason to celebrate the EU NEC common position of June 2000, in spite of the moderate differences in figures between the EU and CLRTAP commitments: 'EU laws "weigh" much more than international agreements. With ceilings prescribed in an EU directive, their implementation can be much better observed'.[306]

In summary, this discussion leads us to conclude that there are in fact *two* puzzles to be solved in this context. First, as the EU NECs *are* a bit more ambitious and not least legally stronger and 'heavier' than the Gothenburg commitments, there is a difference to be accounted for. However, as the difference, at least in numbers, is considerably smaller than expected, why is this? Is this more a matter of coincidence or is it a signal of the EU decision-making system in practice functioning in a much more traditional, inter-governmental way than the impression given by its complex formal institutional structure? With these dual perspectives in mind, let us turn to the explanatory perspectives and first of all to the institutional questions.

Differing Institutional Contexts: Impacts and Paradoxes

As further elaborated in Chapter Two, there are at least four main institutional issues and factors which may throw light upon comparative differences in policy strength: membership scope, administrative strength, decision-making procedures, and issue linkage potential. Let us see how these perspectives stand up when confronted with the empirical evidence.

Membership Scope: Is an Expanding EU Still a Much More 'Handy' Institution than CLRTAP?

In a comparative perspective, the difference in membership is of course an obvious candidate for accounting for possible differences in regulatory strength. Forty six countries, as well as the EC, have now joined CLRTAP and the number of countries/entities participating in the CLRTAP negotiations on the multi-protocol was more than 30; in other words, more than double the present number of EU countries. Moreover, not only is the number of state actors much larger within CLRTAP, but also the heterogeneity of actors is much more striking within CLRTAP. This is related both to the Eastern European and North American participation in CLRTAP. This led us to propose that higher regulatory strength within the EU could be explained by policy-making within the smaller and somewhat more homogenous EU group of countries being less complicated than policy-making within the broader group of CLRTAP countries.

At a cursory glance, this proposition carries substantial explanatory weight. For instance, when the *ENDS Report* in September 1999 compared emissions ceilings within the two contexts, it stated that 'the emission reductions needed to deliver these goals differ from the EC proposals because of the wider geographical scope of the UNECE protocol' (ENDS 296:44). A possible logical extension of this argument is that the non-EU countries had similar or less ambitious policy preferences than the less ambitious EU countries. If they had similar preferences to the EU laggards, then this may have strengthened the 'weight' and negotiating power of the less-ambitious group of countries within CLRTAP compared to the EU.[307] This argument is even more relevant if they held less ambitious preferences than the EU laggards.

Taking a second look at the CLRTAP constellation of preferences in this comparative perspective, the latter 'less-ambitious-than-the-EU-laggards' notion receives little support. For one thing, there are several examples of non-EU countries being clearly more ambitious than the EU laggards, of which Switzerland is a good example.[308] Hence, the former 'similarly unambitious' notion seems far more fitting. Overall, countries such as Russia, Ukraine, Hungary and Poland held quite similar positions to countries such as Greece, Spain and Portugal. Hence, as the EU had a group of quite unambitious countries within its ranks, the difference in membership between the two contexts in terms of the presence of 'laggards' must clearly have been more one of degree than one of fundamental nature.

Overall, membership differences may have contributed to differences in regulatory strength. But a closer scrutiny clearly questions whether they should be seen as the sole or main reason for the policy differences. Let us have a closer look at the other institutional candidates.

Administrative Strength: Who is David and Who is Goliath in Terms of Air Pollution Policy-making?

As elaborated in Chapter Two, in formal terms, the David and Goliath metaphor is clearly a fitting one. The policy-initiating and driving force within the EU system, the Commission, is of course an institution of a totally different kind than the CLRTAP Secretariat. Even if we only count the Environment Directorate, DG ENV, its administrative capacity of around 480 employees compares very favourably with the CLRTAP Secretariat's 9–10 employees. Moreover, in terms of 'systemic institutional forces' backing up decision-making processes, within the EU, there is also the possibility of the green institutional forces within the EU joining forces. In addition to DG ENV, it may be assumed that at the least these forces include the Environment Committee in the Parliament. The difference in terms of budgetary resources is also, of course, quite vast. On this background, the proposition was put forward that higher policy strength within the EU could have something to do with more and stronger institutional resources and forces backing up regulatory propositions within the EU than within CLRTAP.

Comparing the processes within the two institutions, it is soon realised that although the differences in institutional strength are not without significance, they do not very appropriately catch the relationship between the two institutions in practice. Addressing first the main point on which the proposition above hits the nail, this has to do with financial resources. As further described in Chapter Four, it became increasingly problematic to finance the complex scientific modelling work underpinning the ambitious multi-pollutant and multi-effects approach within the limited CLRTAP budgetary resources. A significant part of this work took place at IIASA. In this increasingly difficult situation for CLRTAP, the EU Commission could step in as 'the rich uncle' and ensure the continuing development of the scientific groundwork – and in return, benefit from IIASA's work in its own process of developing a scientifically based Acidification and Ozone Strategy.

However, as indicated, in several other respects the David and Goliath secretarial picture is seriously misleading. This has first and foremost to do with structural differences in the mode of operation of the two institutions. The main point in this connection is what may be called CLRTAP's non-conspicuous 'guerilla' weapon: the scientific-political complex. As further described in Chapter Four, CLRTAP policy-making rests upon a complex web of scientific/technical sub-bodies: Working Groups, International Cooperative Programs and Task Forces. These bodies are financed and manned by a number of nation states; hence complementing the CLRTAP Secretariat's administrative and financial resources many times over.

If we then include the scientific-political complex in CLRTAP's policy-making resources, the comparative picture in terms of such resources looks much more balanced between the two institutions. In fact, comparing the CLRTAP scientific-political complex at work in the Gothenburg Protocol process with the administrative resources commanded by the EU air pollution unit in charge of the Acidification/Ozone Strategy and NEC Directive process, one may even come to the conclusion that *CLRTAP is the stronger institution!* Hence, closer scrutiny within the issue area of air pollution policy seriously questions the proposition that greater policy strength within the EU than CLRTAP can simply be explained by greater administrative strength within the EU.

Decision-making Procedures: Considerable Formal Differences - but Practical Similarities?

In general, the multi-institutions and multi-layered EU is of course a much more complex and, especially in one sense, procedurally stronger institution than the more straight-forward CLRTAP international regime. EU decisions are shaped through intricate bargaining, back-and-forth processes involving the policy-initiating Commission, the consultative Parliament, and the decision-making Council of Ministers. However, as further elaborated in Chapter Two, that aspect which most clearly sets the EU apart from traditional international regimes is the increasing ability to make decisions by some sort of majority. In general, majority decisions increase the ability to cut through aggregation deadlocks easily caused by unanimity requirements, and hence also the ability to vote down policy laggards. If the majority of parties are green in nature, then the use of this procedure may also lead to greener outcomes than under rules of consensus. The 1995 accession of a group of 'rich and green' new Member States probably strengthened the general capacity to form green majorities within the EU. In comparison, in the case of CLRTAP, the requirement for consensus was written into the 1979 Convention, although practised with some flexibility. In summary, higher policy strength within the EU than within CLRTAP could possibly be explained by the capacity to make decisions by majority vote within the EU and voting down laggards.

Revisiting briefly first the CLRTAP process, it is fairly clear that this was a traditional, consensus-driven process. However, this does not mean that reluctant parties were not subjected to political pressure. This happened not least in the final phase between the conclusion of negotiations within the Working Group on Strategies in September 1999, with agreement on draft emission ceilings and the final adoption of the Protocol at the beginning of December. However, the effect was moderate; only Sweden and Belgium lowered their ceilings in this period.[309] Moreover, in line with established practice in connection with earlier protocols, the reluctants were not allowed to block the adoption of the Protocol in December. A small group of parties, including Belgium, Greece, Poland and the EU, simply did not sign the Protocol.[310]

Turning to the EU Acidification/Ozone strategy process and the NEC Directive, the legal base for this Directive opened up for its adoption by the use of majority voting. However, as the process unfolded, a clear North-South split within the EU with regard to the perception of the seriousness of the (in particular) acidification problems, but also the ozone problems, became apparent. This pointed to the need for delicate consensus-building and compromises being struck, and away from a simple voting down of 'Southern laggards' by a 'triumphant and green' Northern majority. As discussed in Chapter Five, we do not know very much about the exact proceedings of the crucially important Environment Council meeting in June 2000. However, from what we do know, the outcome of the meeting must primarily be understood as a complex compromise and package deal. As a result of the building of this compromise, earlier reluctants and potential blockers in this process such as Spain and Greece chose to move to greener positions more acceptable to the majority, instead of being voted down. However, this does not rule out the more indirect impact of majority voting as a sort of 'hidden stick' and a stimulant to the building of an overall acceptable compromise.

Given that both CLRTAP and the EU started the work leading up to multi-pollutant emission ceilings at about the same time in 1995, why then was the EU NEC Directive far from adoption at the time the CLRTAP Gothenburg Protocol was adopted? This may of course have something to do with more co-incidental factors like the resignation of the Commission in the spring of 1999 and the related slowing down of several, on-going decision-making processes. Moreover, it may have something to do with the higher regulatory ambitiousness within the EU context; expressed in the draft NEC Directive put forward by the Commission in 1999. However, it may *also* have something to do with the precise *combination* of higher regulatory ambitiousness and decision-making procedures. Here, it must be remembered that once adopted, EU Directives are automatically binding for the EU states, and subject to compliance procedures as well as the European Court of Justice.

Within CLRTAP (and other international environmental regimes), the adoption of the protocol is, of course, only an important first step in the process of establishing binding international law. As clearly witnessed in connection with the Kyoto Protocol within the climate change context, ratification and entry into force can in no way be taken for granted.[311] Moreover, a compliance mechanism similar to the ECJ is generally not present.[312] Hence, somewhat paradoxically, this comparative decision-making strength of the EU may actually be an impediment in terms of getting regulations adopted, as the 'opting out' possibility of non-ratification is not present and retribution for non-compliance is increasingly becoming more of a practical reality within the EU context.[313]

Summing up, despite considerable formal procedural differences between the two contexts, decision-making practice seems to have been quite consensual in both contexts. However, some 'hidden stick' effects of the formal possibility to resort to majority-voting cannot be ruled out in the EU context. Moreover, the more immediate legal effect and sharper compliance procedures may in fact disadvantage EU policy-making compared to international regimes like CLRTAP. All in all, although the case of the NEC Directive is clouded in some uncertainty, the main proposition guiding the discussion in this section does not throw very much light on the differences between the EU and CLRTAP in terms of policy strength.

Issue Linkage Potential: Another Case of Formal Differences and Practical Similarities?

Compared with CLRTAP, the EU of course covers a much broader set of issues. In contrast to the issue-specific concern about acidification which led to the establishment of CLRTAP, the EU was established for broader economic and trade reasons, with the environment 'incidentally' added to the regulatory focus in the 1970s, and given formal legal footing first with the Single European Act in 1987. Hence, given that the EU spans a wide variety of issue areas, it was suggested that concessions states would be willing to make within an environmental policy-making process could be rewarded by concessions from other states in other environmental policy-making processes and/or even processes within other issue areas. Such possibilities were assumed to be of less relevance within the more narrowly focused CLRTAP. Hence, greater strength of policy within the EU than within CLRTAP could possibly be explained by the greater capacity to put together integrative package deals within the EU than within CLRTAP.

Let us first turn to the EU context. First, in theory, thinking only in terms of air pollution policy-making, there should be plenty of room for striking package deals, given several parallel and somehow related policy processes. In addition to the Acidification Strategy from 1996–97 onwards, work was proceeding with regard to a revision of fuel quality and vehicle emission requirements (i.e. the Auto-Oil I Programme); a revision of the 1988 Large Combustion Plants Directive; a directive on the sulphur content in fuels; and the flushing out of several daughter directives of the 1996 Air Quality Framework Directive. As discussed in more detail in Chapter Five, the relationship between the Acidification Strategy and NEC Directive process and these other processes varied in intensity, and there were also some shifts over time. With regard to the Auto-Oil I process on fuel quality and vehicle emissions, this had only very general links to the Acidification Strategy/NEC Directive process.

However, a central conclusion in Chapter Five was that it is hard to understand the development and outcome of the Acidification Strategy/ NEC Directive process without acknowledging the links especially to the air quality and LCP renegotiation processes. Acknowledging the air quality considerations are essential elements in order to understand the process leading up to the inclusion of the NO_x and VOC NECs in the Commission's proposal of June 1999. After that, the LCP process takes over as the most intimate partner, with Member States increasingly emphasising the need to see NECs and revised LCP requirements as a package. Hence, in order to understand how it was possible to obtain a NEC common position at the crucial June 2000 Environment Council – against the expectations of many insiders and observers – the package perspective is highly relevant.

Turning to CLRTAP, in a vaguely similar fashion to the EU, in the period 1996-98 there were several parallel policy processes. In addition to the negotiations on the Gothenburg Protocol, negotiations on protocols on heavy metals and persistent organic pollutants (POPs) were on-going. However, there is nothing to suggest that developments within these processes 'spilled over' to the Gothenburg Protocol process. Much more so than within the EU, this process seems to have developed according to its own, internal dynamic. Still, the multi-pollutant and multi-effects approach should in theory provide ample room for linkages. Increasing knowledge over time about the relationship and interplay of different pollutants and the related development of multi-pollutant policy approaches should mean possibilities for states to give concessions in the form of stricter reduction requirements for one pollutant in return for more lax requirements in relation to other pollutants. But even such 'internal' linkage seems to have taken place only to a very moderate degree.

In conclusion, issue-linking seems to have been a much more prominent feature of the decision-making processes within the EU than within CLRTAP. This is partly a reflection of the fundamentally different nature of the two institutions. Over time, the EU has developed a variety of different policy types addressing and 'attacking' the air pollution problems from a number of angles, including product standards, emission limits, air quality standards and, most recently, national emission ceilings. This very 'policy density' led to a number of related policy processes from the mid-1990s onward, partly pertaining to a revision of earlier policies, and partly to the development of completely new policies. Hence, the proposition of a higher capacity for package dealing within the EU and related positive effects in terms of policy development is given support by the cases studied in this context.

Challenging the Institutional Perspective: How Similar are the Problems Addressed in Reality?

So far, we have accepted as a premise for the discussion that the fundamental problem characteristics are 'quite similar'; paving the way for an interesting and meaningful comparison of the institutional strengths and weaknesses of the two contexts. However, 'quite similar' in no way means *identical*. The time has come to examine the main rival proposition put forward in Chapter Two, namely that remaining differences in problem characteristics may have led to higher policy strength within the EU than within CLRTAP.

Let us start by recalling the quote from *ENDS Report* in September 1999 comparing emission ceilings within the two contexts. This stated that 'the emission reductions needed to deliver these goals differ from the EC proposals because of the wider geographical scope of the UNECE protocol' (ENDS 296:44). This statement was in part misleading, as the journal compared CLRTAP political bids (from June 1999) with 'scientific' draft EU ceilings. If we instead compare the emission ceilings within the guiding scenarios in both contexts – i.e. the 'H1' scenario in the EU context and the 'G5/2 rev' scenario in the CLRTAP context – the differences are not very dramatic. In the table below, France, Germany and the UK are singled out as an illustration.

Clearing the Air

Table 6.2   Comparison of ceilings within guiding modeling scenarios

	SO$_2$		NO$_x$		VOC		NH$_4$	
	H1/ NEC Draft	G5/2 CLRTAP	H1/ NEC Draft	G5/2 CLRTAP	H1/ NEC Draft	G5/2 CLRTAP	H1/ NEC Draft	G5/2 CLRTAP
France	218	219	679	704	932	989	718	642
Germany	463	463	1051	1081	924	995	413	413
The UK	497	499	1181	1181	964	1101	264	264

Still, as there are slight differences, the *ENDS Report* is on to something which may be seen as correct. Given differences in geographical scope and hence somewhat differing problem characteristics, the modelling exercise came out in some instances with somewhat lower NO$_x$ and VOC ceilings within the EU context than the CLRTAP context. This is primarily related to the targets in terms of ozone. The most substantial ozone breaches take place in Central Europe (i.e. Belgium, the Netherlands, Germany and Northern France). As the modelling for the EU area could not include and benefit from emission reductions for instance in Poland and the Czech Republic (at least not yet!), the modellers had to compensate by lowering the EU emission ceilings somewhat.[314] In addition, it should also be realised that some modelling elements were adjusted in the very final phase within the EU context with the inclusion of the effects of other, proposed EU legislation, and new data from the Member States.[315] These changes also contributed to lowering the EU NEC ceilings compared to the CLRTAP guiding scenario.

In sum, and cutting a much longer story short, somewhat differing problem characteristics led to somewhat different guiding scenarios, and hence differing starting points for the main political wrangles in the two contexts. As further elaborated in the two previous chapters, much political manoeuvring did take place in the final phases of the processes within both contexts, and most so within the EU context. Tuinstra et al. (1999:39) have commented upon the differences between CLRTAP and the EU in the following manner: 'whereas simulations with RAINS were an integral part of the LRTAP negotiations, they are really just the starting point of the EU deliberations'. So when it comes to the NEC outcome of June 2000, RAINS and the 'H1' scenario seem far away. However, as can be recalled from Chapter Four, although simulations may have been 'an integral part of the LRTAP negotiations' and Tuinstra et al. have a point, the distance between the Gothenburg Protocol NECs and the ceilings in the guiding 'G5/2' scenario was not any better than in the case of the EU.

All in all, although it cannot be ruled out that the initial, 'scientific' ceilings were not forgotten in some government offices, it makes much more sense to interpret the final differences between the EU and CLRTAP ceilings as primarily due to politics. This means very little backing for our main rival proposition, although it does deserve credit for making us aware of the fact that problem characteristics *do* partially differ within the EU and CLRTAP contexts. However, at least in this case, these differences 'drowned in the sea of politics'.

Concluding Comments

The relationship between CLRTAP and the EU in terms of policy leadership has been gradually changing. In the mid 1980s, CLRTAP was the clear policy leader. A decade later, the relationship was becoming much more even. For instance, by the time the negotiations on the second sulphur protocol came to an end in Oslo in 1994, policy development within the EU had made it possible for the EU to sign on and later ratify as an entity. By the turn of the century, it may be asked whether the EU has taken over as the leader, in terms of policy strength. Judging at least by the case of the NEC Directive and the Gothenburg Protocol, the answer is a qualified yes. The emission ceilings are a little lower and hence ambitiousness higher within the EU context, and the bindingness and 'political weight' of the EU NECs is most likely higher.

How, then, may this relationship be explained? If we take as a point of departure that the air pollution problems addressed by the EU and CLRTAP share basic similarities (but are not entirely identical in terms of scope), then institutional differences should be good candidates for shedding light on differences in policy strength. Four main institutional propositions were examined to shed light upon such a difference: Fewer and more homogeneous parties in the EU; higher administrative strength within the EU; stronger decision-making procedures in the EU; and a higher issue linkage potential in the EU.

Closer scrutiny produced only limited evidence to back up the first three propositions. In terms of membership scope, there was undoubtedly a somewhat more numerous laggard group within the CLRTAP than within the EU. However, as the EU still had a group of quite unambitious countries within its ranks, the difference between the two contexts in terms of the presence of laggards is more one of degree than one of fundamental nature.

Turning to differences in administrative strength, closer scrutiny indicated that the relationship between the EU and CLRTAP in terms of secretarial and administrative strength to back up air pollution policy-making may be seen as close to the opposite of that suggested. Comparing the CLRTAP scientific-political complex at work in the Gothenburg Protocol process with the administrative resources commanded by the EU air pollution unit in charge of the Acidification/Ozone Strategy and NEC Directive process, one may even come to the conclusion that *CLRTAP* is the stronger institution! So this proposition turned out to be of very little help in shedding light on the policy difference between the EU and CLRTAP.

Moving on to the issue of decision-making procedures, despite con-siderable formal procedural differences between the two contexts, decision-making practice seems to have been quite consensual in both contexts. However, some 'hidden stick' effects of the formal possibility to resort to majority-voting could not be ruled out in the EU context.

With regard to the fourth and final institutional difference high-lighted, related to issue linkage potential, this hit the nail far more on its head. EU's developing air pollution 'policy density' led to a number of related policy processes from the mid-1990s on, partly pertaining to a revi-sion of earlier policies, and partly the development of completely new policies. This made issue interaction and linking a much more prominent feature of the decision-making process within the EU than within CLRTAP. Although the comparative effect should not be exaggerated, in particular the final linking of the revision of the Large Combustion Plant Directive and the NEC Directive contributed both to making a NEC Common Position at all possible in June 2000, and to slightly more ambi-tious emission ceilings.

The challenge to these institutional perspectives by a perspective pinpointing the possible effects of remaining differences in problem char-acteristics did not shed further light on the differences in policy strength, although it did make us aware of the fact that problem characteristics *do* partially differ within the EU and CLRTAP contexts. But these differences 'drowned in politics', so to speak. All in all, in order to explain the some-what higher policy strength within the EU, we are primarily left with institutional explanations.

In addition to issue linkage aspects highlighted above, one should also be aware of the simple aspect of *timing*. As the EU's NEC Common Position was adopted six months after the Gothenburg Protocol, this meant that the Member States had some extra time to discuss and negotiate and to further clarify the domestic possibilities for emission reductions.[316]

Why then, does the final difference in NECs and ambitiousness seem to end up considerably less than expected? Is this more a matter of coincidence, or is it a signal of the EU decision-making system in practice often functioning in a much more traditional, inter-governmental way than the impression given by its complex formal institutional structure? Again, timing may be an important explanatory factor, but almost in the opposite way as that pinpointed above.[317]

As further elaborated in Chapter Five, the plan developed in connection with the preparation of the Acidification Strategy was to first prepare the Ozone Strategy, then – based on both the Acidification and Ozone Strategies – to develop the NEC proposal rather smoothly and quickly. Hence, in such a scenario, the EU could become a helpful, contributory force in the efforts to increase policy ambitiousness in the concluding phase of CLRTAP Gothenburg Protocol negotiations. However, bureaucratic slowness and the resignation of the Commission delayed the proposal by about half a year and, as it turned out, the CLRTAP emission ceilings became an important point of reference in the final phase of the EU decision-making process, instead of the other way around, as intended. The unfortunate effects of this timing of events makes much sense. However, irrespective of timing, some political 'watering down' of the Commission's proposal would presumably have taken place anyway, given the considerable policy reluctance of the Southern Member States in this context.

Notes

[304] I am thankful to Christer Ågren for providing me with these figures. Communication with Christer Ågren, October 2000.

[305] See ECE/CLRTAP (1999:91).

[306] Acid News 3, October 2000, p. 7.

[307] This is *ceteris paribus*, not least with regard to decision-making procedures. The possible effects of differences in such procedures are discussed in the following sections.

[308] Communication with Christer Ågren, October 2000.

[309] Interviews, Autumn 1999.

[310] However, these countries all signed the Protocol before the deadline at the end of May 2000.

[311] See for instance Agarwala and Andresen (1999) on the uncertain prospects of ratification by the key actor the US.

[312] However, like in most other matters, practice in terms of implementation review and compliance reactions is far more similar in EU and international regimes than indicated by formal procedural differences. On the EU 'implementation gap', see Jordan (1998, 1999).

[313] As noted by Weale et al. (2000:325), 'More effective implementation may well have an adverse knock-on effect on policy formulation, since it may reduce the willingness of

some representatives on the Council to more environmental legislation. There is a certain irony in the possibility that consistent policy implementation might lead to a slowing down of decision-making or a dilution of environmental standards'.

[314] I am thankful to Christer Ågren for making this clearer for me (communication, March 2001).

[315] Acid News 2, June 1999, p. 8.

[316] Communication with Christer Ågren, March 2001.

[317] Ibid.

Chapter 7

Implementing Stronger European Air Pollution Policies
Will High Hopes in Brussels and Geneva be Dashed in London?[318]

Introduction

Although this book is primarily focused on the *making* of international policies, the 'proof of the pudding' lies in effective and successful national implementation. Hence, this chapter will make a first, modest cut in terms of assessing the prospects for successful implementation. As substantial cuts in emissions will be required of many countries, the potential environmental improvement will be significant. Moreover, it has generally been suggested that stronger commitments will easily be followed by weaker implementation (cf. e.g. Downs, Rocke and Barsoom 1996). Hence, the topic is of considerable political and theoretical interest.

With regard to the four main substances focused on in recent EU and CLRTAP policy-making (i.e. SO_2, NO_x, VOCs, NH_3), there are certain key countries in terms of size of emissions and contributions to transboundary effects – and hence also a number of countries whose performance matters only marginally. Take SO_2, NO_x and VOC emissions:[319] according to ECE/ CLRTAP (1999) regarding SO_2 emissions, the six largest European emitters in 1995 were Poland, the UK, Germany, Spain, Bulgaria, and Italy.[320] With regard to NO_x, the top five 1995 emitters were the UK, Germany, Italy, France and Spain.[321] Regarding VOC emissions, the top five on which data existed in 1995/96 were as follows: France, Italy, the UK, Germany, and Spain.[322]

Looking at these various groups, *certain key countries stand out, first and foremost the UK, Germany, Italy and France.* Is there one 'really key' country? Norwegians and Swedes would probably point at the British, given the 'vulnerable, net-importer not least from the UK' position of the Scandinavians. The UK, being a big emitter, is a generally interesting country, with its past 'dirty man of Europe' image and record of international stubbornness.[323] This is then the background for the question posed in the title of this chapter: Will the high hopes of emissions reductions in Brussels/EU and Geneva/CLRTAP be 'dashed' in London? In addition to the UK, the two other central countries France and Germany and their implementation prospects are singled out for closer scrutiny in this context.

This does not, however, mean that the performance of the other countries is of no importance or interest. For instance, several of the Eastern European countries are high emitters, and their prospects in terms of air pollution policy takes on added interest in the context of the EU enlargement process. As pinpointed by EU Environment Commissioner Wallström in the wake of the common position on the NEC Directive in June 2000, 'the "NEC" agreement sets an important environmental benchmark for negotiations with candidate countries in the enlargement process'.[324]

In order to understand a country's *past* level of compliance, three main analytical perspectives have been suggested: First, what may be termed 'basic interests', related to the relationship between abatement costs and damage costs; second, 'domestic politics', bringing in not least the societal distribution of costs and benefits; and third, the issue of 'learning' and policy diffusion (Underdal 1998). In order to use these perspectives to look *forward*, the perspectives need to be complemented by a baseline perspective, summing up important achievements and failures so far of the countries in question. On this background, the chapter will be structured in the following manner: The next section will sum up some baseline information about past achievements of the countries singled out, within both the EU and CLRTAP contexts. The third section will form the main part of the chapter, elaborating and discussing the three 'prospective implementation' perspectives of interests, politics, and learning. Section four will sum up main findings and provide some concluding comments.

'The Implementation Baseline': What has been Achieved so Far?

In this context, we can fortunately use a recently published overview of compliance and achievements so far within CLRTAP as a point of departure (ECE/CLRTAP 1999), before adding some notes on the more specific EU context and CLRTAP-EU interplay so far.

Achievements Within the CLRTAP Context: Uneven, but Well-documented

Starting with the issue of sulphur dioxide commitments, as discussed in Chapter Three, SO_2 emissions have the longest and most 'advanced' regulatory history. As can be recalled, the first 1985 CLRTAP protocol called for 30 percent emissions reductions, and the second protocol in 1994 introduced both the critical loads concept and differentiated and more ambitious targets. No surprise then that achievements here are impressive.[325] In relation to the 1980 baseline, European SO_2 emissions had been reduced by 60 percent by 1997.

Second, the main NO_x commitment was established in 1988, calling for a stabilisation of emissions by 1994, with 1987 as baseline. In addition, twelve countries adopted a declaration calling for 30 percent reductions by 1998. Overall, as signalled by lower ambitions, NO_x achievements are less impressive. Between 1987 and 1994, NO_x emissions fell by around 10 percent.

Third, the 1991 VOC Protocol overall called for 30 percent reductions by 1999, with 1988 as the main baseline. Measuring performance here is complicated by lacking baseline and emissions data, but available data indicate around 20 percent reductions between 1988 and 1997. In sum, the overall CLRTAP compliance picture looks pretty good, but in terms of reduction achievements, the SO_2 record is far more impressive than the NO_x and VOC record.[326]

Let us then sum up some main compliance achievements by 1996/97 of the three countries singled out.[327] Turning first to France, its sulphur record is very good (66 percent reductions); NO_x record unimpressive (rough stabilisation); and VOC record unknown (no figures submitted for the base year – but in the period 1990-97 VOC emissions actually increased!).

Germany's sulphur record is also good (50 percent reductions); NO_x record good (22-23 percent reductions); and VOC record fair (20 percent reductions).

Although the UK did not sign the 1985 SO_2 Protocol, sulphur emissions had been reduced by 60 percent by 1996; NO_x emissions had been reduced by 20 percent, and the VOC record is similar to Germany, i.e. 20 percent reductions.

Overall, although VOC developments are less impressive, the countries focused upon have done fairly well in terms of compliance. On one hand, this generally bides well for the future. On the other hand, the recently adopted commitments are generally far more ambitious than in the past. Moreover, having reduced quite a lot already means that achieving further, substantial reductions may become increasingly expensive.

Some Notes on the More Specific EU Context and the Effect of EU-CLRTAP Interplay so Far

It could be argued that there is no need to discuss the EU separately, as the EU as an entity has signed and ratified both the NO_x, VOC and 1994 sulphur protocols.[328] Hence, in a way, CLRTAP commitments are also automatically EU commitments. Moreover, there is little doubt that CLRTAP was the international policy frontrunner in the 1980s and early 1990s. However, as has been discussed earlier, from the mid- 1980s onward the EU increasingly developed its own air pollution policy. Large Combustion Plants (LCPs) and motor vehicles were the main regulatory targets; with the LCP Directive adopted in 1988 and several motor vehicles directives adopted in 1988, 1989 and 1991.[329] Hence, the possibility grew that the implementation of EU policies could support – or, in unfortunate circumstances, hinder – the implementation of the various CLRTAP commitments in the course of the 1990s.

So what has happened? Do we know anything about it? On one hand, the impression of the implementation of EU environmental policies more generally is one of a substantial 'implementation gap'.[330] According to Jordan (1998:39) for instance, 'Until relatively recently, neither EU institutions nor Member States paid much attention to whether or not rules formulated to protect the environment were actually being followed'. On the other hand, in terms of implementation of air pollution policies more specifically, existing contributions indicate a more nuanced picture country-wise.[331] With regard to the implementation of the 1988 LCP Directive, several authors indicate good implementation in the UK, Germany and France – and a less convincing Spanish performance.[332]

In accounting for differences in implementation performance, a central, common factor pinpointed is the degree of match between EU policy style/design and the policy style of the country in question. For instance, in the case of Germany, the central role played by Germany in the acceleration of EU air pollution policy-making in the 1980s is highlighted; this role contributing to a high match between German and EU policy styles.[333] This opens up for interesting perspectives in the NEC context being given primary attention in this book, as the NEC Directive is clearly not of German design. This issue will be further discussed later in this chapter.

Moreover, judging from the recently published Underdal and Hanf volume on CLRTAP policy-making and implementation in nine European countries (up to around 1995/96), EU policies have had some positive effects, sometimes over-shadowing CLRTAP policies: 'Several of the country studies report that EU directives and regulations have had considerably more 'teeth' and therefore greater impact on domestic policies than ECE protocols. The combination of its greater institutional weight and its ability to reward and support as well as to punish gave the EU a major advantage in terms of inducing real changes in the domestic policies and behaviour of member countries – particularly the laggards' (Underdal and Hanf 2000:378). Hence, the EU-CLRTAP interplay perspective should clearly be kept in mind when we now turn to the more forward-looking exercise.

Implementing the NEC Directive and Gothenburg Protocol: The Three Determining Factors of Interests, Politics, and Learning

'Calculating Interests': A Rare Case of Benefits Clearly Exceeding Costs?

This fundamental perspective zooms in on the governments' calculation of the benefits and costs related to compliance.[334] An important aspect of such benefits and costs is simply the domestic monetary dimension of these concepts. Hence, in the context of environmental policy, a main proposition related to this perspective can be formulated as follows: *A party will comply if, and only as long as, its expected marginal abatement costs are lower than expected marginal damage costs.*[335] But as pinpointed by Underdal (1998), costs and benefits also have more international and political dimensions. Being caught cheating may represent a substantial cost for certain governments and, conversely, being a 'best in class' and 'vanguard implementor' may include technology development and export possibilities, and represent substantial reputation benefits. Hence, the proposition above may be restated in the following manner: *An actor will comply if, and only as long as, expected marginal abatement costs minus any implementation benefits are lower than expected marginal damage costs plus any sanction costs incurred by defecting.*[336]

Turning first to the more domestic monetary aspects, consultant reports produced during the EU and CLRTAP policy-making processes give us important inputs for discussing these important issues. As further discussed in Chapter Four, within CLRTAP, specific figures were put on the table in the beginning of 1999. At this stage, it had principally been agreed to base the CLRTAP multi-pollutant protocol on a 'medium' ambitious emissions reductions scenario.[337] The total costs in 2010 for Europe under this scenario was put at 8.5 billion ECU, with the EU countries accounting for two-thirds of the costs. Total benefits were more uncertain, with a low estimate at 26.5 billion and a high estimate at 42.3 billion ECU.[338] Still, these figures indicated that *overall benefits would outweigh costs by a clear margin*. This must be characterised as interesting, although such figures invite a number of critical questions. Moreover, the impression of overall benefits clearly exceeding costs was strengthened when the draft EU NEC Directive was put forward in June, 1999.[339]

However, other country-specific information presented in the EU context was more disturbing, not least in terms of the countries given specific attention in this study. According to EU Commission official Peter Gammeltoft, 'meeting these national ceilings <in the draft EU Directive> will cost little in Finland, but the costs will be higher "elsewhere", especially in the United Kingdom, France, Belgium, and some parts of southern Europe'.[340] With regard to the UK situation, the Commission estimated in June that annual costs for the UK would be 1350 million ECU; 18 percent of the EC total. Towards the end of 1999, the British Department of Environment (DETR) disputed this figure, but not in the direction that one would easily anticipate. In fact, the DETR believed that these cost figures were 'likely to be significant overestimates'.[341] Instead, the DETR put the overall annual costs at around 900 million ECUs; most of these for VOC controls. Moreover, DETR stated that the cost of meeting the CLRTAP ceilings would be 'considerably lower'.[342] However, on the other hand, the DETR also fundamentally doubted whether the Commission's claim that benefits would exceed costs was correct and based on sound valuation methods.[343]

What about Germany, then? This central country was not mentioned in the statement from the Commission official cited above. However, in a table indicating the total implementation costs for each of the EU countries, Germany comes out clearly at the top, with 2146 million Euro per year. This is almost twice as much as number two on the list, the UK.[344] Moreover, reported German 'backtracking' in the concluding negotiations on the CLRTAP multi-pollutant protocol may indicate that the costs of coming reductions worry German decision-makers.[345] Turning very briefly to France, the Commission's June exercise referred to above explicitly identified France as one of the high cost countries. Total annual costs of 916 million euro were indicated.[346]

However, for all three countries we must keep in mind that these costs are related to the attainment of the emission ceilings in the EU NEC directive proposal put forward by the Commission in June 1999. As indicated by British decision-makers, meeting the CLRTAP targets – and hence also the only slightly more ambitious targets adopted by the EU Council of Ministers in June 2000 – will be less costly. This also follows from the simple fact that the CLRTAP targets in many cases are quite close to what the Institute for Applied Systems Analysis (IIASA) has calculated as the 'reference' scenario – in other words, what the countries will probably do anyway, due to other commitments and due to likely developments in energy use etc.[347] Tentatively summing up, this exercise indicates that in the case of the singled out countries, CLRTAP abatement costs will not necessarily be excessive. However, if the final EU NEC Directive is adopted close to the initial Commission proposal, then the cost factor will become much more important.

Is it then possible to say anything more specific about damage costs in the focused countries? As indicated above, the UK authorities generally doubted that the overall cost-benefit ratio was as positive as depicted by the Commission, or even whether it was positive at all. As this was partly due to a greater scepticism in principal about valuation methods, it does not necessarily mean that the UK authorities see the more specific UK cost-benefit scenario as skewed in favour of costs. Taking into account other recent information about the development of the British air pollution conditions and effects (see Chapter Five), there are reasons to assume that perceived damage costs are on the increase in the UK. For instance, a UK workshop on eutrophication and acidification held in December 1998 concluded that conditions throughout the country were more serious than perceived earlier.[348]

Turning to Germany and France, the impression is clearly that German concern over air pollution has decreased somewhat compared to the 1980s heyday. Given Germany's comparatively highest abatement costs, it is more open as to whether damage costs will weigh as heavily as earlier in the German cost-benefit assessment.[349] With regard to the French situation, it was for a long time one of stable, quite low concern. As was noted in Chapter Five, France has never experienced a 'Waldsterben' uproar and the impression is that concern over air pollution (effects) has never been really high on the French agenda.[350] Still, experienced observers point out that that urban air quality has been afforded steadily increasing attention in France in recent years, also at the national, government level. While not as prominent in the public debate as in the UK, it is clearly noticeable in French media and public debate.[351] Hence, there are certain indications of a somewhat growing societal demand for stronger air pollution policies in France in the most recent years. Given uncertain French costs (but substantial in the EU context), the overall impression is still that the French cost-benefit assessment will easily be skewed in the favour of abatement costs.

So far, scattered pieces of evidence about important domestic interest-determining factors have been summed up. However, as can be recalled, this perspective also includes some 'international' factors. What can we say about those? First, with regard to 'implementation benefits' and technology exports etc., the author would be skating on extremely thin ice and this aspect must be left unspecified in this context. However, a bit more can be said about the issue of 'sanction costs' and 'shaming'. Both the EU and CLRTAP have established formal reporting procedures. The CLRTAP Gothenburg Protocol includes a quite elaborated Article 7, spelling out various reporting commitments. Within CLRTAP more generally, reporting practice has so far been mixed, with especially VOC reporting being inadequate.[352] Within the EU, directives usually require the Member States to submit a report to the Commission on national legislation, regulations or administrative measures that give formal effect to the directive. Reporting practice can also here be characterised as mixed.[353]

Moreover, both institutions have seemingly developed somewhat tougher practices with regard to implementation review in recent years. Within CLRTAP, although functioning basically in a consensual and non-confrontational way, a specific Implementation Committee was established in 1997.[354] Within the EU, as indicated, the 'implementation gap' has received increasing attention throughout the 1990s. In terms of enforcement, the EU has in a sense the most advanced system, with the possibility of taking cases of non-compliance to the European Court of Justice. In recent years, there has seemingly been an increasing willingness on the part of the Commission to take states to court over lacking environmental policy implementation.[355] In July 2000, Greece was fined for its failure to comply with an earlier ruling on waste management. This decision marked the first time the Court used its right to fine a country for not complying with its initial ruling.[356]

Hence, all in all, it is possible to envisage the EU in the future acting as a sort of 'compliance cop' for CLRTAP. The crucial question is however: Are the commitments in question really 'verifiable' enough to form the basis for clear determination of non-compliance and ensuing strong EU (or CLRTAP) action? According to Jordan (1998), a central cause of earlier inadequate implementation was 'poor lawmaking', with directives 'peppered with vague phrases and contradictory objectives' (p.39). With regard to the NECs on one hand, the commitments and emissions ceilings are clearly precise enough to allow the determination of compliance/non-compliance. On the other hand, the emission figures are clearly the weakest link in the EU and CLRTAP science-politics systems.[357] Hence, the critical question is if this part of the systems is robust enough to withstand 'creative calculations' if states get into trouble? This is very much an open question. If, however, the answer here is negative, then it may very well be possible that CLRTAP meetings and the looser review atmosphere within that regime may be at least as strong a compliance-strengthening mechanism as the formally stronger procedures within the EU.

Institutions and Politics: Will not-so-high Total Costs Fall Specifically on Powerful Actors and 'Huge Benefits' Disappear into the Air?

This perspective highlights the *complexity* of democratic decision-making. Interests are not only 'calculated', they are shaped through negotiations and political pressure – within and outside the government. Although governments may perceive the benefits of compliance as clearly exceeding costs, they may be *unable* to comply due to societal resistance. Or conversely, they may be pressured to comply due to the strong political position of 'compliance supporters'. Societal resistance may be assumed to be related to the *distribution* of implementation costs and benefits. A main idea here is that implementation policies which need to hit specific, well-organised and powerful societal groups are much less likely to contribute to governmental compliance than policy situations where compliance can be achieved without the need to take on such societal actors. Hence, two important propositions within this perspective can be formulated in the following manner:

- The policy measures that are most easily implemented will be those which offer tangible benefits to some specific sector of the economy or organised segment of society, while costs are widely dispersed (and the other way around);
- Damage or abatement costs that hit the social 'centre' of society will be better articulated and carry more political weight than those that hit the social 'periphery' only, and this bias will be stronger the greater the distance in social and political resources between 'centre' and 'periphery'.[358]

A full-fledged, systematic discussion of these and a number of other, related 'political' propositions is beyond the scope of this chapter.[359] Instead, in addition to some general reflections on the institutional capacity for implementation, including the institutional match between EU policies and regulatory styles of the various countries[360], the following more loose, but clearly relevant question will be addressed: Does the current environmental policy-making development and 'swing' in the countries focused upon bide good or bad for future levels of air pollution compliance?

Turning first to the UK, the impression is that the current air pollution political 'swing' in this country is positive. As further described in Chapter Five, for one thing, a solid, revised national Air Quality Strategy was launched in January 2000.[361] This must be seen as part of the government's response to a deteriorating urban air pollution situation, with traffic going up – like almost everywhere else.[362] Popular concern over these problems seems also to be on the increase. Moreover, as discussed under the previous section, British authorities seem quite confident about the implementation possibilities. With regard to SO_2 emissions, fuel switching or further installation of flue gas desulphurisation equipment has been indicated.[363] Moreover, and not least important, given the 1990 baseline, the UK can again benefit from the 'dash to gas' process which took place in the first part of the 1990s.[364] Several VOC control measures have also been indicated, among them vapour recovery on offshore installations and further controls in refineries.[365]

In addition to these more specific points, one should also keep in mind the improving match between EU environmental policies and British regulatory styles in the 1990s. As noted by Sbragia (2000:309), 'As British legislation now shapes a good deal more of EU legislation, the UK's domestic administrative apparatus sits more easily with it'. The case of NECs is a good example of this development; with the ceilings being very much in line with the British preference for flexible measures and air quality thinking. It is reasonable to assume that this is an element which may contribute positively to British implementation processes. All in all, although a more detailed scrutiny of the UK situation would probably reveal a number of questions and discussion points, the overall picture does look quite promising.

With regard to Germany, a sweeping 70 percent emissions reduction by 2010 (with a 1990 baseline) domestic target has been established for all the four focused substances.[366] Compared with the 1999 Gothenburg Protocol commitments for sulphur, this is actually 20 percent *below* the German CLRTAP commitment (i.e. 90 percent reductions). But for both NO_x and ammonia, this is more ambitious than the CLRTAP targets (i.e. 60 percent NO_x reductions and 'mere' 28 percent NH_3 reductions). This domestic ambitiousness can be counted as a weak but positive implementation signal. In terms of institutional implementation issues and the match between EU policy design and national policy styles, it has generally been noted by

Heretier et al. (1996) that: 'the Germans fiercely combat proposals betraying a quality-orientation...<being> regulatory concepts fundamentally opposed to their philosophy' (p.276). This was clearly seen in the negotiations on the NEC Directive as portrayed in Chapter Five, where the Germans gave much more priority to the renegotiation of the Large Combustion Plant Directive than to the setting of national emission ceilings. However, although this aspect will surely not bolster German NEC Directive implementation, its negative effect should not be exaggerated either.

With regard to the general institutional capacity for implementation, it has been noted that 'decision-making authority on issues of air pollution control in Germany is neither highly centralised nor very decentralised. It rests mainly with the federal government, albeit subject to relatively strong influence of the states as exercised mainly through the Bundesrat' (Sprinz and Wahl 2000:148). However, compared to for instance the UK, there is generally a greater chance for a German 'implementation gap' between the central government and local authorities. The picture that most easily comes to mind is one of a willing government and stubborn local authorities (Lander).[367] Moreover, the seemingly decreasing governmental concern and 'supply' and public 'demand' in the climate change context may not bide well for the air pollution context either, especially the climate-related transport and NO_x /VOC context.[368]

Finally, a few words about France. Going back to the French CLRTAP compliance performance so far – very good on sulphur and far more modest with regard to NO_x and VOCs – NO_x and VOC politics will most probably be the two issues and sectors to watch. A glance through the two chapters and 60 pages on 'national strategies and policy measures' in the 1999 ECE/CLRTAP review, reveals very little information on France's current activities and policy plans ahead.[369] This *may* be a sign that the French government does not give very high priority to this issue area. A counteracting trend is the recent increase in concern about urban air pollution, as described in the previous section. Reports about air pollution choking Paris surely point towards 'damage costs that hit the social centre of society'.[370]

Learning and Policy Diffusion: Will Knowledge Provided by 'Epistemic Communities' and Diffusion of 'Smart Policies' Energise the Implementation Processes?

This perspective sensitises us to the inherently more diffuse processes of social learning and policy diffusion. In a stark version, although costs may exceed benefits, and supporters of compliance may be weak, governments may still comply due to convincing knowledge provided or policy pressure exerted by 'epistemic communities' – or due to learning about smart and less costly policies and technologies from other policy actors.[371] Hence, in relation to the previous, domestic perspective, this perspective is more transnational by nature. Moreover, it is also clearly less elaborated than the two previous perspectives.[372] Hence, the discussion of this perspective will be very tentative and probing.

Is there an epistemic community, including both scientists and policy-makers, in the international air pollution context?[373] It can be argued that several characteristics of the air pollution issue point in this direction. First, there is the comparatively long scientific and political history of the acid rain/air pollution issue. Second, there is the strong emphasis given to scientific cooperation and monitoring within the regime, manifested for instance in the well-functioning EMEP monitoring program (Cooperative Programme for Monitoring and Evaluation of Long-range Transmissions of Air Pollutants in Europe).[374] Third, there is the increasingly closer science-politics interface within the CLRTAP regime.[375] In sum, there should then be a strong reason to expect that an epistemic community exists in this issue area.

An implication of this is that there are good reasons to believe that there are groups of quite centrally placed people in all the focused countries which can be expected to voice their concern in a situation where implementation of the air pollution commitments clearly lags behind. This should be good news for the prospects of compliance in general, but it says nothing about the possibly more specific impacts in specific countries. A rough guess here would be that the British part of the transnational epistemic community will be most influential (of the three countries singled out in this context) on the domestic air pollution scene, given the active role of the British in the scientific work within CLRTAP. The German part of the community may also be quite influential, as Germany for instance has been the lead country in CLRTAP's scientific work on forests.[376] In comparison, the French part of the community can be assumed to be least influential.

What about the prospects for the diffusion of smart technologies and policies? As indicated, this is a field this author knows very little about. However, given the 'maturity' of the air pollution control issue (compared for instance to the climate change issue), the general hunch would be that main technological and political options are quite well known by now, and that radical progress and breakthroughs in the field of technology are less likely than in the mid 1980s.

Concluding Comments: Positive Prospects, but Much Uncertainty

Based on the reasoning above, it does not seem reasonable to assume that the 'high hopes' in Geneva/CLRTAP and Brussels will be dashed in London. The UK as 'the dirty man of Europe' seems to be history. The prospects for German implementation are more uncertain, but it seems reasonable to assume that the Germans will do quite well, but less impressive than in the past. France is even more of an uncertain card here, and unimpressive NO_x and VOC performance so far does not bide well. The following table sums up the overall picture and important areas of uncertainty with regard to implementation prospects:

Table 7.1 Central factors determining compliance in the UK, Germany and France

	The UK	Germany	France
'Interests'	Substantial possible abatement costs in the EU context, but increasing damage costs. Seemingly relaxed policy-makers	Highest abatement costs and decreasing damage costs? Past leader reputation to uphold, though.	Substantial abatements costs at least in the EU context and uncertain damage costs.
'Politics'	Increasing concern over air pollution; a National Air Quality Strategy recently published	Decreasing concern over air pollution? More ambitious domestic NO_x and NH_3 targets than international commitments	Low, but somewhat increasing, concern about air pollution? Little information on planned air pollution policies
'Learning'	Influential British part of 'epistemic community'?	Quite influential German part of 'epistemic community'?	Moderately influential French part of 'epistemic community'?

On the condition that these countries are among the most central ones both in the EU and CLRTAP contexts, even though there are huge uncertainties to be clarified further, the implementation prospects for the new EU and CLRTAP commitments are overall quite promising.

Bringing in the estimates of the overall relationship between costs and benefits, some would even say that implementation of the CLRTAP and EU commitments is a 'piece of cake'. As indicated earlier, figures produced both within the CLRTAP and EU context indicate that overall benefits will outweigh costs by a clear margin. Moreover, IIASA has indicated that the Gothenburg targets point to very moderate additional reduction costs for the key countries – as considerable emission reductions are already in the pipeline due to other international commitments and planned national policies. If the implementation of these other commitments progresses smoothly, relatively low additional and particularly Gothenburg/NEC implementation costs could mean smooth 'piece of cake' implementation processes.

In addition, the effects of the implementation of climate commitments agreed to in Kyoto in 1997 have so far not been included in this discussion at all. Such an inclusion will lower the specific, necessary air pollution abatement costs even further.[377] It can in this context be noted that an EU policy integration effort was launched in 1998 under the banner of 'Clean Air for Europe' (CAFE).[378] One of the main aims of this process is a closer linking of climate and air pollution policies. CAFE will be further discussed in the following and concluding Chapter Eight.

However, a more troubling 'tall order' scenario can also be envisioned. In the case of slow progress of the implementation of other international and national measures, including a non-ratification of the Kyoto Protocol and stalling of the climate processes, then particularly the NEC implementation costs could become more important. For instance, according to the French Environment Institute (IFEN) these costs, seen in isolation, should not be looked upon as insignificant.[379]

Notes

[318] This title is of course inspired by Pressman and Wildavsky's classic 1973 implementation study, *Implementation: How Great Expectations in Washington are Dashed in Oakland.*

[319] The following are Central European emitters. Other large emitters are Russia and Ukraine.

[320] Poland (2376 000 tons), the UK (2343 000), Germany (2102 000), Spain (2061 000), Bulgaria (1497 000) and Italy (1322 000).

[321] The UK (2104 000 tons), Germany (1946 000), Italy (1768 000), France (1666 000), and Spain (1223 000).

[322] France (2620 000 tons), Italy (2368 000), the UK (2120 000), Germany (1981 000) and Spain (1120 000).

[323] See for instance Rose (1990).

[324] This quote from a June 22, 2000 press conference is lifted from International Environment Reporter, July 5, 2000, p.521.

[325] For overview discussions of the protocols and the CLRTAP regime, see Wettestad (1991; 1996; 1999); Levy (1993; 1995); and Gehring (1994).

[326] This has of course to do with the SO_2 problem having a longer scientific and regulatory history than the others and also being a more easily targeted 'power stations' problem. See Wettestad (1998).

[327] The baselines are as set in the protocols: SO_2 1980; NOx 1987; VOC 1988. Note here that we talk about *compliance* achievements, which say absolutely nothing about the *causes* of emission reductions.

[328] With regard to the VOC Protocol, the EU has signed it, but still not ratified it.

[329] See here for instance Chapter 11 in Weale et al. (2000).

[330] See for instance Jordan (1998; 1999).

[331] See Chapter 8 in Weale et al (2000) for a country-by-country overview.

[332] See Knill (1997); Knill and Lenschow (2000); and Boerzel (2000).

[333] See Sbragia in Wallace and Wallace (2000:306) and contributions referred to in footnote 316.

[334] The perspective builds upon three basic assumptions: 1) states are unitary, rational actors; 2) decision-makers evaluate options in terms of costs and benefits to their nation, and only in those terms, and choose whichever option (is believed to) maximize(s) net national gain; 3) states are in full control of 'their' societies. See Underdal (1998:7-12).

[335] Ibid.:8.

[336] Ibid.:9. 'Sanction costs' will here be interpreted broadly and include softer 'shaming' and reputation effects.

[337] See summary of these developments in Acid News 1999 A: 1, 4-5.

[338] According to Christer Agren, the estimated benefits are clearly underestimated for the simple reason that they only take account of what is judged to be possible to estimate in monetary terms (i.e. primarily health) – thus excluding some of the main objectives of the legislation, i.e. reduced acidification, reduced 'damage' to the natural and cultural environment, etc.

[339] See International Environment Reporter, June 23, 1999:518-519.

[340] Ibid.

[341] ENDS Report 299, December 1999:41.

[342] Ibid:42.

[343] Ibid.

[344] International Environment Reporter, op.cit.:519.

[345] See Chapter Four.

[346] International Environment Reporter, op.cit.:519.

[347] See ENDS Report 296, September 1999:44-45.

[348] Interviews with CLRTAP negotiators, Autumn 1999.

[349] For an interpretation of the dynamics of German air pollution politics, see Boehmer-Christiansen and Skea (1991); Wettestad (1996); and Sprinz and Wahl (2000).

[350] See for instance Skea and Du Monteuil, in Underdal and Hanf (2000).

[351] Communication with Christer Ågren, October 2000.

[352] See Acid News, December 1999, pp.12-13.

[353] See e.g. Jordan (1998:39).

[354] See Wettestad (1999), Ch.4.

[355] See for instance International Environment Reporter, February 3, 1999, pp.96-97.

[356] See Environment Watch, September 1, 2000, 'Environment main area for failures to comply with EU law', pp.14-19.

[357] Interviews with CLRTAP negotiators Autumn 1999.

[358] Underdal (1998, p.14, 16).

[359] See Underdal (ibid., pp.12-20), for an overview of such propositions.

[360] In a more deep-diving effort, the OECD Performance Reviews contain useful institutional and political background information. See e.g. the UK report (OECD 1994).

[361] A consultation document was published in 1999; see DETR (1999). Note, however, that the final strategy was immediately attacked by environmentalists, especially the government's targets on particles; see Reuter/Planetark, January 20, 2000.

[362] See for instance ENDS Report 272, 1997, 'Royal Commission warns of looming transport crisis', pp.11-12.

[363] ENDS Report 296, September 1999, p.42.

[364] See Collier (1997) and Boehmer-Christiansen's chapter in Underdal and Hanf (2000).

[365] ENDS Report 296, September 1999, p.42.

[366] ECE/CLRTAP (1999:12).

[367] However, in the global climate change context, the political dynamics have been rather the opposite. See Hasselmeier and Wettestad (2000).

[368] Ibid.

[369] For instance, quite opposite to what one would expect, there is much more information on Turkey than on France.

[370] See for instance Reuter/Planetark, July 31, 2001, 'Smog covers Paris, drivers told to slow down'. See also *New Scientist* July 29 1995, 'Paris chokes while officials fiddle', p.9.

[371] The classic reference with regard to the concept of 'epistemic communities' is of course Haas (1990). I am grateful to Arild Underdal for pointing out to me that such communities may influence policy-making both by the more 'passive' production of new knowledge and more 'active' knowledge-based policy pressure.

[372] See Underdal (1998:20-23) for an overview of central assumptions and somewhat mixed propositions which can be derived from this perspective.

[373] Peter Haas defines 'epistemic communities' as 'transnational networks of knowledge based communities that are both politically empowered through their claims to exercise authoritative knowledge and motivated by shared causal and principled beliefs'.

[374] See for instance di Primio (1996).

[375] For the development of this interface, see Wettestad (2000 B).

[376] Germany has chaired the International Co-operative Programme on forests under CLRTAP.

[377] See for instance Ågren (1999).

[378] See Discussion Paper on the Future Development of Air Quality in the European Union, Environment Directorate/DG XI, October 5, 1998.

[379] See International Environment Reporter, May 24, 2000, pp.419-420.

Chapter 8

Summing Up and Looking Ahead

Constructive Interplay between the EU and CLRTAP

Introduction: The Central Questions Revisited

As laid out in Chapter One, four clusters of questions have formed the point of departure for this study: first, using air pollution politics and policies from the 1980s and early 1990s as a rough comparative benchmark, how can a closer, separate scrutiny of central and recent EU and CLRTAP policy outcomes substantiate the impression of a substantial strengthening of policy over time, thinking in terms of both political and environmental indicators of strength?

Second, assuming that such a policy strengthening has taken place within the two contexts, which factors can best shed light on this development? Given that the further development of abatement measures were becoming increasingly expensive and environmental concern was on the decrease again, and hence important issue characteristics did *not* favour policy strengthening, it became natural to focus attention on several interesting institutional changes in terms of membership and decision-making procedures within both contexts. For instance, in the EU context, an interesting increase in the opportunity for majority voting took place in the 1990s. Moreover, three relatively green new Member States were added to the EU in 1995; their accession possibly influencing the operation of all major EU institutions. Within the CLRTAP context, regime-induced improvement in the knowledge of the interplay of pollutants and their effects has paved the way for a new, broader and a potentially more integrative decision-making approach.

Third, adopting a comparative perspective, when directly comparing the emission ceilings in the CLRTAP Protocol and the parallel EU NEC Directive, the EU ceilings are overall somewhat more ambitious. Given the fact that the problems addressed by both institutions are quite similar, this provides a good opportunity to scrutinise the impact of several institutional differences between the EU and CLRTAP. Given the wide-spread percep-

tion of the EU as a considerably stronger institution than traditional regimes, why are the differences in strength still so moderate?

Fourth, on the basis of the foregoing, what are the prospects for
crucially important successful implementation of recent policies within the
EU and CLRTAP, and what are the future institutional implications of the
increasing interplay and parallel policy-making witnessed within the two
contexts throughout the 1990s? Will the EU 'take over' and CLRTAP fade
away?

In the next section of this chapter, main findings in relation to the
three first clusters of questions will be provided. The third and fourth sections will then look at perspectives ahead.

How CLRTAP and the EU have Contributed Significantly to 'Clearing the Air' in the 1990s

Let us first sum up the most important findings, before winding up this section with a discussion of some limitations related to the analytical framework applied in this study.

Substantially stronger policies, but still not strong enough

Even a rather crude comparative venture like the one carried out in this
context reveals that policy strength has increased substantially both within
the EU and CLRTAP contexts – most conspicuously in terms of ambitiousness and 'behavioural bite'. Within the EU context, national emission
ceilings for EU countries codified within the CLRTAP context have been
replaced by ceilings codified within the EU institutional structure; flat rate
reductions have been replaced by a complex net of differentiated commitments; new substances such as ammonia have been drawn into the
regulatory picture; and emission targets have generally been tightened. The
implication of this development is that the gap between adopted policies
and 'acceptable' emission levels has been substantially reduced. However,
current policies even faithfully implemented, will still leave a significant
gap in 2010.

Within CLRTAP, the agreed emission cuts of both SO_2, NO_x and
VOCs are considerably more ambitious than earlier CLRTAP commitments. Moreover, including ammonia means that an important first step has
been taken also within CLRTAP in closing what has been referred to as a
regulatory gap in European air pollution policy. The overall implication of
this development is that the gap to environment-friendly emissions levels

has been substantially reduced. But like the case within the EU context, current policies will still leave a significant gap in 2010. Hence, an overall score in terms of the development of policy strength within both contexts would be something like 'substantially stronger, but still not strong enough'.

Shedding light upon CLRTAP developments: The integrative multi-pollutant approach – and a greener UK

In order to shed light upon the strengthening of policy, prime and initial emphasis was put on more fundamental institutional changes having taken place within the two contexts related to membership, decision-making procedures and interplay with other institutions. A rough comparison with CLRTAP as an institution during the NO_x negotiations a decade earlier reveals both similarities and differences. On one hand, the basic functioning of the institution was quite similar. Both processes functioned on the basis of a consensus principle, and both processes developed on the basis of a close science-politics dialogue.

On the other hand, Chapter Two drew attention to three potentially important institutional developments: First, in terms of membership, the break-up of the old Soviet bloc and the changes in Eastern Europe were focused upon. It was suggested that these changes have made CLRTAP parties more homogenous and led to more East-West coalition building. Combined with the 'pulling-effect' of the EU accession process, this may have led to more constructive CLRTAP decision-making and possibly contributed to increasing CLRTAP policy strength.

With regard to the first element here, there seems to be widespread consensus on the notion that the general decision-making atmosphere has certainly become more open and relaxed than in the old Cold War days. In this context, it was noted that a Trust Fund for Assistance to Countries in Transition (TFACT) established by the Executive Body in 1994, contributed to wide participation in the negotiations. However, these generally positive developments seem to have had very little effect on the main positions adopted in the negotiations. Moreover, given the enlargement process within the EU, one might have expected greater negotiation flexibility and more progressive positions in primary EU candidates such as Poland and Hungary. At least with regard to Poland, this does not seem to hold true. All in all, although the general development of the East-West negotiating atmosphere seems to have been captured well by this proposition, the anticipated effects on positions did not follow suit.

With regard to changes in decision-making procedures and approaches, the development of a multi-pollutant approach in the 1990s was focused upon. This development could mean an increasing ability to address several pollutants together and develop broader, integrative policy packages, thereby generally improving decision-making capacity and possibly contributing to increasing CLRTAP regulatory strength. Although the NO_x process in the 1980s was also underpinned by rapid knowledge improvement, the multi-pollutant process was marked by a unique and close interplay between scientific and technological bodies and institutions and negotiating bodies. As one element in this, for the first time in CLRTAP negotiating history there was an explicit scrutiny of abatement costs.

Moreover, the multi-pollutant and multi-effects approach driving the negotiations gave the negotiations a different institutional flavour from the process in the 1980s. It was possible to quantify the damage and compare to the ultimate target of 'no exceedance'. This comprehensive approach – apart from making the whole package more rational and cost-effective – was an important key for encompassing (geographically) varying interests. The main driving forces in terms of impacts in Scandinavia and the Netherlands have been acidification and eutrophication; in many Central European countries and Southern Europe, it is increasingly air quality and public health. Thus, by linking several types of effects, virtually everyone would be able to find some benefits that suited their interests. Hence, this logic may help us understand why a number of countries proposed and ended up with somewhat more ambitious ceilings than in a business-as-usual scenario, providing some support for the second institutional proposition put forward.

As the third institutional perspective, the possible positive spill-over effects from the parallel EU acidification/NEC process were pinpointed. It is clear that the relationship between the two institutions grew far closer from the mid 1990s. From the CLRTAP point of view, the EU's financing of IIASA's modelling work after 1996 was a clear, positive interplay effect. Without the EU financial contribution to IIASA's work, the progress of the CLRTAP process could have been seriously slowed down. But CLRTAP did not benefit from parallel, stronger policies and positions developed within the less comprehensive and more homogenous EU context.

This had something to do with an unfortunate timing of events. 'Progressive' EU/CLRTAP actors hoped to be able to reach political agreement within the EU context *prior to* the final negotiation phase within CLRTAP. In this way, anticipated more ambitious EU NEC ceilings and positions could have been 'transposed' into the CLRTAP context and contributed new political energy into this context. However, the EU process did not proceed as quickly as hoped for, and the resignation of the Santer Commission on March 16 1999, the day before the NEC Directive was to be launched, meant an additional delay. Hence, instead of what some had hoped for, the CLRTAP process 'got ahead of' the EU process. Moreover, although the NEC Directive *was* put forward by the Commission in June, and pointed towards relatively ambitious ceilings for countries such as France, Germany, and the UK, the EU countries did not enter the final CLRTAP meetings on the background of ceilings politically rubber-stamped in the Council. There is, however, little evidence to suggest that EU policy dynamics in any way impeded CLRTAP progress. Hence, all in all, the EU had a mild positive influence on CLRTAP policy-making, primarily through the financing of modelling work at IIASA.

The institutional change perspective was then mildly challenged by two perspectives laid out initially in Chapter Two as essentially rival and independent. The first of these perspectives pinpointed parallel, relevant policy development within CLRTAP, with attention primarily given to the possibility of positive and policy-enhancing spill-over from the development of several other air pollution policy processes. Although two other protocol negotiation processes were concluded during the negotiations on the Gothenburg Protocol, neither of these had any noticeable effect upon the process given prime attention in this context.

So attention could quickly be shifted to a limited opening up of the 'black box' of domestic politics. As the most notable development, the big emitter and earlier laggard, the UK, moved closer towards the 'progressive' camp, partly related to increasing domestic concern over air pollution. In the concluding rounds of the negotiations, the UK was one of the countries which showed greatest negotiation flexibility. Apart from that, few conspicuous changes in the positions of earlier laggards and indifferents took place which called for a closer scrutiny of domestic developments.

All in all, the single most important factor accounting for the strengthening of CLRTAP policy is the regime-induced knowledge improvement and the development of the multi-pollutant and multi-effects approach. As this development is the fruit of activities dating back to the 1980s, there is clear merit in seeing the Gothenburg Protocol as the jewel in the crown for CLRTAP as a dynamic regime. Hence, this study offers clear support to a process perspective, emphasising the importance of 'getting the ball rolling' in the first place. So including specific clauses and timetables for policy reviews and revisions may turn out to be of far greater importance than the often lax more substantial policy content of the initial commitments. It should here be recalled that a central foundation for the

CLRTAP Gothenburg Protocol was the review clauses established in earlier protocols, and especially the 1988 NO_x Protocol.

Shedding light upon developments within the EU: Nordic pressure, package deals and the CRLTAP effect

Within the context of the EU, the first proposed explanation centred around how the 1995 accession of a group of 'rich and green' new Member States specifically concerned with air pollution, greened the staffing of both the Environment Directorate and other Directorates within the Commission, and also the composition of the Parliament and the Council. This subsequently and together may have led to a more benign constellation of preferences in the Council and ultimately to increasing EU air pollution policy strength. This proposition made a lot of sense in this specific context. Particularly interesting and influential developments seemed to have taken place within the Commission and the DG ENV, with several influential Scandinavian experts succeeding each other. But the Nordic dominance in terms of relevant Rapporteur positions acquired in the Parliament is also striking, and the strengthening of the green frontrunner coalition in the Council was also assumed to be of importance.

The next institutional propositions suggested looking beyond the 1995 accession and focusing on the effects of other institutional changes. First, an increased possibility for majority-voting in the Council has led to a more powerful aggregation of preferences and may have given the 1995 enlargement a more decisive effect in the Council proceedings, ultimately leading to increasing policy strength. As a second development, a more prominent role for the Parliament in decision-making and the added weight of Parliament amendments could have contributed to a greening of preferences in the Council, and the final round of conciliation in particular could have forced the Council to move in a policy-strengthening direction.

Neither of these propositions seemed to hit the nail on the head in this context. Although the functioning of the Council in specific processes is shrouded in secrecy, and 'hidden stick' effects of majority-voting can never be ruled out, the outcome of the crucial June 2000 Council meeting stands out as a classic EU compromise – with concessions to all camps and clear winners hard to identify. With regard to the Parliament, it clearly placed itself in the camp within the EU system pushing for the most ambitious strengthening of EU policy in this area. Basically, it has supported the targets and ambitiousness expressed in the Commission's various inputs to this process. Hence, although the Parliament has surely contributed to the strengthening of policy which has taken place, it cannot be counted as a crucially important driving force in this process. This is partly due to the simple fact that the Commission and the Parliament have been in basic agreement in most of this process. But also the very complexity of NEC modelling and decision-making has complicated the task of justifying calls for tighter emission ceilings.

As the final institutional element, the greening effect due to a changing organisational environment was pointed out, with developments within CLRTAP specifically focused upon. The substantial knowledge improvement and policy development in the 1990s within the CLRTAP context could have functioned as a regulatory inspiration and stimulant, strengthening the position of EU policy entrepreneurs in the field of air pollution and leading to a more benign constellation of preferences and ultimately increasing policy strength. This proposition clearly highlighted important aspects. CLRTAP experience and expertise had a major impact on the Acidification and Ozone Strategies, which in themselves introduced a new way of working and thinking within the Commission. Moreover, the idea of setting National Emission Ceilings emanated from the 1994 Sulphur Protocol; the very multi-pollutant and multi-effects approach emanated from within the CLRTAP system, and the over time, shared use of IIASA's services proved beneficial to all parties involved. Hence, the more general CLRTAP system influence on the shape of the EU process should be seen as significant.

As in the case of CLRTAP, the institutional change perspective was then mildly challenged by two rival perspectives. The first of these perspectives pinpointed parallel, relevant policy development in the EU, with attention primarily given to the possibility of positive and policy-enhancing spill-over from the development of several other air pollution policy processes. This relates both to the fuel quality and vehicle emissions issue, air quality standards, and strengthened requirements to Large Combustion Plants. Such spill-over could take the form of policy goals being adopted in one context, logically pointing to the need for stricter emission reduction goals. It could also take the form of specific, integrative package deals being formed. Of the three processes discussed in this context, the Auto-Oil I fuel quality and vehicle emissions process had only very general links to the Acidification Strategy and NEC Directive process. The air quality considerations were more important and are essential elements in order to understand the background for determining the NO_x and VOC emission ceilings in the Commission proposal put forward in June 1999. Still, these considerations seem to have glided more into the background in the subsequent political debacles.

So in terms of impact in the final phases, the renegotiation of the LCP Directive is the one to watch. This process was in the pipeline before work started on the Acidification Strategy, but picked up speed after the renegotiation was moved into the broader Acidification Strategy context. Nevertheless, the relationship between these processes did not become really intimate until the spring of 1999. After that, Member States increasingly emphasised the need to see national emission ceilings and revised large combustion plant requirements as a package. Hence, in order to understand how it was possible to obtain a common position on the NEC Directive at the crucial June 2000 Environment Council – contrary to the expectations of many insiders and observers – the package perspective is highly relevant. Furthermore, it cannot be excluded that some countries' acceptance in this final phase of somewhat lower (and hence stronger) NECs – such as the UK – had something to do with the final wording of the LCP compromise.

In sum, it is hard to understand the development and outcome of the Acidification Strategy/NEC Directive process without acknowledging the links especially to the air quality and LCP renegotiation processes. However, although air quality improvements in a general sense presuppose reduced emissions, the very *establishment* of the Acidification Strategy process did not come about due to these other processes.

Finally, a limited opening up of the 'black box' of domestic politics was put forward as the main logical alternative perspective to the internationally focused institutional and policy perspectives. More specifically, it was suggested that a domestically induced greening of laggards and the indifferent nations could have led to a more benign constellation of preferences and subsequently higher policy strength. With regard to France, Italy, Greece, Portugal and Spain, they have all experienced a disturbing situation, particularly in terms of ozone concentration and urban pollution, and public concern has been growing in these countries in recent years. However, this has had limited effects hitherto in terms of strengthened policies and positions, and several of these countries do not favour stronger *EU* policies as a response to these problems.

With regard to the earlier 'Dirty Man of Europe', the UK, both switching from coal to gas for energy, resulting in reduced British sulphur emissions 'for free', and increasing concern over both rural and urban problems related to air pollution, must be taken into account in this context. No less important, it was realised during the first part of the 1990s that at least half of the UK's problems were 'imported' from abroad, providing a powerful incentive to adopt a more positive attitude towards the strengthening of European policies in this field. Hence, such a domestic perspective stands out as simply essential in order to understand the more flexible and progressive positions taken by the UK on these issues in recent years.

All in all, thinking counterfactually, the most important institutional changes behind the strengthening of EU air pollution policies is, first, the 1995 accession and the effects of this within all of the EU bodies. Such an effect has been indicated in relation to other environmental issue areas and processes.[380] Through detailed process tracing, this study hence augments existing knowledge on this point significantly. Moreover, this part of the study gives support to the general importance of the ability to identify and constructively take advantage of political 'windows of opportunity'.[381] It is here instructive to recall how the Swedes, soon after being included in the good EU company, picked up on the acidification target established in the 1992 Environmental Action Programme. These non-binding targets could have easily been silently forgotten if the Swedes had not realised the window of opportunity which this target offered.

The second key institutional determinant is the increasingly closer interplay with CLRTAP and the reaping of the benefits of the multi-pollutant approach also within the EU context. In order to understand this strengthening more fully, both parallel EU policy development and domestic greening developments, not least in the UK, need to be brought into the picture. These developments have served to counteract a number of forces in the 1990s not favourable for policy strengthening – ranging from generally decreasing environmental concern to the subsidiarity debate and deregulation processes within the more specific EU context.

Why the EU is more ambitious than CLRTAP – but not very much more

Let us then turn to the third intention of this study, namely to shed light upon the comparative policy differences between the EU and CLRTAP. When directly comparing the emission ceilings in the CLRTAP Protocol and the parallel EU NEC Directive, the EU ceilings are overall somewhat more ambitious. As the problems addressed are fairly similar, could it be that this difference stems from institutional contexts which differ in a number of ways? Given the wide-spread perception of the EU as a considerably stronger institution than traditional regimes, why are the differences in strength still so moderate?

In order to study the difference in policy strength, four main institutional propositions were examined: fewer and more homogeneous parties in the EU; higher administrative strength within the EU; stronger decision-making procedures in the EU; and a higher issue linkage potential in the

EU. Closer scrutiny produced only limited evidence to back up the three first propositions.

In terms of membership scope, there was undoubtedly a somewhat more numerous laggard group within the CLRTAP than within the EU. However, as the EU still had a group of quite unambitious countries within its ranks, the difference between the two contexts in terms of the presence of laggards is more one of degree than one of fundamental nature.

Turning to differences in administrative strength, comparing the CLRTAP scientific-political complex at work in the Gothenburg Protocol process with the administrative resources commanded by the EU air pollution unit in charge of the Acidification/Ozone Strategy and NEC Directive process, one may even come to the conclusion that *CLRTAP* is the stronger institution! So this proposition turned out to be of very little help in shedding light on the policy difference between the EU and CLRTAP.

Moving on to the issue of decision-making procedures, despite considerable formal procedural differences between the two contexts, decision-making practice seems to have been quite consensual in both contexts. However, some 'hidden stick' effects of the formal possibility to resort to majority-voting could not be ruled out in the EU context.

With regard to the fourth and final institutional difference highlighted, related to issue linkage potential, this hit the nail far more on its head. EU's developing air pollution 'policy density' led to a number of related policy processes from the mid-1990s on; partly pertaining to a revision of earlier policies, and partly the development of brand new policies. This made issue interaction and linking a much more prominent feature of the decision-making process within the EU than within CLRTAP. Although the comparative effect should not be exaggerated, in particular the final linking of the revision of the Large Combustion Plant Directive and the NEC Directive contributed both to making a NEC Common Position at all possible in June 2000 and also to slightly more ambitious emission ceilings.

The challenging of these institutional perspectives by a perspective pinpointing the possible effects of 'remaining' differences in problem characteristics did not shed further light on the differences in policy strength, although it did sensitise us to the fact that transboundary movements of pollutants, sensitive areas and hence problem characteristics *do* differ a bit between the EU and CLRTAP contexts. Overall, explaining the somewhat higher policy strength within the EU in addition to issue linkage aspects highlighted above, the simple aspect of *timing* was pinpointed. As the EU's NEC Common Position was adopted six months after the Gothenburg Protocol, this meant that the Member States had some extra time to discuss and negotiate and to further clarify the domestic possibilities for emission reductions.

Timing also turned out to be a central key to understanding why the final difference in national emission ceilings and their ambitiousness between the two contexts has ended up considerably smaller than expected. The plan was to have the EU NEC Directive adopted before the final phase of the CLRTAP negotiations. In such a scenario, the EU could become a helpful, contributing force in the efforts to increase policy ambitiousness in the concluding phase of CLRTAP Gothenburg Protocol negotiations. However, bureaucratic slowness and the resignation of the Commission delayed the proposal with about half a year and, as it turned out, the more lax CLRTAP emission ceilings became an important point of reference in the final phase of the EU decision-making process, instead of the intended other way around.

How Robust are These Findings? Ways to Further Develop the Analytical Framework

So far the main findings. How robust are they? On the one hand, the analytical framework has functioned well. Perhaps just because the framework has been somewhat simplistic and crude, it has been very helpful with regard to unravelling and making sense of processes with a number of forces and processes simultaneously at work. Furthermore, interviews and communication with central participants in and observers of the studied processes have convinced me that central determinants within both the EU and CLRTAP contexts have been captured in this study.

On the other hand, work on this study has also revealed a number of limitations of the framework applied and hence ways to improve and develop the framework further. Turning first to the central concept of policy strength, it has been argued that the emphasis on the level of reduction commitments and the top-down 'behavioural bite' should be complemented by more attention to the attributes of 'who will be bitten' and the relationship between the regulator and the regulated in general.[382] The Auto-Oil I Programme and the resulting strengthened EU fuel and vehicle emissions standards, as further described in Chapter Five, has been pinpointed as a good example of how the very policy-making approach, with extensive involvement of various stakeholders, can be seen as a strengthening of 'behavioural bite' – 'totally irrespective of the exact level of standards achieved in the Programme'.[383] This is a valid point. However, as it is very likely that the involvement of stakeholders influences the very level and stringency of standards, such involvement can clearly defend a position both as a dependent and independent variable.

Turning to the explanatory perspectives applied in this study, as pointed out in Chapter Two, given the complexity of the institutions and policy problems under scrutiny, there are clearly factors and linkages which have received only superficial attention in this study. For one thing, the EU system is so rich and complex in terms of institutions and policies that the risk of overlooking influential factors and interplay is very high. For instance, although the impact of broader EU debates and developments expressed in keywords such as 'subsidiarity' and 'deregulation' has not been totally ignored, it is clear that the relationship between such more general EU developments and the specific air pollution policy development has not been given adequate attention.

Moreover, as an obvious omission, the fascinating and comprehensive 'black box' of domestic politics has been opened just a crack. As an important element in explaining the strengthening of policy over time, central analysts have pointed to 'the gradually increasing level of knowledge and awareness of environmental issues among the public all over Europe (although the starting point was different in the various parts of Europe), which in turn has raised the "public pressure" for action'.[384] In order to evaluate the merit of such claims, the 'black box' of domestic politics, not least in Southern Europe, must be opened and assessed much more fully.

Finally, getting a solid grip on the interconnectedness of international and domestic policy-making is a tough challenge in all studies of this sort. This interconnectedness is especially intricate in the EU context. The interplay in practice between the three perspectives, here initially set out as largely independent factors, has turned out to be considerable. Hence, the following, slightly revised model can be launched as a more accurate indication and summary of the relationships in practice:

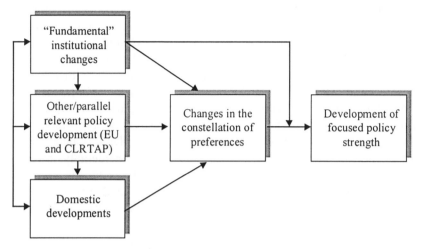

Figure 8.1 Revised model

Looking Ahead: The Prospects for implementing stronger European Air Pollution Policies

Although this book is primarily focused on the *making* of international policies, the 'proof of the pudding' lies in effective and successful national implementation. Hence, Chapter Seven made a first, modest cut in terms of assessing the prospects for successful implementation. With regard to countries given specific attention, such attention was given to three key-emission countries: the UK, Germany and France. Given their size of emissions and contributions to transboundary effects, their performance is both environmentally and politically of specific importance. Generally, in order to evaluate countries' prospects with regard to compliance and implementation, four main analytical perspectives were suggested and further elaborated in Chapter Seven:

- A baseline perspective, summing up important achievements and failures so far of the countries in question
- 'Basic interests', related to the relationship between abatement costs and damage costs
- 'Domestic politics', bringing in not least the distribution of costs and benefits
- 'Learning' and policy diffusion.

Summing up first the UK picture, 'the dirty man of Europe' seems to be history. The CLRTAP compliance record is quite good. In terms of probable abatement costs, the EU Commission estimated in June 1999 that annual costs for the UK would be 1350 million ECU; 18 percent of the EU total. Towards the end of 1999, the British Department of the Environment, Transport and the Regions (DETR) disputed this figure. In fact, the DETR believed that these cost figures were 'likely to be significant overestimates'. Instead, the DETR put the overall annual costs at around 900 million ECUs; most of these for VOC controls. Moreover, DETR stated that the cost of meeting the CLRTAP ceilings would be 'considerably lower'. In terms of damage costs, as was noted in Chapter Five, concern over acidification and urban pollution is on the increase, and so is probably the government's estimate of damage costs. Hence, the overall balance between costs and benefits does not look that bad.

Turning to the more political side of things, as was also discussed in Chapter Five, the impression is that the current air pollution political 'swing' in this country is positive. Quite recently, a revised national Air Quality Strategy was launched. This must be seen as part of the government's response to a deteriorating urban air pollution situation, with traffic going up – like almost everywhere else. Moreover, popular concern over these problems seems to be on the increase. All in all, there are good reasons to believe that the 'high hopes' in Geneva/CLRTAP and Brussels will not be dashed in London.

The prospects for German implementation are more uncertain. The German CLRTAP compliance record is good. However, in terms of implementation and abatement costs, Germany comes out clearly at the top, with an estimated 2146 million euro per year. This is almost twice as much as number two on the list, the UK. Moreover, the German backtracking in the concluding negotiations on the CLRTAP Gothenburg Protocol described in Chapter Four may indicate that the costs of coming reductions worry German decision-makers. In addition to this, the impression is that concern over air pollution has decreased somewhat compared to the 1980s heyday. Given Germany's comparatively highest abatement costs, it is more open if damage costs will weigh as heavily as earlier in the German cost-benefit assessment. All in all, there are reasons to believe that the Germans will do quite well, but less impressive than in the past.

France is even more of an uncertain card here, and unimpressive NO_x and VOC performance so far does not bide well. In terms of abatement costs, the Commission's June 1999 exercise explicitly identified France as one of the high cost countries. Total annual costs of 916 million euro were indicated. With regard to damage costs, France has never experienced a

'Waldsterben' uproar and the impression is that concern over air pollution has never been very high on the French agenda. Still, over the last few years there has been an obvious increase in concern in France about (urban) air pollution problems and health impacts. Nevertheless, given uncertain French costs (but substantial in the EU context), the guess would be that the French cost-benefit assessment will easily be skewed in favour of abatement costs.

Hence, even if there are huge uncertainties to be clarified further, the implementation prospects related to these particular countries seem overall to be on the promising side. Bringing in estimates of the overall relationship between costs and benefits, some would even say that implementation of the CLRTAP and EU commitments is a 'piece of cake'. Figures produced both within the CLRTAP and EU context indicate that overall benefits will outweigh costs by a clear margin. Moreover, IIASA has indicated that the Gothenburg targets point to very moderate additional reduction costs for the key countries – as considerable emission reductions are already in the pipeline due to other international commitments and planned national policies. If the implementation of these other commitments progresses smoothly, relatively low additional and particularly Gothenburg Protocol/NEC Directive implementation costs could mean smooth 'piece of cake' implementation processes. On top of all of this, the effects of the implementation of climate commitments agreed to in Kyoto in 1997 have so far not been included in this discussion at all. Such an inclusion will lower the specific, necessary air pollution abatement costs even further.

However, a more troubling 'tall order' scenario can also be envisaged. In the case of slow progress of the implementation of other international and national measures, including non-ratification of the Kyoto Protocol and stalling of the climate processes, then the more particular NEC implementation costs could become more important. For instance according to the French Environment Institute (IFEN), these costs, seen in isolation, should not be looked upon as insignificant.

CAFE and Enlargement: Is the EU Taking Over and CLRTAP Fading Away?

This study has described increasing interplay and parallel policy-making in the wider CLRTAP and more narrow EU contexts. As signalled by the higher policy ambitiousness within the EU NEC context than in the very parallel CLRTAP process, the institutionally more advanced EU context – not least with its comprehensive spanning of sectors and related potential for pro-active environmental policymaking – has the general potential for becoming the policy frontrunner in European air pollution politics.

One central building-block in fulfilling this potential is a successful outcome of *the Clean Air for Europe (CAFE) programme*.[385] As noted earlier, this initiative was launched in 1998. On May 4 2001 the Commission then published the Communication on the programme (COM(2001) 245). The CAFE programme is meant to deliver 'an integrated strategy to effectively combat air pollution' by 2004.[386] This will then form one of the thematic strategies under the EU's Sixth Environmental Action Programme. CAFE can be seen as a sort of 'one step back in order to make two new steps forward'. As described earlier in this book, the NEC Directive means a significant further step in the development of EU air pollution policy – and the Directive has developed in parallel and interplay with policy development on air quality, large combustion plants and vehicle emissions. The time has now come for an 'in-depth review of the adequacy and effectiveness of existing Community legislation', in order to underpin the review in 2004 of air quality standards and national emission ceilings. One central gap already singled out in the current legislation pertains to the issues of particulate matter and ground-level ozone.

Work will be conducted in a number of working groups and contracts will be issued for research relating to the review of existing legislation.[387] The principles of stakeholder involvement and transparency are established as guides to the participation in and mode of this work. In light of EU enlargement, CAFE 'will include candidate countries within its geographical scope from the beginning'. Enhanced cooperation with CLRTAP is also a mechanism in this connection, as candidate countries are all parties to CLRTAP.

All in all, CAFE is an important and promising initiative, but also clearly a challenging one. Unclear financing of the programme has been pointed out as a weakness.[388] So has lacking specification of the work programme which must be rapidly established in order to meet the 2004 deadline.[389] In addition, there are clearly organisational challenges. Within the context of stakeholder involvement, industrial participation needs to be balanced by environmentalist participation. Moreover, as pinpointed by *Environment Watch*, 'most if not all the key sectoral areas of policy making required to build the strategy remain the responsibility of those same parts of the Commission that ran them previously. They have not been brought into the grasp of policy makers running the CAFE programme, so it remains to be seen if the requisite linkages can be made to work in practice as well as they may look in theory'.[390]

Another central determinant for the EU's potential for further success in the field of air pollution is a successful enlargement process. As well known, thirteen new countries are knocking on EU's door, with a possibility of a sizeable group consisting of up to ten countries being included in 2004.[391] Enlargement 'success' in the environmental policy-making context can be defined as extending the EU's span of central European polluters without stalling environmental policy-making, diluting standards, and aggravating the 'implementation gap' within the Union.

With regard to the extension of geographical span, the scope of the EU in the more specific air pollution context has so far not been ideal. As pinpointed by Weale et al. (2000), 'for many environmental problems, of which acidification is a good example, <the EU's> boundaries are insufficiently wide to internalise the relevant externality' (p.445). Enlargement will obviously improve this situation. Getting significant emitters such as Poland and Bulgaria into the EU institutional machinery will be good news, not least for vulnerable countries such as Sweden and Norway.

However, the critical question is the extent to which this beneficial extension of geographical scope can be achieved without stalling policy-making on new standards and aggravating the implementation gap. Giving extensive and well-founded answers to this challenging question goes far beyond the scope of this study. According to analysts such as Homeyer (2001), there is a clear danger that enlargement will undermine the leader-laggard dynamic in the Council, 'because most Accession Countries will probably oppose relatively strict environmental standards once they have joined the EU' (p.36). Moreover, the implementation gap may also widen, as 'Accession Countries lack the financial resources and administrative capacities to achieve full practical implementation of EU environmental legislation by the date of accession' (ibid.).[392]

Finally, as the EU expands eastwards, and the membership overlap increases even further, will there be a rationale left for upholding the CLRTAP forum? Within the community of policy-makers, the view is clearly that such a rationale exists.[393] This is also emphasised in the EU Communication on the CAFE programme, viz: 'The need to enhance co-operation with ..CLRTAP.. has been one of the strongest messages arising from discussions with national and stakeholder representatives'.[394]

First of all, it is positive that problems are 'attacked' by several and different institutions – with differences in membership. Countries such as Russia and Ukraine will not become members of the EU in the foreseeable future. Moreover, the EU enlargement process is quite probably going to take a while, and in the meantime it will become necessary to broaden the CLRTAP regulatory scope to include new substances (such as particulate matter), and to renegotiate the Gothenburg Protocol.[395] In the scientific process underpinning such a renegotiation process, it is very well possible that a similar fruitful collaboration as witnessed recently between CLRTAP and the EU could take place – with the 'richer' EU financing IIASA and CLRTAP modelling work, and in return taking advantage of the modelling results in EU policy development.

In the long haul, it is possible that CLRTAP can develop into a forum primarily for inter-regional harmonisation of policies, leaving it primarily to an expanded EU to handle the more specific European matters. When policy attention gradually turns to the issue of particulate matter, where trans-Atlantic transport of pollutants seems to be taking place, the European-American CLRTAP context will be a strength.

Notes

[380] See for instance Young and Wallace (2000); Chapter 5, and particularly p.116.

[381] The classic reference here is Kingdon (1984).

[382] This was a central comment of one of the reviewers of this manuscript.

[383] Statement of the reviewer.

[384] Communication with Christer Ågren, October 2000.

[385] On the launching of CAFE, see EU Communication (COM (2001) 245); EU Press Release, May 7, 2001, 'Commission launches 'Clean Air for Europe' programme'; Europe Environment, May 8, 2001, pp.22-23; Environment Watch, May 11, 2001, pp.5-6; and Acid News 2, June 2001, p.2.

[386] The CAFE Programme has the following specific objectives: to develop, collect and validate scientific information concerning air pollution, including projections, inventories, integrated assessment modelling and cost-effectiveness analysis studies, leading to the development of air quality and deposition objectives and indicators and identification of measures required to reduce emissions; to support the implementation of legislation and develop new legislation, especially the air framework Directive daughter Directives and contribute to the review of international protocols; to ensure that measures in different sectors needed to achieve air quality objectives are taken in a cost-effective manner at the relevant policy level through the development of effective structural links with the relevant policy areas; to develop an overall integrated strategy to achieve air quality objectives in a cost-effective way; to disseminate widely information and results from the programme.

[387] The following working groups have been indicated: health effects; non-health effects; air quality assessment, including implementation of air quality directives; policy measures; scenario development; and strategy development.

[388] See Acid News 2, June 2001, op.cit.

[389] See Environment Watch, May 11, 2001, op.cit.

[390] Environment Watch, May 11, 2001, op.cit., p.6.

[391] These ten countries are Hungary, Poland, Slovakia, Latvia, Estonia, Lithuania, The Czech Republic, Slovenia, Cyprus and Malta. The three other applicants are Bulgaria, Romania and Turkey. See Christiansen and Tangen (2001).

[392] On these points, see also Holzinger and Knoepfel (eds, 2000).

[393] This is based on interviews with policy-makers in Sweden, Denmark and the UK in the autumn of 1999.

[394] EU Communication (COM (2001) 245), p.14.

[395] Article 10 in the Gothenburg Protocol states that the first review of the Protocol shall start no later than one year after entry into force.

Bibliography

Acid News (1995), 'Action Should Mean It', no. 3, June, p. 2.
- (1996), 'Protocols in the Making', no. 2, April, pp. 5-6.
- (1996), 'Full Package Revealed', no. 4, October, p. 1, 3.
- (1996), 'Developing a Strategy', no. 5, December, pp. 1-4.
- (1997), 'Acidification: Advancing Plans for a Strategy, no. 1, April, pp. 6-7.
- (1997), 'New Protocol – Facing Problems', no. 2, June, p. 6.
- (1997), 'Fuels and Vehicles: Stricter Standards to Come', no. 3, October, pp. 6-7.
- (1997), 'Acidification Strategy', no. 3, October, p. 7.
- (1997), 'Targets and Trends', no. 3, October, p. 11.
- (1998), 'LCPs – New Directive Surprisingly Excludes Existing Plants', no. 1, March, p. 6.
- (1998), 'Benefits of Reduction Assessed', no. 2, June, pp. 16-18.
- (1998), 'For a Multi-pollutant Protocol', no. 3, October, pp. 4-5; 18.
- (1998), 'Air Quality – Some Standards Ready', no. 3, October, p. 7.
- (1998), 'Emission Ceilings: Four Pollutants Targeted', no. 4, December, pp. 1-5.
- (1998), 'LCP Directive: Old Plants are the Problem', no. 4, December, pp. 8-9.
- (1999), 'Multi-effects: Towards a Protocol', no. 1, March, p. 1; 4-5.
- (1999), 'Air Quality Work: Coordination Proposed', no. 1, March, p. 6.
- (1999), 'Multi-effect Protocol: Negotiations are Continuing', no. 2, June, p. 5.
- (1999), 'Almost at a Standstill', no. 2, June, pp. 8-9.
- (1999), 'New Protocol on the Way', no. 3, October, p. 1; 4-5.
- (1999), 'Strange Behaviour', no. 3, October, p. 2.
- (1999), 'Multi-effects: Clear Shortcomings of New Protocol', no. 4, December, p. 5.
- (1999), 'Varied Response to Commitments', no. 4, December, pp. 12-13.
- (2000), 'Ground-level Ozone – High levels Ignored Further South', no. 1, March, p. 15.
- (2000), 'NEC Directive: Clashing Over Ceilings', no. 3, October, pp. 6-7.
- (2000), 'Large Combustion Plants Directive – Limits also for Existing Plants', no. 3, October, pp. 8-9.
- (2000), 'Air Quality: Muddle Over Ceilings and Standards for Ozone', no. 4, December, p. 12.

- (2001), 'Editorial: Should have Learnt', no. 2, June, p. 2.
- (2001), 'NECs and LCPs – Moving towards a Compromise', no. 2, June 2001, pp. 1, 3-5.
Agrawala, S. and Andresen, S. (1999), Indispensibility and Indefensibility? The United States in the Climate Treaty Negotiations, *Global Governance*, vol. 5, no. 4, pp. 457- 82.
Amann, M. and Lutz, M. (2000), The Revision of the Air Quality Legislation in the European Union Related to Ground-level Ozone, working paper, IIASA/DG ENV.
Andersen, M.S. and Liefferink, D. (eds) (1997), *European environmental policy – The pioneers*, Manchester University Press, Manchester.
Andresen, S., Skjærseth, J.B. and Wettestad, J. (1995), Regime, the State and Society: Analyzing the Implementation of International Environmental Commitments, Laxenburg, IIASA Working Paper WP–95–43, June.
Andresen, S., Skodvin, T., Underdal, A. and Wettestad, J. (2000), *Science and Politics in International Environmental Regimes - Between Integrity and Involvement*, Manchester University Press, Manchester.
Arp, H. (1993), Technical Regulation and Politics: The Interplay between Economic Interests and Environmental Policy Goals in EU Car Emission Legislation, in Liefferink, J.D., Lowe, P.D., and Mol, A.J.P. (eds), *European Integration and Environmental Policy*, Belhaven Press, London.
Bjørkbom, L. (1998), Transboundary Cooperation for Cleaner Air. Rationale for an International Multi-effects and Multi-pollutant Protocol, note, October 16, 1998.
Boehmer-Christiansen, S. (2000), The British Case: Overcompliance by Luck or Policy?, in Underdal, A. and Hanf, K. (eds) (2000), *International Environmental Agreements and Domestic Politics: The Case of Acid Rain*, Ashgate, Aldershot, pp. 279-313.
Boehmer-Christiansen, S. and Skea, J. (1991), *Acid Politics: Environmental and Energy Policies in Britain and Germany*, Belhaven Press, London.
Boehmer-Christiansen, S. and Weidner, H. (1995), *The Politics of Reducing Vehicle Emissions in Britain and Germany*, Pinter, London.
Boerzel, T. (2000), Why there is no Southern Problem. On Environmental Leaders and Laggards in the European Union, *Journal of European Public Policy*, vol. 7, no. 1, pp. 141-62.
Castells, N. (1999), International Environmental Agreements – Institutional Innovation in Transboundary Air Pollution Policies, Dissertation, European Commission Joint Research Centre, Ispra.
Christiansen, A.C. and Tangen, K. (2001), The Shadow of the Past: Environmental Issues and Institutional Learning in EU Enlargement Processes, FNI Report 1/2001, The Fridtjof Nansen Institute.

Coffey, C., Jordan, A. and Wettestad, J. (2000), 'Can We Measure and Explain the Effectiveness of International Environmental Regimes and EU Policies Using the Same Theoretical and Methodological Tools? Some Reflections and Impressions', an agenda setting paper prepared for the third year Conference of the 1998-2000 *EU Concerted Action Project on the Effectiveness of International Environmental Agreements*, Barcelona, 9-11 November 2000. The Fridtjof Nansen Institute, Lysaker (published at http://www.fni.no).

Collier, U. (1997), Sustainability, Subsidiarity and Deregulation: New Directions in EU Environmental Policy, *Environmental Politics*, vol. 6, no. 2, summer 1997, pp. 1-23.

- (1998, ed), *Deregulation in the European Union – Environmental perspectives*, Routledge, London.

Dahl, A. and Sverdrup, L.A. (1996), Lobbying the European Parliament – Some Early Experiences in the Field of Environmental Policy, FNI-Report R:004-1996, The Fridtjof Nansen Institute, Lysaker.

DETR (1999), The Air Quality Strategy for England, Scotland, Wales, and Northern Ireland – A Consultation Document, Department of the Environment, Transport and the Regions, London.

- (2000), The Air Quality Strategy for England, Scotland, Wales, and Northern Ireland, Cm 4548, Department of the Environment, Transport and the Regions, London.

di Primio, J. (1996), Monitoring and Verification in the European Air Pollution Regime, Laxenburg, IIASA Working Paper WP–96–47.

Downs, G.W., Rocke, D.M., and Barsoom, .P.N. (1996), Is the Good News about Compliance Good News about Cooperation?, *International Organization*, vol. 50, pp. 379-406.

Earnshaw, D. and Judge, D. (1995), Early days: the European Parliament, Co-decision and the European Union Legislative Process Post-Maastricht, *Journal of European Public Policy*, vol. 2, p. 4, December, pp. 624-49.

- (1996), From Co-operation to Co-decision – The European Parliament's Path to Legislative Power, in Richardson, J. (ed), *European Union: Power and Policy-making*, Routledge, London, pp. 96-126.

Edwards, G. and Spence, D. (1997), *The European Commission*, Cartermill Publ., London.

ENDS Report (1987), A Change of Rules for the EEC's Environmental Policy, no. 145, February, pp. 9-11.

- (1987), Major Rifts over NO_x Controls, no. 152, September, p. 3.

- (1992), Brussels to Propose New Targets for SO_2, NO_x, no. 205, February, pp. 34-5.

- (1993), Brussels Drafts Framework Law on Air Quality, no. 219, April, pp. 38-9.

- (1994), Framework Directive opens New Phase in EU Air Quality Policy, no. 234, July, pp. 41-2.
- (1995), Commission Throws SO₂ policy Back in Melting Pot, no. 246, July, pp. 33-4.
- (1996), Environment Ministers Push Ozone back onto EU Agenda, no. 256, May, p. 43.
- (1996), Government's Air Quality Strategy puts Transport on the Spot, no. 257, June, pp. 15-8.
- (1996), Car Industry Lashes out at Auto-Oil Proposals, no. 257, June, pp. 41-3.
- (1997), EC Move on Acidification Leaves UK Strategy Adrift, no. 264, January, pp. 37-8.
- (1997), Acidification Plan Spells End for High-sulphur Fuel Oil, no. 266, March, pp. 40-1.
- (1997), Row Over Combustion Plant Spells Trouble for Acidification Plan, no. 268, May, pp. 40-1.
- (1997), Accelerated Review for Air Quality Strategy, no. 270, July, pp. 34-5.
- (1997), Royal Commission Warns of Looming Transport Crisis, no. 272, pp. 11-12.
- (1997), New Drinking Water Rules Agreed, but Trouble for UK on Landfills, no. 273, October, pp.34-7.
- (1998), Ministers Agree Air Pollution Rules, Lengthy Deadline on Water Quality, no. 281, June, p. 47.
- (1998), Compromise Reached on Auto/Oil Fuel, Emission Standards, no. 281, June, p. 48.
- (1998), Combustion Plant Proposal Takes Heat Off Existing Plant, no. 282, July, pp. 49-50.
- (1999), Air Quality Management and the Art of the Possible, no. 288, January, pp. 17-21.
- (1999), Commission Suggests Umbrella Strategy for Clean Air, no. 288, January, pp. 46-7.
- (1999), National Emissions Ceiling Proposal Points to New Squeeze on VOCs, no. 293, June, pp. 45-6.
- (1999), New Emissions Protocol Falls far Short of EC Proposals, no. 296, September, pp. 44-5.
- (1999), Ministers Divided over Emission Ceilings, Press for Action on Climate, no. 297, October, pp. 52-3.
- (1999), UK Firms up Opposition to Emissions Ceilings Directive, no. 299, December, pp. 41-2.
- (1999), Ministers Row over Combustion Plants, but Agree Strategic EIA Directive, no. 299, December, pp. 43-4.
- (2000), No Surprises in Air Quality, no. 300, January, pp. 37-8.

- (2001), Treaty Reform brings Little Change for Environment, no. 312, January, pp. 42-3.
- (2001), Air Pollution Directives Head for Conciliation, no. 315, April, p. 55.
- (2001), Ministers and Parliament Agree Air Pollution Directives, no. 319, August, p. 52.

ENDS Environment Daily (2000), Clash Looms over Watered Down Plan to Curb Ozone, October 5.

Environment Update/Euractive (2001), European Parliament Wants Stronger Ozone Directive, June 15, EurActiv.com Portal News.

Environmental Policy and Law (1988), NO$_x$ Protocol Signed, vol. 18, no. 6, p. 196.

Environment Watch: Western Europe (1999), Revision of EU Combustion Plants Faces Possible Spanish Veto, February 19, pp. 6-7.
- (1999), EU Assembly Votes Narrowly for Stricter Combustion Plant Emissions Curbs, May 7, pp. 10-11.
- (1999), Executive Finalizes EU Proposals on Emissions Ceilings, Ozone Pollution, June 18, pp. 7-8.
- (1999), Environment Ministers Unwilling to Lower National Emissions Ceilings, October 15, pp. 1-3.
- (1999), LCP Directive Now Unlikely to Include Existing Plants, November 12, pp. 1-2.
- (2000), Parliament Supports Commission Call for Strict Air Pollution Measures, March 31, pp. 2-3.
- (2000), Large Combustion Plant Talks Reopen Making NEC Deal Likely, May 26, pp. 9–10.
- (2000), Ministers Move to More Ambitious Air Pollution Targets, July 7, pp. 5-6.
- (2000), Environment Main Area for Failures to Comply With EU Law, September 1, pp. 14-19.
- (2001), Commission Launches Clean Air for Europe Programme, May 11, pp. 5-6.

Europe Environment (1996), Auto-Oil: Commission Proposes New Emission and Fuel Standards, no. 480, June 27, p.1.
- (1997), Acidification: Commission Unveils New Strategy and Specific Actions, no. 496, March 25, pp. 1-3.
- (1997), European Commission: New Community Strategy to Combat Acidification, Supplement to no. 497, April 8, 19 pages.
- (1997), Environment Ministers Tackle Pollution from Cars and Vans, no. 509, October 28, pp. 12-13.
- (1998), Air Pollution: Parliamentary Reports on Air Quality, Acidification and Sulphur, no. 522, May 12, pp. 4-5.

- (1998), Air Pollution: European Parliament Hardens the Tone, no. 523, May 26, pp. 3-4.
- (1998), Air Pollution: Commission in New Clampdown on Power Plant Emissions, no. 527, July 21, pp. 1-4.
- (1999), Member States Split on Large Combustion Plants, no. 541, March 16, pp. 14-15.
- (1999), Acidification: MEPs Urge Crackdown on Power Plant Emissions, no. 542, March 30, p. 9.
- (1999), Air Pollution: European Parliament Urges Crackdown on Power Plants, no. 544, April 27, p. 19.
- (1999), Air Quality: National Emission Ceilings and Ozone Concentration Limits Proposed, no. 547, June 15, pp. 1-13.
- (1999), Environment Council: North/South Opposition on Acidification and Ozone, no. 544, October 19, pp. 24-5.
- (1999), Amended Proposal on Large Combustion Plant Tabled, no. 558, December 14, p. 13.
- (2000), Environment Council: Ministers Fail to Reach Agreement on Large Combustion Plants, no. 559, January 7, p. 3.
- (2000), Air Quality: MEPs Committed to Combating Ozone and Acid Rain, no. 563, March 7, p. 2.
- (2000), Environment Council: Portuguese Presidency Revives Air Quality Debate, no. 565, April 4, p. 4.
- (2000), Environment Council: 22 June Session to Focus on Air Quality and Climate Change, no. 570, June 20, pp. 30-1.
- (2000), Environment Council: Ministers Clinch Deal on Large Combustion Plants & National Emission Ceilings, no. 571, July 4, pp. 3-5.
- (2000), Environment Council: Ministers Agree Common Position on Ozone, no. 576, October 17, p. 3.
- (2000), Air Pollution: Commission Backs Council on LCPs and Emissions Ceilings, no. 579, November 28, pp. 14-5.
- (2001), Commission Backs Council Ozone Position, no. 586, March 20, p. 12.
- (2001), Air Pollution: MEPs get Tough on Large Combustion Plants and National Emission Ceilings, no. 586, March 20, pp. 13-4.
- (2001), 'CAFE': A new Strategy, no. 589, May 8, pp. 22-3.
- (2001), Ozone: MEPs Seek to Force States to Clean up Air, no. 591, June 12, pp. 17-8.
- (2001), MEPs Committed to Improving Ozone Agreement, no. 592, June 26, p. 30.
- (2001), Atmospheric Pollution: Agreement on Combustion Plants and Emission Ceilings, no. 593, July 10, p. 15.

European Environmental Bureau (2001), National Emission Ceilings and Large Combustion Plants Directives: Conciliation Agreement Could have been Better!, press release, July 7.

Friedrich, A., Tappe, M., and Wurzel, R. (1998), The Auto-Oil Programme: Missed Opportunity or Leap Forward?, research paper 1/98, The University of Hull.

- (2000), A New Approach to EU Environmental Policy-Making? The Auto-Oil I Programme, *Journal of European Public Policy*, vol. 7, no. 4, October, pp. 593-612.

Gehring, T. (1994), *Dynamic International Regimes - Institutions for International Environmental Governance*, Peter Lang, Berlin.

Golub, J. (1996), 'Sovereignty and Subsidiarity in EU Environmental Policy', *Political Studies*, vol. 44, no. 4, pp. 686-703.

- (ed) (1998), *New Instruments for Environmental Policy in the EU*, Routledge, London.

- (1999), In the Shadow of the Vote? Decision Making in the European Community, *International Organization*, vol. 53, no. 4, Autumn, pp. 733-64.

Haas, P.M. (1990), *Saving the Mediterranean: The Politics of International Environmental Cooperation*, Columbia University Press, New York.

Haigh, N. (ed) (1992), *Manual of Environmental Policy: The EC and Britain*, Longman/IEEP, London. Updates 1997/98/99/2000/2001.

Hasselmeier, G. and Wettestad, J. (2000), German Climate Policy Ambitiousness: Just a Side-Effect of Reunification?, FNI-Report no. 2/2000, The Fridtjof Nansen Institute, Lysaker.

Heretier, A, Knill, C., and Mingers, S. (1996), *Ringing the Changes in Europe – Regulatory Competition and Redefinition of the State. Britain, France, Germany*, Walter de Gruyter, Berlin.

Holzinger, K. (1997), The Influence of New Member States on EU Environmental Policy-making: A Game Theoretic Approach, in Liefferink, D. and Andersen, M.S. (eds), *The Innovation of EU Environmental Policy*, Scandinavian University Press, Copenhagen, pp. 59-83.

Holzinger, K. and Knoepfel, P. (2000), *Environmental Policy in a European Union of Variable Geometry?*, Helbing & Lichtenhahn, Basel.

Homeyer, I. (2001), Enlarging EU Environmental Policy, paper presented at the workshop on 'Environmental Challenges of EU Eastern Enlargement', May 25-26, 2001, European University Institute, Florence.

International Environment Reporter (1994), European Union: Commission Proposes Framework Directive to Create Single Approach to Air Quality, July 13, pp. 589-90.

- (1997), EU Proposes Air Quality Standards for Sulfur Dioxide, Other Pollutants, October 15, pp. 953-54.

- (1998), 'Environment Ministers Sign Protocols on Heavy Metals, Organic Pollutants', July 8, p. 663.
- (1998), Legislation Setting Auto Emission, Fuel Quality Standards Approved by Union, July 8, p. 671.
- (1999), European Union: Commission Acts Against Belgium, U.K., France for alleged Breach of Directives, February 3, pp. 96-7.
- (1999), European Union: Commission Proposes National Ceilings for Sulfur Dioxide, NO_x, VOCs, Ammonia, June 23, pp. 518-19.
- (1999), European Union: Commission Proposes New Air Quality Index to Address High Levels of Urban Smog, June 23, pp. 520-21.
- (1999), European Union: Wallstrom Faces First Political Battle Over SO_2, Other Emission Ceilings, September 29, p. 785.
- (2000), European Union: Wallström Warns Against Moves to Weaken National Emission Ceilings, March 29, pp. 269-70.
- (2000), French Institute Says Each EU Nation Faces Cost of $55 million to Curb Acid Rain, May 24, pp. 419-20.
- (2000), Ministers Set National Emission Ceilings, Standards for Large Combustion Plants, July 5, p. 521.
- (2000), EU Environment Ministers Agree on Ozone Monitoring Directive, Alert System, October 11, p. 779.
- (2001), Parliament to Press for Tougher Limits on Emissions by Large Combustion Plants, March 28, pp. 236-37.
- (2001), European Parliament Demands Talks with Member States on Emissions Limits, March 28, p. 248.
- (2001), European Parliament Votes to Challenge State Attempts to Weaken Ozone Legislation, June 20, p. 512.
Jordan, A. J. (1998), 'EU Environmental Policy at 25: The Politics of Multinational Governance', *Environment*, vol. 40, no. 1, pp. 14-20, 39-45.
- (1999), 'The Implementation of EC Environmental Policy: A Policy Problem Without a Political Solution?' *Environment and Planning C (Government and Policy)*, vol. 17, no. 1, pp. 69-90.
Judge, D. (1992), 'Predestined to Save the Earth': The Environment Committee of the European Parliament, *Environmental Politics*, vol. 1, no. 4, pp. 186-212.
Kerremans, B. (1996), Do Institutions Make a Difference? Non-Institutionalism, Neo-Institutionalism, and the Logic of Common Decision-Making in the European Union, *Governance*, vol. 9, no. 2, pp. 216-40.
Kingdon, J.W. (1984), *Agendas, Alternatives, and Policy Alternatives*, Little and Brown, Boston.
Knill, C. (1997), The Europeanisation of Domestic Policies: The Development of EC Environmental Policy, *Environmental Policy and Law*, vol. 27, no. 1, pp. 48-57.

Knill, C. and Lenschow, A. (2000), New Concepts – Old Problems? The Institutional Constraints for the Effective Implementation of EU Environmental Policy, paper presented at the Annual International Convention of the International Studies Association, March 14-18, 2000, Los Angeles.

Kotov, V. and Nikitina, E. (1998), Implementation and Effectiveness of the Acid Rain Regime in Russia, in Victor, D., Raustiala, K. and Skolnikoff, E. (eds), *The Implementation and Effectiveness of International Environmental Commitments*, MIT Press, Cambridge, Massachusetts, pp. 519-49.

Kronsell, A. (1997), Sweden. Setting a Good Example, in Andersen, M.S. and Liefferink, D. (eds), *European Environmental Policy – The Pioneers*, Manchester University Press, Manchester, pp. 40-81.

Kutting, G. (1998), The Critical Loads Approach and International Relations – Effective International Environmental Policy Making?, *International Environmental Affairs*, vol. 10, no. 2, pp. 98-122.

Lammers, J.G. (1988), The European Approach to Acid Rain, in Magraw, D.B. (ed), *International Law and Pollution*, University of Pennsylvania, Philadelphia, pp. 265-309.

Levy, M. (1993), European Acid Rain: The Power of Tote Board Diplomacy, in Haas, P.M., Keohane, R. and Levy, M. (eds), *Institutions for the Earth*, MIT Press, Cambridge, Massachusetts and London, England, pp. 75-133.

- (1995), International Co-operation to Combat Acid Rain, *Green Globe Yearbook 1995*, Oxford University Press, pp. 59-69.

Levy, M., Young, O.R. and Zürn, M. (1994), The Study of International Regimes, Laxenburg, IIASA Working Paper WP–94–113.

Lewanski, R. (2000), Italy: Learning from International Co-operation or Simply 'Following Suit'?, in Hanf, K. and Underdal, A. (eds), *International Environmental Agreements and Domestic Politics: The Case of Acid Rain*, Ashgate, Aldershot, pp. 255-79.

Liberatore, A. (1993), The European Community's Acid Rain Policy, draft for the project on 'Social Learning in the Management of Global Environmental Risks'.

Liefferink, D. (1996), *Environment and the Nation State - The Netherlands, the European Union and Acid Rain*, Manchester University Press, Manchester.

Liefferink, D. and Andersen, M.S. (eds) (1997), *The Innovation of EU Environmental Policy*, Scandinavian University Press, Copenhagen.

McCormick, J. (1997), *Acid Earth – The Politics of Acid Pollution*, Earthscan, London.

- (1998), Acid Pollution – The International Community's Continuing Struggle, *Environment*, vol. 40, no. 3, April, pp. 17-20, 41-45.

180   *Clearing the Air*

Miles, E.L., Underdal, A., Andresen, S., Wettestad, J., Skjærseth, J.B. and Carlin, E.M. (forthcoming 2001), *Environmental Regime Effectiveness: Confronting Theory with Evidence*, MIT Press, Cambridge, Massachusetts.

New Scientist (1995), 'Paris Chokes while Officials Fiddle', July 29, p. 9.

Nollkaemper, A. (1993), The Legal Regime for Transboundary Water Pollution: Between Discretion and Constraint, Martinus Nijhoff/Graham & Trotman, Dordrecht.

OECD (1994), OECD Environmental Performance Reviews – United Kingdom, OECD, Paris.

Peters, B.G. (1992), Bureaucratic Politics and the Institutions of the European Community, in Sbragia, A.M. (ed), *Euro-Politics: Institutions and Policymaking in the 'New' European Community*, Brookings Institution, Washington, pp. 75-122.

Pressman, J.L. and Wildavsky, A. (1973), *Implementation: How great Expectations in Washington are Dashed in Oakland,* University of California Press, Berkeley.

Reuters/Planetark (2000), 'Environmentalists Attack New UK Air Quality Plan', January 20.

- (2000), 'EU States Agree to Cut Smog and Acid Rain', June 23.

- (2001), 'Smog Covers Paris, Drivers Told to Slow Down', July 31.

Rose, C. (1990), *The Dirty Man of Europe. The Great British Pollution Scandal,* Simon and Schuster, London.

Sbragia, A.M. (2000), 'Environmental Policy', in Wallace, H. and Wallace, W. (eds) *Policy-Making in the European Union*, Oxford University Press, Oxford, pp. 293-317.

Sebenius, J.K. (1990), Negotiating a Regime to Control Global Warming, report, Harvard University, Boston.

Selin, H. (2000), *Towards International Chemical Safety – Taking Action on Persistent Organic Pollutants (POPs)*, Linköping Studies in Arts and Science 211, Linköping.

Skea, J. and Du Monteuil, C. (2000), What's This Got to do with Me? France and Transboundary Air Pollution, in Hanf, K. and Underdal, A. (eds), *International Environmental Agreements and Domestic Politics: The Case of Acid Rain*, Ashgate, Aldershot, pp. 211-39.

Skjærseth, J.B. (1998), The Making and Implementation of North Sea Pollution Commitments: Institutions, Rationality and Norms, doctoral dissertation, Department of Political Science, University of Oslo/The Fridtjof Nansen Institute, Oslo/Lysaker.

Skjærseth, J.B. and Wettestad, J. (2000), 'The Study of EC Environmental Policy: Can Regime Theory Further Our Understanding?', draft, March 2000, The Fridtjof Nansen Institute, Lysaker.

Sprinz, D. and Wahl, A. (2000), 'Reversing (Inter)National Policy – Germany's Response to Transboundary Air Pollution', in Hanf, K. and Underdal, A. (eds), *International Environmental Agreements and Domestic Politics: The Case of Acid Rain*, Ashgate, Aldershot, pp. 130-55.

Stenstadvold, M. (1991), The Evolution of Cooperation: A Case Study of the NO_x Protocol (in Norwegian), unpublished thesis, University of Oslo.

Tsebelis, G. (1994), The Power of the European Parliament as a Conditional Agenda-Setter, *American Political Science Review*, vol. 88, no. 1, pp. 128-42.

Tuinstra, W., Hordijk, L. and Ammann, M. (1999), Using Computer Models in International Negotiations – The Case of Acidification in Europe, *Environment*, vol. 41, no. 9, pp. 33-42.

Underdal, A. (1990), Negotiating Effective Solutions: The Art and Science of Political Engineering, unpublished paper, the University of Oslo.

- (1998), Explaining Compliance and Defection: Three Models, *European Journal of International Relations*, vol. 4, no. 1, pp. 5-30.

- (1999), Methodological Challenges in the Study of Regime Effectiveness, paper prepared for the workshop on 'The Study of Regime Consequences: Methodological Challenges and Research Strategies', 19-20 November, 1999, Oslo.

- (2000), One Question; Two Answers, draft chapter for Miles, E.L., Underdal, A., Andresen, S., Wettestad, J., Skjærseth, J.B. and Carlin, E.M. (forthcoming 2001), *Environmental Regime Effectiveness: Confronting Theory with Evidence*, MIT Press, Cambridge, Massachusetts.

Underdal, A. and Hanf, K. (eds) (2000), *International Environmental Agreements and Domestic Politics: The Case of Acid Rain*, Ashgate, Aldershot.

Van Deveer, S. (1998), European Politics with a Scientific Face: Transition Countries, International Environmental Assessment, and Long-Range Transboundary Air Pollution, Report E-98-09, Global Environmental Assessment Project, Belfer Center for Science and International Affairs, Harvard University, Boston.

Vogel, D. (1995), 'Environmental Regulation and the Single European Market' in *Trading Up. Consumer and Environmental Regulation in a Global Economy*, Harvard University Press, Cambridge, Massachusetts and London, pp. 56-98.

Wallace, H. and Wallace, W. (eds) (2000), *Policy-Making in the European Union*, Oxford University Press, Oxford.

Weale, A. (1996), 'Environmental Rules and Rule-making in the European Union', *Journal of European Public Policy*, vol. 3, no. 4, December, pp. 594-611.

- (1999), 'European Environmental Policy by Stealth: the Dysfunctionality of Functionalism?, *Environment and Planning C. Government and Policy 1999*, vol. 17, pp. 37-51.

Weale, A., Pridham, G., Cini, M., Konstadakopulos, D., Porter, M., and Flynn, B. (2000), *Environmental Governance in Europe*, Oxford University Press, Oxford.

Wetstone, G. and Rosencrantz, A. (1983), *Acid Rain in Europe and North America*, Environmental Law Institute, Washington, DC.

Wettestad, J. (1991), The effectiveness of LRTAP, in Wettestad, J. and Andresen, S., *The Effectiveness of International Resource Cooperation: Some Preliminary Findings*, Report 007/1991, The Fridtjof Nansen Institute, Lysaker, pp. 74–94.

- (1996), *Acid Lessons? Assessing and Explaining LRTAP Implementation and Effectiveness*, WP-96-18 March, IIASA Working Paper. A revised version was published as 'Acid Lessons? Assessing and Explaining LRTAP Implementation and Effectiveness' in *Global Environmental Change*, vol. 7, no. 3, 1997, pp. 235-49.

- (1998), Participation in NO_x Policy-Making and Implementation in the Netherlands, UK, and Norway: Different Approaches, but Similar Results?, in Victor, D., Raustiala, K. and Skolnikoff, E. (eds), *The Implementation and Effectiveness of International Environmental Commitments*, MIT Press, Cambridge, Massachusetts, pp. 381-431.

- (1999), *Designing Effective Environmental Regimes - The Key Conditions*, Edward Elgar, Cheltenham.

- (2000 A), 'Implementing Stronger European Air Pollution Commitments – Will High Hopes in Brussels and Geneva be Dashed in London?', Paper presented at the 41st Annual ISA Convention, Los Angeles, 14-18 March.

- (2000 B), 'From Common Cuts to Critical Loads : The ECE Convention on Long-range Transboundary Air Pollution (CLRTAP)', in Andresen, S., Skodvin, T., Underdal, A. and Wettestad, J., *Science and Politics in International Environmental Regimes - Between Integrity and Involvement*, Manchester University Press, Manchester, pp. 95-122.

Wurzel, R. (1999), Britain, Germany and the European Union: Environmental Policy-making from 1972-97, Ph.D. thesis, London School of Economics.

Young, A.R. and Wallace, H. (2000), *Regulatory Politics in the Enlarging European Union*, Manchester University Press, Manchester.

Young, O.R. (1979), *Compliance and Public Authority: A Theory with International Applications*, Johns Hopkins University Press, Baltimore.

Ågren, C. (1999), Getting More for Less – An Alternative Assessment of the NEC Directive, no.13, Air Pollution and Climate Series, The Swedish NGO Secretariat for Acid Rain, Gothenburg.

EU and CLRTAP Documents

EU:

Commission Communication IP/97/205, March 12, 1997. Commission adopts strategy and two specific actions to combat acidification.

Commission Communication, COM (2001) 245. The Clean Air for Europe (CAFE) Programme: Towards a Thematic Strategy for Air Quality. May 4, 2001.

Commission of the European Communities (1993), 'Towards sustainability – A European Community programme of policy and action in relation to the environment and sustainable development'.

Commission Reports on the Concentration Levels of Tropospheric Ozone, 1998, 1999.

Commission Staff Working Paper on Acidification, November 27, 1995. SEC(95) 2057.

Council Conclusions, Acidification, December 20 1995, 13006/95.

Council Conclusions on a Community Strategy to Combat Acidification, December 19, 1997, 13622/97.

Council Directive 88/76/EEC of 3 December 1987 amending Directive 70/220/EEC on the approximation of the laws of the Member States relating to measures to be taken against air pollution by gases from the engines of motor vehicles (OJ L036 09.02.1988).

Council Directive 89/458/EEC of 18 July 1989 amending with regard to European emission standards for cars below 1,4 litres, Directive 70/220/EEC on the approximation of the laws of the Member States relating to measures to be taken against air pollution by emissions from motor vehicles (OJ L226 03.08.1989).

Council Directive 91/441/EEC of 26 June 1991 amending Directive 70/220/EEC on the approximation of the laws of the Member States relating to measures to be taken against air pollution by emissions from motor vehicles (OJ L242 30.08.1991).

Council Directive 1999/30/EC of 22 April 1999 relating to limit values for sulphur dioxide, nitrogen dioxide and oxides of nitrogen, particulate matter and lead in ambient air (OJ L163 29.06.1999).

Council Directive 96/62/EC of 27 September 1996 on ambient air quality assessment and management (OJ L296 21.11.1996).

Discussion Paper on the Future Development of Air Quality in the European Union, Environment Directorate/DG XI, October 5, 1998.

EU Press Release June 22, 2000, 'EU Commission welcomes agreement to curb air pollution', IP/00/657.

EU Press Release, May 7, 2001, 'Commission launches 'Clean Air for Europe' programme', IP/01/647.

EU Press Release, July 3, 2001, 'Large Combustion Plants' and National Emission Ceilings Directives/ Agreement', 10244/01.

European Commission (1999), 'What do Europeans think about the environment? The main results of the survey carried out in the context of Eurobarometer 51.1', DG XI/DG X, Brussels.

European Environment Agency (1999), *Environment in the European Union at the Turn of the Century*, Copenhagen.

European Parliament Document A5-0063/2000, Proposal for a European Parliament and Council directive on national emission ceilings for certain atmospheric pollutants, suggested amendments by the Parliament.

European Parliament (2000), Draft Recommendation for Second Reading on the Council Common Position for Adopting a European Parliament and Council Directive on National Emission Ceilings for Certain Atmospheric Pollutants (10674/1/2000-C5-0563/2000-1999/0067 /COD), Committee on the Environment, Public Health and Consumer Policy, December 8.

European Parliament Resolution A4-0162/1998, Resolution on the Communication to the Council and the European Parliament on a Community Strategy to Combat Acidification (Com(97)0088 – c4-0436/97).

Proposal for a Directive of the European Parliament and of the Council on national emission ceilings for certain atmospheric pollutants; Proposal for a Directive of the European Parliament and of the Council relating to ozone in ambient air, COM (1999) 125 final.

CLRTAP:

ECE/CLRTAP (1999), Strategies and Policies For Air Pollution Abatement, UN/ECE, Geneva.

EB.AIR/WG.5/R.32, 11 June 1992, Second generation abatement strategies for SO_2, NO_x, NH_3 and VOC – Note submitted by the delegations of Norway, Sweden and United Kingdom.

EB.AIR/WG.5/R.64, 17 June 1996, WGS, 'Integrated assessment of abatement strategies for nitrogen and volatile organic compounds', status report by the Chairman of the Task Force on Integrated Assessment Modelling.

ECE/EB.AIR/49, 10 December 1996, Report of the fourteenth session of the Executive Body.

EB.AIR/WG.5/R.69, Working Group on Strategies, Integrated assessment modelling, Progress report by the Chairman of the Task Force.

EB.AIR/WG.5/42, 3 April 1997, Working Group on Strategies, Report of the twentieth session.

EB.AIR/WG.5/R.80, 30 May 1997, Draft composite negotiating text for a protocol on nitrogen oxides and related substances.

ECE/EB.AIR/53, 7 January 1998, Report of the fifteenth session of the Executive Body.

EB.AIR/WG.5/R.97, 21 January 1998, Economic assessment of benefits, progress report by the Chairman of the Task Force on Economic Aspects of Abatement Strategies.

EB.AIR/CRP. 19/Add.1, 8 December 1998, draft report of the sixteenth session, p. 2.

EB.AIR/WG.5/62, 16 June 1999, WGS-30, Report of the thirtieth session.

UN/ECE Press Release ECE/ENV/99/11, 24 November 1999.

NME Notes:

March 9, 1995, WGS-15 meeting summary.

February 22, 1996, WGS-16 meeting summary.

August 29, 1996, WGS-18 meeting summary.

March 24, 1997, WGS-20, meeting summary.

September 30, 1997, WGS-22, meeting summary.

January 1, 1998, EB 1997 meeting summary.

September 15, 1998, WGS-27, meeting summary.

February 3, 1999, WGS-28 meeting summary.

April 7, 1999, WGS-29, NO_x -negotiations, meeting summary.

June 8, 1999, NO_x -negotiations, meeting summary.

List of Interviews

(Chronological order)

Lars Bjørkbom, Swedish Environmental Protection Agency and Chairman of the Working Group of Strategies, CLRTAP, October 21, 1999.

Lars Lindau, Swedish Environmental Protection Agency, October 21, 1999.

Svante Bodin, Swedish Ministry of Foreign Affairs, October 21, 1999.

Malcolm Ferguson, Institute of European Environmental Policy (IEEP), November 5, 1999.

Andrew Farmer, IEEP, November 5, 1999.

Ian Yarnold, Bernie Frost, Tony Baker, Department of the Environment, Transport and the Regions (DETR), UK, November 8, 1999.

Graham Davis, Martin Williams, DETR, November 9, 1999.

Per B. Suhr, Danish Environmental Protection Agency, November 10, 1999.

Erik Iversen, Danish Environmental Protection Agency, November 10, 1999.

Christer Ågren, Swedish NGO Secretariat on Acid Rain, February 15, 2000; and November 21, 2000.

Mari Sæther, Norwegian Ministry of Environment, February 29, 2000.

Anneli Hulthen, Swedish representative, European Parliament, and EP Rapporteur for the Acidification Strategy, May 2, 2000.

Peter Gammeltoft, DG ENV/D3, European Commission, May 2, 2000.

Martin Lutz, DG ENV/D3, European Commission, May 2, 2000.

Erik Pegazzano, European Parliament, May 2, 2000.

Sarah Blau, European Parliament, May 2, 2000.

Per Bergman, Swedish Delegation to the EU, May 3, 2000.

Magnar Ødelien, EFTA Secretariat, May 19, 2000.

Riita Mueller, Finnish representative, European Parliament, and EP rapporteur for the NEC Directive, January 9, 2001.

Index

Clearing the Air